John Ashbery

Selected Prose

Edited by Eugene Richie

THE UNIVERSITY OF MICHIGAN PRESS
Ann Arbor

A CIP catalog record for this book is available from the British Library.

Library of Congress Cataloging-in-Publication Data

Ashbery, John.
    [Prose works. Selections]
    Selected prose / John Ashbery ; edited by Eugene Richie.
        p. cm. — (Poets on poetry)
    Includes index.
    ISBN 0-472-11439-5 (alk. paper)
    1. Ashbery, John—Authorship.   2. Poetry—Authorship.
3. Poetry.   I. Richie, Eugene.   II. Title.   III. Series.
PS3501.S475A6   2004
818'.5408—dc22   2004012109

Selected Prose

Preface

This book collects miscellaneous prose pieces written over the last half-century. They have various reasons for existing. Some were written for money, to help subsidize my poetry habit. (Dr. Johnson said, "No man but a blockhead ever wrote, except for money"; perhaps he would have exempted poets, who do write for other reasons.) Others were written because I liked someone's work, felt it unjustly neglected, and wanted to call attention to it. Sometimes both these factors came into play, as when an editor would commission me to write about some subject she knew I was interested in—this was the case with an article on the poets John Wheelwright and A. R. Ammons, which Barbara Epstein asked me to write for the *New York Review of Books*. Also I spent many years as an art critic, and though much of this writing has been collected in another volume, the present one contains a few pieces on art that weren't included in it. The texts on Raymond Roussel are fragments of an abandoned doctoral dissertation. There are two pieces on film, the only ones I've ever written—again, I wanted to single out works I thought deserved notice.

The very format of the University of Michigan Press Poets on Poetry series ought to shield one from the criticism invariably leveled at reviewers who are unwise enough to gather their scattered writings between covers. Presumably the series is aimed at readers who like poetry, want to learn more about the poets in question, and think that prose is usually easier to understand than poetry. Mary McCarthy once complimented me on my art criticism, and was about to add something like, "Why can't your poetry be like that?" but stopped herself at the last minute. Other keen-witted people have felt the same. I hope that some of them will enjoy the assembled results of an activity that has always been something more than a hobby, if less than a calling.

—John Ashbery

Contents

Introduction by Eugene Richie

In the late eighties, when I was preparing John Ashbery's archives to be sent to the Houghton Library at Harvard, I first saw many of his early manuscripts and a newspaper clipping of his 1967 *New York Times* review of *The Complete Poems of Marianne Moore*. Shortly after we sent these papers to Harvard, I began to wonder how many other people who admired his poetry knew as little about his reviews, essays, introductions, and presentations as I did at that time.

With the help of David Kermani's wonderful annotated bibliography of Ashbery's early literary activity, I soon learned how much I'd been missing.[1] The problem, of course, was that most of this work was simply not available in one place, and some pieces were still in manuscript in Ashbery's own archives. In fact, during the years from 1984 to 1994, when I worked as Ashbery's secretary, other pieces were being produced before my eyes. So, in the early nineties, when David Lehman wrote to me with the idea that I collect and edit a volume of Ashbery's prose work for the University of Michigan Press Poets on Poetry series, I gladly accepted his invitation.

In the works collected in this volume, a reader can trace the development of Ashbery's literary career as well as his sensibility, based on his reading and thinking about some of the authors, artists, and filmmakers whose creations have been of particular interest to him. These pieces comprise a half-century's worth of critical perceptions and judgments, but it is important to note that Ashbery's approach to criticism has always been to spend time writing about work that he considers important. To best exhibit parallels between his poetry and prose, the texts have been arranged chronologically by date of presentation or first publication, with all successive publication dates noted.

In the publication note at the end of each piece, full bibliographical references give the publication history and other vital information for interested readers. For works that were published before their appearance in this volume, I have selected the most recent or most complete of sometimes quite a few published versions, since Ashbery has occasionally made minor changes of phrasing in subsequent publications or even added notes or postscripts. I have retained whatever titles appeared in the latest published versions. Some of these were Ashbery's original titles, while others were supplied by the editors of the publications. If a piece was an untitled review, comment, preface, foreword, introduction, or address, I have myself provided a brief descriptive title, such as "Introduction to a Reading." I have also given descriptive titles to two untitled, published essays on poets: "On the Poetry of F. T. Prince" and "On the Poetry of Joan Murray." Seven pieces in the book are published here for the first time. I have supplied descriptive titles for six of these. Four are introductions to readings and are noted as such. The fifth is an unpublished review of Ted Berrigan's *The Sonnets.* The sixth is the "Robert Frost Medal Address." The seventh, a panel presentation, was originally titled "The New York School of Poets."

Like most writers, Ashbery has always written about other writers. The early poetry of W. H. Auden was the topic of his undergraduate English honors thesis at Harvard. Henry Green was the focus of his master's thesis in English at Columbia University. Gertrude Stein and Michel Butor are the subjects of this collection's earliest pieces, which date from 1957. Ashbery has also written several pieces on the work of Raymond Roussel: his most recent work on Roussel (the foreword to Mark Ford's *Raymond Roussel and the Republic of Dreams*) is reprinted here along with his groundbreaking 1962 essay, initially titled "Re-establishing Raymond Roussel" and retitled "On Raymond Roussel."[2] Of the original title Ashbery notes, "This title wasn't mine and I tried unsuccessfully to get *ARTnews* to change it, arguing that it was incorrect because Raymond Roussel had never been established."

This book, however, is not a complete collection of all of Ashbery's prose works, which could fill a multivolume set. His many introductions to other writers' books or to readings would alone form a single volume. The pieces we have included focus on some of the many writers whose work he admires, as do his Charles Eliot Norton Lectures, collected in *Other Traditions* (Harvard University Press, 2000). The numerous interviews he has given would also make a book themselves, not to mention the most recent interview with Mark Ford, which *is* an entire book.[3] A single volume too could be dedicated to a representative selection of the creative prose Ashbery has produced.[4] Such pieces as *Architectural Digest*'s "Guest Speaker: John Ashbery—The Poet's Hudson River Restoration" were not included; again, the abundant material connected with the creative environment of his house—by Ashbery, critics and journalists, the American artist Archie Rand, and the English composer Robin Holloway, for example—could easily make up another volume, compact disc, or documentary like Mel Stuart's recent film (*John Ashbery—A Poet's View*, Academy of American Poets, 2002).[5] Pieces by Ashbery published only in French, such as "Reverdy en Amérique" and an article on Roussel—"Les versions sceniques d'*Impressions d'Afrique* et de *Locus Solus*"—have not been reprinted.[6] Also awaiting some future collection are four of Ashbery's rare pieces on composers, which are, however, available in major newspaper archives or as recent program notes.[7]

This book does include Ashbery's only two articles on film; notable pieces of art criticism on Jasper Johns and Louisa Matthiasdottir, not collected elsewhere; and key pieces on artists written after the publication of *Reported Sightings: Art Chronicles 1957–1987* (Knopf, 1989; Harvard University Press, 1991). Also this collection contains some of the most important literary reviews, introductions, essays, and presentations that Ashbery has written thus far during his career as a poet. As editor of this volume, I have made every effort to locate critical writings that are most representative of his poetic sensibility and literary insights.

Mark Ford has aptly described the significance of the literary criticism in this collection:

> This volume will form the third part of a triptych of Ashbery's critical writings, which will, I am sure, end up seeming as vital to the history of twentieth-century poetry as the critical prose of T. S. Eliot. *Reported Sightings: Art Chronicles 1957–1987, Other*

Traditions, and *Selected Prose* will be seen to embody a critical sensibility, which, though seemingly so elusive, has in fact been as influential on the development of poetry in English over the last thirty-five years as Eliot's was during the period 1922–1965.

Ford also suggests that "this collection will not only expand the general poetry reader's understanding of Ashbery's take on literature but will offer a compelling general alternative reading of twentieth-century American and European culture."[8]

The critical prose of a great poet necessarily reflects and impacts upon the poet's own poetry. We may read the prose to learn more about Ashbery's opinion of other writers, his guidelines for reading other writers, and his aesthetic criteria. The definitions of poetry and the poem noted in his reviews and articles on Gertrude Stein, Antonin Artaud, Marianne Moore, Elizabeth Bishop, and Frank O'Hara are themselves a rich poetic mine to explore. In his introduction to the *Collected Poems* of O'Hara (in this collection), for example, Ashbery notes, "Frank O'Hara's concept of the poem as the chronicle of the creative act that produces it was strengthened by his intimate experience of Pollock's, Kline's and de Kooning's great paintings of the late forties and early fifties, and of the imaginative realism of painters like Jane Freilicher and Larry Rivers." But then Ashbery immediately gives James Schuyler's opinion that the influence of painting on O'Hara's concept of the poem has been too highly emphasized. Schuyler's response suggests that "the kindest (and it may even be true) way of seeing it would be along the lines of what Pasternak says about life creating incidents to divert our attention from it so that it can get on with the work it can only accomplish unobserved." Ashbery preserves here a controversial discussion between poets who were not only members of a vibrant and innovative artistic community, but also close friends, on the very essence of poetry and on what, for them, poetry and the artistic process are all about.

Also, what a poet reads and the prose a poet writes may inspire or be inspired by poetic work. This was certainly true, for example, of W. H. Auden and his own prose on Ashbery. Just before he chose Ashbery's *Some Trees* as the 1956 winner in the

Yale Series of Younger Poets and wrote the foreword to it, he composed and gave his inaugural address as newly elected Professor of Poetry at Oxford University, England. Many of the ideas for the lecture were still in his mind, and Edward Mendelson believes that "Auden wrote a prose manifesto . . . in the form of his foreword to John Ashbery's book." The foreword addressed one of the key issues Auden was concerned about in several of his own earlier poems and which Mendelson believes he avoided in his Oxford lecture: how "to solve the double problem of finding subjects worth writing about and in a language they deserve." Mendelson further suggests that in the foreword to Ashbery's book, Auden "named the many difficulties a modern poet faces that he had studiously ignored in his Oxford lecture a few weeks earlier."[9]

In the foreword, Auden's last words come back to this issue: "Is it not surprising, then, that many modern poems, among them Mr. Ashbery's entertaining sestina 'The Painter,' are concerned with the nature of the creative process and with posing the question 'Is it now possible to write poetry?'"[10] Shortly afterward, Mendelson explains, Auden wrote the poem "First Things First," "in an attempt to confront these issues."[11] When Ashbery and I went to the book party for Mendelson's *Later Auden* (New York: Farrar, Straus and Giroux, 1999), at the apartment of the editor Elisabeth Sifton and her husband, the historian Fritz Stern, Mendelson told us he felt confident that the foreword and the poem were interconnected because of the similar ideas and because this was, from his experience, the way Auden truly worked. Such connection between reading and writing underscores how useful an anthology of a poet's prose can be to a reader searching for a poet's thematic development.

Ashbery tells of a similar experience of influence from his own reading of Elizabeth Bishop. On January 11, 2003, he appeared on a panel for a Key West literary seminar called "Poets and Their Work: Poetry as Its Own Biography (Personal I versus Poetic Eye)." In a statement too brief to include in this collection, he discusses Bishop's "Over 2,000 Illustrations and a Complete Concordance." Ashbery recalls, "I wrote her a fan letter in 1948 when I first read it in *Partisan Review,* and was rewarded with a postcard from Maine—one of the many coastlines she cultivated, sandpiper-wise. The poem was the inspiration for a poem of mine called 'Soonest Mended,' which I have called my OSFA (i.e., 'one size fits all') confessional poem." In his 1969 review of Bishop's *The Complete Poems,* included here, Ashbery uses the same Bishop poem to explain an element of her method of poetic composition:

> This quality which one can only call "thingness" is with her throughout, sometimes shaping a whole poem, sometimes disappearing right after the beginning, sometimes appearing only at the end to add a decisive fillip. In "Over 2,000 Illustrations and a Complete Concordance," which is possibly her masterpiece, she plies continually between the steel-engraved vignettes of a gazetteer and the distressingly unclassifiable events of a real voyage.

Many years later, in an essay dedicated to Jane Freilicher's painting *View over Mecox (Yellow Wall),* from *Voices in the Gallery: Writers on Art* (University of Rochester Press, 2001), Ashbery notes, "The painting sings a song of thingness, whether that of the swatch of nature sitting for its portrait or the paint that's helping it to become itself even as it casually poses for its own portrait." Over a period of more than thirty years, the notion of "thingness" in poetry and art has stayed with him, changing mediums, transforming from "the steel-engraved vignettes of a gazetteer" to "the swatch of nature sitting for its portrait." In a kind of Rilkean or Keatsian sense, this idea of "thingness" celebrates the earthly life that opens before us every day like a landscape of nature or a tapestry of worldly artifacts in dissonance or harmony. I, too, have always associated the earthly objects in the domestic tapestry and meditative landscapes of Jane Freilicher with those in the often domestic or seaside terrain of Bishop's poetry.

Though such influences and associations may not always be so obvious, it is certainly true that if we are interested in the origins of a poet's ideas, there is no better place to look than in what the poet is reading and in his own prose and poetry being written at the time. Ashbery's often affectionate, always exquisite perceptions about artists and other writers reveal his own ideas and methods. To encourage the reader to compare these works and to make such connections or associations, this collection of Ashbery's prose was arranged chronologically. However, one may read individual selections simply for the delight of Ashbery's insights on that particular occasion. That imagination and wit which are so much part of his poetry are also very much evident in these generous performances in observation, taste, and judgment.

This book would not have been possible without the assistance of many individuals. I would like to express my gratitude first of all to John Ashbery for making this difficult task a pleasure to accomplish, with his entertaining anecdotes and informative recollections about the genesis of these works. David Kermani has my gratitude and admiration for his invaluable bibliography on Ashbery's early work and for his steadfast dedication to Ashbery's archives. My research was greatly facilitated by Kermani's work in organizing Ashbery's archives and his recent creation of The Ashbery Resource Center (ARC), a project of The Flow Chart Foundation for Bard College (see www.flowchartfoundation.org). He has also continually supported, encouraged, and advised me while I was tracing obscure pieces, negotiating contracts, and choosing and arranging materials.

At Pace University, I would like to thank my dedicated assistant Wai-Wan Lam for initially typing and editing a majority of the texts in the book and for helping me with library research and permissions work. She began working with me when she was a freshman and has continued through her graduation to work with me with outstanding competence and extraordinary personal initiative on this book and on many of my other administrative and academic projects. I am also grateful to my English Department chairs, Professor Sherman Raskin and Dr. Walter Srebnick, for their support; my friend and colleague, Dr. Martha Driver, for her generous advice and encouragement; our research librarians, Elisabeth Birnbaum and Michelle Fanelli, for helping me find the published texts that were the most difficult to locate; my assistants Maria Torres and Alicia Knights, who started this project with me; and my poet colleagues Tom Breidenbach and Charles North for our discussions of Ashbery's work. In addition, grants from the Dyson College of Arts and Sciences Summer Research Fund and the University Scholarly Research Committee helped me with my expenses for research and manuscript preparation.

David Lehman initiated this collection of Ashbery's selected prose with his timely invitation to me to act as editor, and has been both generous and gracious with his editorial advice and literary expertise on Ashbery and other writers, throughout the decade I have worked on this project. I would also like to thank Mark Ford for his advice and perceptions about Ashbery's work and for his continued encouragement during the years I was gathering and editing this material. Miles Champion, the program coordinator at the Poetry Project at St. Mark's, and John Ashbery's dedicated assistants, Marcella Durand and Micaela Morrissette, helped me with texts and bibliographic information. I appreciate as well the support and encouragement of LeAnn Fields, senior executive editor at the University of Michigan Press, and the assistance of Allison Liefer, acquisitions editorial associate, as well as Marcia LaBrenz, senior copyediting coordinator.

I am most grateful to my wife, the poet Rosanne Wasserman, for her literary advice and meticulous editing of each piece in this collection. She has worked with me at every stage of the preparation process—verifying the accuracy in transcription from the originals to the final drafts, discussing and entering Ashbery's own corrections, editing phrasing and facts for clear meaning, and generating the manuscript. This book would not have been possible without her devoted daily support of my efforts and her loving friendship. My son, Joseph, has my undying affection for his love and understanding.

—Eugene Richie

NOTES

1. David Kermani, *John Ashbery: A Comprehensive Bibliography* (New York: Garland Publishing, 1976).

2. John Ashbery, "Re-establishing Raymond Roussel," *Portfolio and ARTnews Annual* 6 (Autumn 1962), pp. 88–92, 97–104, 106.

3. John Ashbery and Mark Ford, *John Ashbery in Conversation with Mark Ford* (London: Between the Lines, 2003).

4. There are many prose works that would be seminal texts in a representative selection of Ashbery's prose poetry and fiction, including the innovative *Three Poems* (1972); and, with James Schuyler, *A Nest of Ninnies*, the novel which they started in 1952 and published in 1969, and which W. H. Auden called extraordinary. The prose poem "A Dream" was Ashbery's first-ever recorded contribution to an anthology, written in 1950, published in "A Little Anthology of the Poem in Prose," edited by Charles Henri Ford, in *New Directions in Prose and Poetry* 14 (New York: New Directions, 1953). "The Egyptian Helen," written in 1952, is a short story that I found in a folder in Ashbery's desk drawer in his apartment in Chelsea and that was subsequently published, first as an appendix to Rosanne Wasserman's doctoral thesis, "Helen of Troy: Her Myth in Modern Poetry" (Ph.D. diss., CUNY, 1986, UMI), and later in the English-Russian magazine *Gnosis* 11 (Winter 1995), edited by the poet Victoria Andreyeva and the fiction writer Arkady Rovner. Another prose experiment, "Novel," written in 1954, was discovered due to the detective work of David Lehman, who unearthed it in the library of the University of California at San Diego, when he was examining James Schuyler's archives while researching his book on the New York School, *The Last Avant-Garde* (New York: Doubleday, 1998). "Novel" was first published by the Grenfell Press in 1998 with ten drawings by the English artist Trevor Winkfield, in a limited edition of one hundred, bound by hand, with silkscreen covers, signed by author and artist.

5. John Ashbery, "Guest Speaker: John Ashbery—The Poet's Hudson River Restoration," *Architectural Digest* 51, no. 6 (June 1994), pp. 36, 40, 44.

6. John Ashbery, "Reverdy en Amérique," *Mercure de France* 344, no. 1181 (January–April 1962), pp. 109–12; John Ashbery, "Les versions scéniques d'*Impressions d'Afrique* et de *Locus Solus*," *Bizarre* 34–35 (May 1964), pp. 19–25.

7. John Ashbery, "Chamber Music Composed by IBM Computer Played [on Iannis Xenakis]," *New York Herald Tribune, European Edition* (May 29, 1962), p. 3; "Composer Gian Carlo Menotti—Busiest Man in Italy Now," *New York Herald Tribune, European Edition* (July 3–4, 1965), p. 10; Program Note to *Ariane et Barbe-Bleue* (Paul Dukas, 1907), American Symphony Orchestra, conducted by Leon Botstein, at Avery Fisher Hall, Lincoln Center, New York City (April 25, 1999); Program Note to *Le Roi Arthus* (Ernest Chausson, 1895), American Symphony Orchestra,

conducted by Leon Botstein, at Avery Fisher Hall, Lincoln Center, New York City (December 27, 2001).

8. Mark Ford, letter to the author, November 20, 2000.

9. Edward Mendelson, *Later Auden* (New York: Farrar, Straus and Giroux, 1999), p. 408.

10. W. H. Auden, foreword to *Some Trees,* by John Ashbery (New Haven: Yale University Press, 1956), p. 14.

11. Mendelson, *Later Auden,* p. 409.

The Impossible: Gertrude Stein

Stanzas in Meditation (1956) is the latest volume in the series of Gertrude Stein's unpublished writings which Yale University Press has been bringing out regularly for the last decade. It will probably please readers who are satisfied only by literary extremes, but who have not previously taken to Miss Stein because of a kind of lack of seriousness in her work, characterized by lapses into dull, facile rhyme; by the over-employment of rhythms suggesting a child's incantation against grownups; and by monotony. There is certainly plenty of monotony in the 150-page title poem which forms the first half of this volume, but it is the fertile kind, which generates excitement as water monotonously flowing over a dam generates electrical power. These austere "stanzas" are made up almost entirely of colorless connecting words such as "where," "which," "these," "of," "not," "have," "about," and so on, though now and then Miss Stein throws in an orange, a lilac, or an Albert to remind us that it really is the world, our world, that she has been talking about. The result is like certain monochrome de Kooning paintings in which isolated strokes of color take on a deliciousness they never could have had out of context, or a piece of music by Webern in which a single note on the celesta suddenly irrigates a whole desert of dry, scratchy sounds in the strings.

Perhaps the word that occurs oftenest in the *Stanzas* is the word "they," for this is a poem about the world, about "them." (What a pleasant change from the eternal "we" with which so many modern poets automatically begin each sentence, and which gives the impression that the author is sharing his every sensation with some invisible Kim Novak.) Less frequently, "I" enters to assess the activities of "them," to pick up after them, to assert her own altered importance. As we get deeper into the poem, it seems not so much as if we were reading as living a rather long period of our lives with a houseful of people. Like people, Miss Stein's lines are comforting or annoying or brilliant or tedious. Like people, they sometimes make no sense and sometimes make perfect sense or they stop short in the middle of a sentence and wander away, leaving us alone for a while in the physical world, that collection of thoughts, flowers, weather, and proper names. And, just as with people, there is no real escape from them: one feels that if one were to close the book one would shortly re-encounter the *Stanzas* in life, under another guise. As the author says, "It is easily eaten hot and lukewarm and cold / But not without it."

Stanzas in Meditation gives one the feeling of time passing, of things happening, of a "plot," though it would be difficult to say precisely what is going on. Sometimes the story has the logic of a dream:

> She asked could I be taught to be allowed
> And I said yes oh yes I had forgotten him
> And she said does any or do any change
> And if not I said whom could they count.

while at other times it becomes startlingly clear for a moment, as though a change in the wind had suddenly enabled us to hear a conversation that was taking place some distance away:

> He came early in the morning.
> He thought they needed comfort
> Which they did
> And he gave them an assurance
> That it would be all as well
> As indeed were it
> Not to have it needed at any time

But it is usually not events which interest Miss Stein, rather it is their "way of happening," and the story of *Stanzas in Meditation* is a general, all-purpose model which each reader can adapt to fit his own set of particulars. The poem is a hymn to possibility; a celebration of the fact that the world exists, that things can happen.

In its profound originality, its original profundity, this poem that is always threatening to become a novel reminds us of the late novels of James, especially *The Golden Bowl* and *The Awkward Age,* which seem to strain with a superhuman force toward "the condition of music," of poetry. In such a passage as the following, for instance:

> Be not only without in any of their sense
> Careful
> Or should they grow careless with remonstrance
> Or be careful just as easily not at all
> As when they felt.
> They could or would would they grow always
> By which not only as more as they like.
> They cannot please conceal
> Nor need they find they need a wish

we are not far from Charlotte's and the Prince's rationalizations. Both *Stanzas in Meditation* and *The Golden Bowl* are ambitious attempts to transmit a completely new picture of reality, of that *real* reality of the poet which Antonin Artaud called "une réalité dangereuse et typique." If these works are highly complex and, for some, unreadable, it is not only because of the complicatedness of life, the subject, but also because they actually imitate its rhythm, its way of happening, in an attempt to draw our attention to another aspect of its true nature. Just as life seems to alter the whole of what has gone before, so the endless process of elaboration which gives the work of these two writers a texture of bewildering luxuriance—that of a tropical rain-forest of ideas—seems to obey some rhythmic impulse at the heart of all happening.

In addition, the almost physical pain with which we strive to accompany the evolving thought of one of James's or Gertrude Stein's characters is perhaps a counterpart of the painful continual projection of the individual into life. As in life, perseverance has its rewards—moments when we emerge suddenly on a high plateau with a view of the whole distance we have come. In Miss Stein's work the sudden inrush of clarity is likely to be an aesthetic experience, but (and this seems to be another of her "points") the description of that experience applies also to "real-life" situations, the aesthetic problem being a microcosm of all human problems.

> I should think it makes no difference
> That so few people are me.
> That is to say in each generation there are so few geniuses
> And why should I be one which I am
> This is one way of saying how do you do
> There is this difference
> I forgive you everything and there is nothing to forgive.

It is for moments like this that one perseveres in this difficult poem, moments which would be less beautiful and meaningful if the rest did not exist, for we have fought side by side with the author in her struggle to achieve them.

The poems in the second half of the book are almost all charming, though lacking the profundity of *Stanzas in Meditation*. Perhaps the most successful is "Winning His Way," again a picture of a human community: "The friendship between Lolo and every one was very strong / And they were careful to do him no wrong." The bright, clean colors and large cast of characters in this poem suggest a comic strip. In fact one might say that Miss Stein discovered a means of communication as well-suited to express our age as, in their own way, the balloons (with their effect of concentration), light bulbs, asterisks, ringed planets, and exclamation marks which comic-strip characters use to communicate their ideas. In "Winning His Way," for example, she experiments with punctuation by placing periods in the middle of sentences. This results in a strange syncopation which affects the meaning as well as the rhythm of a line. In the couplet

> Herman states.
> That he is very well.

the reader at first imagines that she is talking about a group of states ruled over by a potentate named Herman; when he comes to the second line he is forced to change his ideas, but its ghost remains, giving a muted quality to the prose sense of the words.

Donald Sutherland, who has supplied the introduction for this book, has elsewhere quoted Miss Stein as saying, "If it can be done why do it?" *Stanzas in Meditation* is no doubt the most successful of her attempts to do what can't be done, to create a counterfeit of reality more real than reality. And if, on laying the book aside, we feel that it is still impossible to accomplish the impossible, we are also left with the conviction that it is the only thing worth trying to do.

Review of Gertrude Stein's *Stanzas in Meditation* (New Haven: Yale University Press, 1956). From *Gertrude Stein Advanced: An Anthology of Criticism,* edited by Richard Kostelanetz (Jefferson, N. C.: McFarland and Co., 1990). First published in *Poetry* 90, no. 4 (July 1957). Portions were reprinted in *A Library of Literary Criticism: Modern American Literature,* compiled and edited by Dorothy Nyren (New York: Frederick Ungar, 1960).

Review of Michel Butor's
La modification

"What is the worst thing you can think of?" asks a young girl of her lover in Strindberg's play *The Ghost Sonata.* "Counting the laundry," he replies. The girl then mentions other terrors— making the bed, buying soap and matches, getting up in the night to close the windows—arguing that it is these minutiae which constitute the real torment of existence, nibbling away at and ultimately destroying any happiness which comes our way. Michel Butor's *La modification,* latest winner of the Prix Renaudot and a close contender for the Prix Goncourt (which was won by Roger Vailland's *La loi*), is a novel about "ces minimes désagréments, si insupportable à la longue," which through sheer weight and number cause a man finally to change his mind about seeing his mistress and thus seal himself off from future happiness.

This novel is an immense interior monologue, told in the present tense (the solitary character addressing himself as "vous" throughout) in endless run-on sentences which can go on for more than two pages and are often broken up into Péguy-like strophes. It begins as the hero, a middle-aged Paris representative for a large Italian typewriter firm, boards a train at the Gare de Lyon, and it ends as he arrives in the Stazione Termini in Rome. During the trip his eye has automatically registered whatever there is to see (the stations passed, the passengers who come and go, even the bits of paper on the floor of the train and the motion of raindrops on the window), and his mind has just as automatically reflected on his past and future. A comfortably well-off bourgeois, he has four sullen, secretive children and a wife, Henriette, whose silent contempt for him (which she can neither express nor effectively subdue) erodes every day a little more of what remains of his youth. For some time he has been having an affair with Cécile, a young secretary at the French embassy in Rome. They have been able to meet only furtively during his trips to Rome, and the purpose of this journey (which he has pretended to Henriette is just another business trip) is to tell Cécile that he has at last succeeded in finding her a job in Paris and has decided to leave his wife. This, he feels, will redeem him in Cécile's eyes, for she has lately begun to grow caustic about his continual hedging and postponements.

As the trip wears on, as night falls and he becomes increasingly the prey of nightmares and the discomforts of the train, he grows dimly aware that Cécile's nagging has come to resemble Henriette's, that their love has begun to wane. Once, he recalls, he introduced Cécile to Henriette as a business acquaintance, and the two got on famously together: he even felt that they were somehow in league to destroy him. And it dawns on him that the city of Rome (that symbol of eternal youth and glory which he and Cécile have so often explored together) has come increasingly to supplant the image of her in his mind. By the time he leaves the train he has decided not to see Cécile this trip, but to visit the city only. He will never tell her about the post in Paris; little by little she will come to understand the futility of their attachment, and they will separate slowly and painfully since there is no other way open to them.

Butor belongs to what has been called the school of the *roman blanc* (unconsummated novel) or *roman du regard;* that is to say he employs a naturalist approach like that of Flaubert, carried to incredible lengths. The inability of man to perform the simplest act for himself is assumed from the beginning; his desperation is no longer recognizable as such, having changed to a strangely calm resignation to his fate, which is merely to sit observing the appearance of the objects around him. Yet Butor does not go as far in this direction as his colleague Alain Robbe-Grillet, whose thoroughly de-humanized "objective" novels are considered the masterpieces of this new school. Behind the methodical noting of details of landscape, dress and behavior there is in Butor's work the echo of a scream, the raw terror of a human being held incommunicado in a world of indifferent and even hostile objects. He has been compared to Joyce by some French critics, and it is true that his hero's monologue bears a superficial resemblance to that of Leopold Bloom, and that he introduces an esoteric symbolism reminiscent of Joyce's especially in the dreams that complicate the texture of the latter part of the book. But Butor's photographic realism (the outstanding feature of his work) is far from the verbal preoccupation and mythmaking of Joyce, who seldom dwelt on the visual aspect of things. It seems to stem in part from the style of Raymond Roussel, who around 1900 wrote a seventy-five-page poem entitled *La source* which is merely a description of the view of a spa on the printed label of a bottle of mineral water looked at by a man lunching in a restaurant; in the last line he glimpses a couple at another table: "Qui chuchote toujours des choses qu'on n'entend pas." And probably Butor has read as well Emmanuel Bove, author of *Armand* (1927), whose detailing of the minute-to-minute life of the body, imperceptible changes of light, temperature and so on seems to announce the tone of *La modification*.

It is perhaps Butor's talent for minute observation which renders *La modification* so singularly attaching. It is true that his final message is one of agony: his hero can move spiritually neither forward nor backward, nor can he remain where he is. But the richness of detail (including almost humorous descriptions of the minor ennuis of the trip and dazzling evocations of scenery and the play of light and shadow which at times suggest a painting by Degas or Carrière, or a dim drawing by Seurat) causes one to put down the book feeling rewarded rather than *aplati*. Here is an example of Butor's descriptive power:

> Il pleuvait sur le Jura comme il y a plu aujourd'hui; la vitre se
> recouvrait de gouttes de plus en plus grosses qui de-
> scendaient lentement en diagonales sinueuses et comme
> haletantes, secousse par secousse, et dans les tunnels le reflet
> de votre visage faisait comme un trou d'ombre au travers
> duquel vous aperceviez la fuite furieuse du roc. (185)

or again (at breakfast in the dining car):

> Tout d'un coup, dans une vive échancrure soudaine de
> l'horizon, vous avez vu le soleil poindre, balayant de ses
> rayons horizontaux la table à laquelle vous étiez assis, en dé-
> tachant superbement tous les objets, même les miettes, les
> soulignant de longues ombres. (208)

Butor places his whole novel under the sign of "le regard" in a
significant passage in which the hero remembers a visit to the
Louvre:

> Ce que vous avez amoureusement détaillé, ce vers quoi vos
> pas vous avaient mené, ce sont deux grand tableaux d'un
> peintre de troisième ordre, Pannini, représentant deux col-
> lections imaginaires exposées dans de très hautes salles large-
> ment ouvertes où des personnages de qualité, ecclésiastiques
> ou gentilshommes, se promènent parmi les sculptures entre
> les murs couvert de paysages, en faisant des gestes d'admira-
> tion, d'intérêt, de surprise, de perplexité, comme les visiteurs
> dans la Sixtine, avec ceci de remarquable qu'il n'y a aucune
> différence de matière sensible entre les objets représentés
> comme réels et ceux représentés comme peints, comme s'il
> avait voulu figurer sur ses toiles la réussite de ce projet com-
> mun à tant d'artistes de son temps: donner un équivalent ab-
> solu de la réalité, le chapiteau peint devenant indiscernable
> du chapiteau réel, à part le cadre qui l'entoure . . . (55)

What Butor does not say, but allows to be understood, is that the
hero himself, looking at the pictures, becomes part of an even
larger picture in which there is room also for the reader. We all
might as well be objects skillfully painted to give the illusion of
reality, he implies, indistinguishable in kind from the furniture
of the rooms we inhabit, unable to speak or to act. This seems

to be the final message of this strangely beautiful novel whose epigraph could well be T. S. Eliot's famous lines, "Between the idea and the reality / falls the shadow."

Review of Michel Butor's *La modification* (Paris: Editions de Minuit, 1957). From *The French Review* 32, no. 1 (October 1958).

A Note on Pierre Reverdy

We have little biographical information about Reverdy, who has lived since 1926 in almost monastic seclusion near the Abbey of Solesmes, in the Maine region of France. We know that he was born September 13, 1889, in Narbonne, a city in southern France near the Mediterranean and not too far from the Spanish border. After studying at the lycée of Toulouse and the college of Narbonne, he came to Paris in 1910, where he became friendly with Picasso, Braque, Matisse, Juan Gris and Max Jacob. (Picasso, Matisse and Gris have illustrated books by Reverdy, and Picasso's deep admiration for his poetry is well known.) Around 1916 he began editing the excellent review *Nord-Sud* (named after the Métro line that links Montmartre and Montparnasse), publishing among other things the early work of Aragon, Breton and Soupault.

He was only vaguely associated with the Dadaist movement, which reached its peak around 1920. Though his work appeared in some Dadaist reviews, there is nothing to indicate that he subscribed to the Dadaist program of the abolition of all artistic and aesthetic values. One wonders, in view of how beautiful and aesthetically pleasing much of the Dadaist work seems today, whether the artists themselves believed in their own negative program. Perhaps they would have secretly agreed with Reverdy when he said, in his pamphlet *Self-Defense:* "The beautiful does not emerge from the artist's hands, but what emerges from the artist's hands *becomes* the beautiful."

19

We do not know what crisis caused Reverdy to leave the brilliant Paris literary world for a solitary existence within sound of the bells of Solesmes and of its famous choir. But no doubt in 1926 the air of that world was becoming difficult to breathe, especially for someone like Reverdy who was associated more with the generation immediately previous, in which the leading names were those of Cocteau, Apollinaire, Picasso, Satie, Max Jacob. Civil war had broken out among the Surrealists. Manifestos, excommunications and anathematizations were flying thick and fast, and failure to agree on all issues with the small directing group could result not only in a writer's literary exile, but in his being beaten up as well. Though the Surrealists had been admirers of Reverdy in the days when he published their work in *Nord-Sud,* he seems later on to have lost favor with them. In 1933 André Breton remarked wryly in an interview that in his more recent poetry, Reverdy had been "putting water in his wine." Perhaps it was his memory of the early days of Surrealism, which must then have seemed a marvelous possibility, that prompted Reverdy to write years later in *Le livre de mon bord:* "The little magazines edited by the young give off a fragile perfume, full of freshness. For a moment one has the impression that they alone represent what is alive, important in that moment. If one opens them a few years later, nothing could seem deader. Maturity and mastery are the concern of only a few rare survivors."

Though Reverdy seems to us a Surrealist poet, we must remember that the Surrealists insisted on automatic writing, that is, poetry written down as rapidly and unthinkingly as possible and which could not be altered later. While this discipline might seem to abolish all rules and to bring back spontaneity into poetry, one important rule was retained: the poets were careful to observe the conventions of grammar and syntax. "Take care," wrote Breton. "I know the meaning of each of my words and I observe syntax *naturally:* syntax is not a discipline, as certain oafs believe." But does one always observe these rules when one is writing automatically? And what, in fact, is automatic writing? Isn't all writing automatic? If one corrects a poem after writing it, doesn't one happen automatically on the correction? Automatic writing as practiced by the Surrealists seems to have been merely a euphemism for extreme haste. In any case, most Surrealist poetry (with the exception of some of Éluard's and of a handful of transparent gems by Aragon and Breton which are beautiful precisely because they do not seem to have been written according to the formula) is uninteresting from the standpoint of language, and language is poetry, as Mallarmé knew—the frozen shipwreck of his *Coup de dés* still looms larger than anything else on the horizon of French poetry. Recording their unconscious thoughts in correct lycée French, the Surrealist poets were forced into mere lists of exotic and goofy images, more monotonous in the long run than the celebrated *Catalogue d'armes et cycles* of St. Etienne, which comes up so often in discussions of modern French literature.

Reverdy's poetry avoids the disciplines of Surrealist poetry, and is the richer for it. He is not afraid to experiment with language and syntax, and it is often difficult to determine whether a particular line belongs with the preceding sentence or the one following it. The lines drift across the page as overheard human speech drifts across our hearing: fragments of conversation, dismembered advertising slogans or warning signs in the Métro appear and remain preserved in the rock crystal of the poem. And far from banishing poetry to the unconscious, he lets it move freely in and out of the conscious and the unconscious. Since we do not inhabit either world exclusively, the result is moving and lifelike. Sometimes his preoccupations seem infinitesimally small—the shadow of a coin on a book of matches, for instance. And Reverdy has written: "One has said almost nothing about man's misfortunes after one has spoken only of the major ones, about which he thinks or feels only rarely. The worst are the small ones, which are constant, always present and tailored to his size." But the small object can suddenly become enormous, be "all there is," by means of a split-second crescendo like the ones that occur in Webern's music. Reading a poem by Reverdy, one can have the impression one moment of contemplating a drop of water on a blade of grass; the next moment one is swimming for one's life.

It is a disconcerting kind of poetry, but one feels it must be very close to life as it is actually lived. For good or evil, one is near the heart of nature: infinitesimal fluctuations of light and

shade, warm and cold, become determining factors in the outcome of the poem. Reverdy has written in his journal: "Last
night a gust of wind drew back the curtains of mist by blowing
on them, like curtain rings on a rod. And the whole weight of
the gray sky is raised. A little more, a little less heart and light
and everything changes: the mind, the sensibility. We react with
a whole section of our secret being to outside circumstances, as
plants do." And behind their apparent simplicity of texture, the
poems are recorded and composed with a botanist's precision.
Even such a poem as the following one from *Plupart du temps*,
which seems as quiet as a breeze, as simple as a glass of water:

> On the threshold no one
> Or your shadow
> A memory which would remain
> The road passes
> And the trees speak nearer
> What is there behind
> A wall
> Voices
> The clouds rising up
> The moment I was passing there
> And the fence all the way along
> Where those who will not enter are.

is a highly complex organism; like a plant's, its growth obeys
hidden pressures and atmospheric changes, the subtle alter-
ation of the tense of a verb, the introduction of a new pronoun
are like very fine traps constructed to catch something invisible
which was passing.

Reverdy's presentation of reality often seems cinematic, and
the Frenchman whose work most resembles his is perhaps not a
poet but the film director Robert Bresson. Like Reverdy, Bresson
in his few films (especially *Les dames du Bois du Boulogne, Le journal d'un curé de campagne* and *Un condamné à mort s'est échappé*) has
created an ascetically transparent world. Like Reverdy he has a
keen ear for *le langage de la tribu* and a deep feeling for nature.
Trees, clouds, lakes, automobiles, the texture of a woman's skin
and of her dress are shown for what they are and are also unde-
tachable from the story being told; they are like electrodes in the

limpid bath of a precise context. Reverdy too has given us unforgettable moments like these, in which nature seems part of
what is happening to us:

Surprise

> There is no one left in the city
> We go up through the woods
> Some fall
> And those who will arrive too late
> It's you
> It's me
> The chimney is smoking behind
> He stayed in bed downstairs
> And you kneel down forever
> His head and heart are heavy
> And the song is forgotten
> The hours skipped over
> Sleeping with our eyes open
> Don't look at that picture
> It's a broken mirror
> And your eye
> Your eye that hasn't gotten used to it yet

Reverdy has written novels (*Le voleur de talan, La peau de
l'homme*) which are like extensions of his poems. And perhaps
the poems were already enough like novels, novels compressed
into a tiny space by some supernatural force. We are left with
only the mysterious essentials of a story; we see a man walking
down a dark road, the reflections of a candle in a window; we
have the feeling that something enormous has happened, but
we will never know any more of the drama than this. And so
many novels, so many real adventures finally end in one's mind
as two or three apparently trivial details. "It is not at all life as it
is that we love," writes Reverdy, "but a fleeting, dazzling reflection on the façade across the street." A remark which suggests
the *petit pan de mur jaune* and what it symbolized for Proust, who
is with Reverdy one of the rare writers of our time in whose work
despair seems beautiful.

Those who wish to become acquainted with Reverdy's poetry
can best do so through his volume *Main d'oeuvre* (Mercure de
France, 1949), a collection of his poetry from 1925 to 1949,

which also includes some poetry written from 1913 to 1915. Another book, *Plupart du temps* (Gallimard, 1945), is a collection of his poetry from the important period 1915–22. The three volumes of prose fiction mentioned are out of print. He has written several books of aphorisms and reflections, of which two remain in print: *Le livre de mon bord* (Mercure de France, 1948) and *En vrac* (Editions du Rocher, Monaco, 1956). The volume *Pierre Reverdy*, number 25 in Seghers's Poètes d'Aujourd'hui series, is an anthology of his work with interesting illustrations and two over-long essays on Reverdy.

From *Evergreen Review* 4, no. 11 (January–February 1960). Published with six translations of poems by Reverdy.

Antonin Artaud: Poet, Actor, Director, Playwright

More than any other modern writer, Antonin Artaud is the poet of death, horror, impossible melancholy shot through with the sickening excitement of being alive.* What is perhaps more important is that he discovered new forms, that is, new ways of being exact about what he felt. He was a mystic endowed with an almost Jamesian sense of precision in analyzing his turbulent states of mind. The first thing to notice about him is that, unlike the Surrealists, with whom he was briefly identified, he never used their technique of automatic writing, although he was engaged in a similar search. He was not a Surrealist, but really an early Abstract-Expressionist.

His contempt for writing and his refusal to submit to it unconsciously are consequences of his will to create nothing less than reality itself—not literature about it. The late, long poem *Artaud le mômô* is less a poem than a shriek, a horrible crippled

---

*Some of the translations of titles of Artaud's works have been corrected by Ashbery in a letter at the end of this article.

attacking thing, the breath of reality. He left no neat body of work, but several series of letters, manifestos, poems, swatches of writing in which his thought is unevenly distributed. And the extreme disorder and difficulty of access of the writing he left are part of the idea of Artaud. The first volume of his *Oeuvres complètes* (Gallimard, 1956) has not been followed by a second, apparently because of disputes between his family and the editors; many presumably important works such as his play *The Cenci* have not been published, or have been lost, like his short play *The Spent Womb or the Mad Mother,* or his adaptation of Seneca's *Thyestes.* One must look for him in out-of-the-way places, in translations of *The Monk* or of Ludwig Lewisohn, in letters to publishers, in prefaces to Maeterlinck or articles on Van Gogh. Everything—including the fact that part of what he wrote was literature, and marvelous; that some of it is equally marvelous and something other than literature; and that sometimes he degenerates into mere ranting—points to the violence and exemplary disorder of his life.

He was born in Marseille in 1896 of middle-class parents—his mother was of Greek origin and he may have visited Greece as a child. In adolescence he first began suffering from a kind of extreme mental depression which tortured him physically, and which continued throughout his life. In Paris in the twenties he took up acting, and for a number of years made a living as an actor on the stage and in films. Among the latter are Pabst's *Threepenny Opera* (in which he played Mr. Peachum's assistant), Fritz Lang's *Liliom,* Dreyer's *The Passion of Joan of Arc* and Abel Gance's *Napoleon,* in which Artaud played Marat. He was influenced by the theories of Charles Dullin, in whose troupe he acted, and his interest in the theater led him to write and produce a play, *The Cenci,* based on themes of Shelley and Stendhal, to illustrate his ideas about the theater, which are given full expression in his book *The Theater and Its Double.* In 1936, he traveled to Mexico in order to discover the secrets of the Tarahumaras, a race of Indians who use peyotl in their religious rites. In 1937, returning to France from Dublin on an American ship, he was interned as insane, and thereafter was to spend long, miserable years, especially during the occupation, in a series of mental hospitals. Released in 1946, thanks to the efforts of his friends who organized theatrical galas and auctions of paintings so as to guarantee him enough money to live on, he finally returned to Paris. The last two years of his life were certainly brightened by the devotion of these many friends and by the gradual awakening of the public to the importance of his work. Unfortunately the horror of the years in asylums could not be effaced so easily, nor could that of the terrible cancer from which he had been suffering for some time and which was to kill him on March 4, 1948.

Significantly, his literary career is marked at its beginning and end by two series of letters—the early *Correspondence with Jacques Rivière* and the final, terrible *Letters from Rodez*. It is true that before the Rivière correspondence he had published a book of poems, *Tric-Trac of Heaven*, in limited edition, poems of which the French critic Maurice Saillet says, "they breathe a disturbing sweetness, that of a spirit caught between heaven and hell, which will find only in its own ruin the meaning and completion of its perfection." But the essence of Artaud appears first in the letters.

In 1923 Artaud had submitted some poems to Rivière, the editor of the *Nouvelle revue Française*. Rivière rejected the poems, but found them interesting enough to ask their author to call on him at his office. Thus began the correspondence, which Artaud seized upon as a means of expressing himself, and in which his clangorous voice, alive with a horrible precision and knowledge of his *mal*, almost drowns out the cultivated, gently refusing one of Rivière, who is seeking to encourage him:

> I suffer from a frightful disease of the mind. My thought abandons me at every step. From the simple fact of thinking to the external fact of its materialization into words . . .

> There is something that destroys my thought, something which doesn't prevent me from being what I might be, but which leaves me, so to speak, in suspense. Something furtive which robs me of the words *I found,* which diminishes my mental tension, which gradually destroys the substance of the mass of my thought.

Artaud was unable to concentrate on an object; he was "nonobjective" rather than Surrealist. With his editorial gift for uprooting heresy, Rivière tracks down and reproves this tendency:

As long as you let your intellectual force wander in the absolute, it is subject to perturbations, riddled by impotence . . . But as soon as your anguish brings you back to your own mind, you direct it on that nearby enigmatic object and it condenses, intensifies itself, makes itself useful and penetrating and brings you positive benefits, that is, truths expressed with all the relief that can render them communicable, accessible to others, something then which goes beyond your suffering, your very existence, which makes you greater and consolidates you, which gives you the only reality man can reasonably hope to conquer by his own forces—reality in other people.

Rivière had considered him a Surrealist. But Artaud replies, speaking of Tzara, Breton and Reverdy:

They do not suffer, and I suffer, not only in my mind, but in my flesh and in my everyday soul. This inattention to the object, which characterizes that whole literature, is in my case an inattention to life.

The correspondence closes, with nothing solved—not even the question of whether Rivière is or is not going to publish the poems. And one cannot help feeling that the precise ambiguity of Artaud is far less ambiguous in its essence than Rivière's certainty, especially when the latter ambiguously states at one point that he is "keeping" one of the poems, to which Artaud replies: "One thing in your letter remains slightly obscure to me—the use to which you intend putting the poem I sent you."

Artaud's refusal even to leave a body of work is another quality of his that distinguishes him from the Surrealists and that seems like a taste of hot acid after the purity of Surrealism. Despite the aggressiveness and the "revolt" they were constantly proclaiming, the Surrealists were masters of the French art of "knowing just how far it is possible to go too far." With all their horror of everything sacred or traditional they somehow managed to produce works, such as Breton's *Nadja* or Aragon's *The Peasant of Paris,* that have become classics. Artaud did not cheat. For him there was no possibility of withdrawing a few chestnuts from the holocaust that was consuming him:

There where others propose works, I claim to do nothing more than to show my mind.

Life means to burn with questions.

I conceive of no work detached from life.

I don't like detached creation. Nor do I conceive of the mind as detached from itself. Each of my works, each of the maps of myself, each of the glacial flowerings of my internal soul drools on me.

I see myself as much in a letter written to explain the intimate shrinking of my being and the insane castration of my life, as in an essay external to myself, like a pregnancy of the mind that means nothing to me. (*The Umbilical of Limbo*)

Excluded and anathematized by the Surrealists, Artaud answered them in a pamphlet entitled *In the Depths of Night, or The Surrealist Bluff,* in which he states his position still more rigidly:

I scorn life too much to think that any change at all that might develop in the world of appearances could change any part of my detestable condition. What separates me from the Surrealists is that they love life as much as I scorn it. To enjoy on every occasion and with all their pores is their central obsession. But isn't asceticism part and parcel of true magic, even the filthiest, the blackest? Even the diabolical orgiast has ascetic aspects, a certain spirit of self-humiliation.

In the following years Artaud engaged in activities of varied kinds—translating, acting, stage directing, scenario writing—and even began a scenario based on Stevenson's *The Master of Ballantrae.* He had always dreamed of founding a theater, and for a while his "Théâtre Alfred Jarry" managed to survive. Here Artaud produced, among other plays, *Victor, or Children in Command* by his friend Roger Vitrac, the Surrealist writer whose ferociously comic anti-bourgeois plays are too little known today and have almost certainly influenced those of Ionesco and Adamov.

After translating *The Monk* for the publisher Denoël (1931), Artaud obtained a commission from him to write the life of the

Emperor Heliogabalus. The choice of these two subjects, both distinguished by the horror and obscenity of their stories, shows that he was thinking already of figures with which to people the stage of the "theater of cruelty." For once he is concentrating on a subject, but in *Heliogabalus, or The Anarchist Crowned* he gives the facts of the emperor's life in a marvelous way, often quoting the ancient historians and then going on to give his own spiritual, and no doubt the true, interpretation of them. As Paule Thévenin says in her valuable biographical essay on Artaud (in the *Cahiers de la Compagnie Madeleine Renault—Jean-Louis Barrault,* May 1958), this book that crops up so bizarrely in the list of Artaud's works actually prefigures in many ways *The Theater and Its Double:*

> Hence the innumerable chambers consecrated to one action, or even to a simple gesture, and with which the cellars of the temple, its swarming entrails, were stuffed. The rite of ablution, the rite of abandoning, the rite of complete nudity in every sense of the word; the right of the corrosive force and the unforeseen leaping up of the son corresponding to the appearance of the wild boar; the rite of the rabies of the wolf of the Alps and the ram's obstinacy; the rite of emitting lukewarm heat waves and that of the great solar crackling at the time when the masculine principle marks its victory over the serpent; all these rites, throughout the ten thousand chambers, reply daily to each other, or from month to month, or from two-year period to two-year period—they reply as a robe answers to a particular ceremony, or a step to a spurting of blood.

There is no doubt that long before the appearance of *The Theater and Its Double* (1938), which is probably Artaud's most famous work, he had begun thinking of the theater as a kind of absolute expression. The value of *The Theater* lies not so much in its practical advice about stage direction (which, surprisingly, has never really been taken in spite of considerable lip service and half-hearted pretenses) but in its being a superb incendiary poem about life.

> The real theater, because it is moving and because it makes use of living instruments, continues to stir up the shadows in

which life has never ceased to stumble about. The actor who never repeats the same gestures twice, but who makes gestures, is moving, and of course he brutalizes forms, but behind these forms, and through their destruction, he rejoins what survives forms and produces their continuation.

. . . Thus when we pronounce the word life, we are not to understand life intuited from the external aspect of things. But rather that kind of fragile, moving center which forms do not touch. If there is something infernal and truly accursed at this present time, it is the lingering artistically over forms, instead of behaving like victims being burnt at the stake, who gesture out of the flames.

But the practical means of inducing this all-important horror on the part of the spectator remain up in the air, and Artaud's program of masks, stilts, music, shrieks, the magic gestures designed to induce a kind of primeval terror, the elaborate lighting and costuming and the secondary importance of decor and written text, etc., seem to be not *necessarily* the recipe for success. Everything depends on the talent of the individuals involved and the ambience of the moment, and as soon as one admits this, recipes are of secondary importance. Artaud is aware of this when he says:

To break language so as to move the spectator is to make or remake the theater, and the important thing is not to believe that this act must become sacred, that is, reserved. But the important thing is to believe that not just anyone can do it, and that preparation is necessary.

There is no doubt that *he* knew how to do it, and that his own productions, especially *The Cenci,* were unforgettable experiences. But neither is there any doubt that the more dogmatic parts of *The Theater and Its Double* are useless for his successors, who might succeed in other ways. These passages seem to be a result of the French liking for systems, manifestos and pre-existing programs for action, and often sound as quaint as Diderot's precise specifications for the *drame bourgeois.*

Letters from Rodez was written during the blackest period of his life, during his internment in the insane asylum in Rodez, in southwestern France, just after the war. They were written to Henry Parisot, whom Artaud wished to persuade to publish *Journey to the Land of the Tarahumaras*. But the real subject of the letters appears on the very first page:

All this is well and good, my friend, but a little old-hat. There is something else in the world at this moment besides literature, publishing and reviews . . . It is an affair of general voodoo, in which everyone participates more or less, now and then, but trying to hide from himself that he participates in it sometimes consciously and sometimes unconsciously, but more and more in all consciousness.

He feels a prey to the collective hatred of the human race. Far from being an invisible spiritual force this ill will takes on concrete forms, especially that of mass sex orgies staged in Paris in order to "bewitch" him in Rodez:

There was one two weeks ago in the Avenue de la Motte-Picquet; the promoters of this obscene orgy shut themselves up in a café almost opposite the Labrunie tavern, from which they carried on their voodooing with the aid of a group of Parisian men and women on the sidewalk. There was an absolutely sensational one of these voodooings of obscene and criminal pus last night near the post office on the Avenue de Ségur. It was between eleven and midnight. The result for me was deathly anguish, and a rat, who lodged himself in a piece of bread I had near me on a table and ate out the inside of it, covered my books with rat dung.

What is so overwhelming is that Artaud in his madness should have come upon such precise, hallucinating images to translate the feeling of anguish and cosmic hatred that all of us have felt at one time. And his pronouncements, even when they are not literally true, are spiritually true, as when he says of Poe:

If Edgar Poe was found dead one morning in a gutter in Baltimore, it was not because of acute delirium tremens but because of a few bastards who hated his genius and wanted to squelch his poetry, and poisoned him to prevent his living and displaying the strange, horrifying magic potion that flows through his work.

As in *Heliogabalus,* Artaud supplants true history with spiritual truth. This constitutes his chief importance.

His final works as far as we can know them are invaded by the blackness brewed by his disease and his internment, but which had always been the background of his work, as in the paintings of Cranach and Uccello, whom he so much admired. The terrible seething poem *Artaud le mômô* is among his most important works, and indeed when all of Artaud has been published it may well turn out that he was one of the greatest of modern French poets—in spite of his contempt for "detached creation," this creation is, alas, all we have of him. His famous pamphlet on Van Gogh (*Van Gogh, or The Man Suicided by Society*) is great not because Artaud was a great art critic (which he wasn't because fortunately he could only create, not criticize) but because of what it says about all artists:

> Thus strange forces are stirred and brought beneath the dome of the stars, in that sort of somber cupola that is constituted over all human breath by the venomous aggressiveness of the evil spirit of most people.

This was Artaud's view of the world just before his death. But the dome, though dark and built of hate, is lit by stars and astir with forces. Horror inspires creation. The feeble ray of the stars is all the more important because it is so slight, because it is wrung from blackness, like the almost invisible light falling from the window at the end of Kafka's *The Trial.* As he had said in *To the Depths of Night:*

> A certain kind of pessimism carries its lucidity with it. The lucidity of despair, of the senses agonized and pushed to the edge of the abyss. And beside the horrible relativity of human action, lies that unconscious spontaneity that in spite of everything pushes you to action.

N. B. The French titles of Artaud's works, as translated into English above, are: *Ventre brûlé, ou la mère folle (The Spent Womb, or The Mad Mother); Tric-trac du ciel (Tric-Trac of Heaven); L'ombilic des limbes (The Umbilical of Limbo); À la grande nuit, ou le bluff Surréaliste*

(To the Depths of Night, or The Surrealist Bluff); Voyages aux pays des Tarahumaras (Journey to the Land of the Tarahumaras); Eliogabale, ou l'anarchiste couronné (Heliogabalus, or The Anarchist Crowned).

From *Portfolio and ARTnews Annual* 2 (1960). Published along with "Fragments from *A Journal in Hell*," translated by Kenneth Koch. Copyright © 1959 *ARTnews* LLC, reprinted courtesy of the publisher.

Letter to the Editor (*ARTnews* [January 1960] 58, no. 9, p. 6. Copyright © 1960 *ARTnews* LLC, reprinted courtesy of the publisher) by John Ashbery.

Sir:

In my article on Antonin Artaud [*Portfolio and ARTnews Annual* 2], there are several inexact translations of titles of works by Artaud, for which I am not responsible, since to avoid possible confusion I purposely left in French the titles of all works which do not exist in English translation. *Ventre brûlé* would be better translated as *Burnt Womb* or *Burnt-out Womb* than as *The Spent Womb*, but there is also no doubt an allusion to the expression "tête brulée," meaning a hot-headed person, a daredevil. *Tric-trac du ciel* should be translated *Click-Clack of the Sky*. *L'ombilic des limbes* means *The Navel of Limbo*. *À la grande nuit* does not mean *To the Depths of Night* as stated in the note at the end of the article. It refers to *Au grand jour,* the title of a Surrealist pamphlet which attacked Artaud and to which he was replying. "Au grand jour" means "in broad daylight" or "publicly," with the idea of a scandal being made public, hence a more correct title of Artaud's counter-attack might be *In Total Darkness*.

On Raymond Roussel

Raymond Roussel's name does not yet mean very much in America; it means almost as little in France, where he is remembered as an amiable eccentric, the author of naïve plays which intrigued the Surrealists. And yet in spite of the fact that the public has always regarded him as a curiosity, some of France's leading modern writers and artists, from Gide and Cocteau to Duchamp and Giacometti, from the Surrealists to the school of the *nouveau roman,* have considered him a genius.

Who was the writer capable of arousing such diverse enthusiasms, and why, in spite of it all, does Roussel remain an obscure figure known only to a few initiates? Perhaps there is a kind of answer in Cocteau's remarks about him in *Opium:* "Raymond Roussel, or genius in the pure state. . . . In 1918 I rejected Roussel as likely to place me under a spell from which I could see no escape. Since then I have constructed defenses. I can look at him from the outside." It is true that there is hidden in Roussel something so strong, so ominous, and so pregnant with the darkness of the "infinite spaces" that frightened Pascal, that one feels the need for some sort of protective equipment when one reads him. Perhaps the nature of his work is such that it must be looked at "from the outside" or not at all.

Though Roussel died only in 1933, at the age of fifty-six, there exists little biographical information about him. What little we do know is contained chiefly in his short memoir published posthumously in *Comment j'ai écrit certains de mes livres,* and in the articles of Michel Leiris, the leading authority on Roussel. Luckily for us, Leiris, a former Surrealist who is one of France's most brilliant and original writers, knew Roussel from childhood, since his father was Roussel's lawyer. If it had not been for this fortunate coincidence, our knowledge of Roussel's life would be slight indeed.

Roussel was born on January 20, 1877, in Paris in his parents' apartment at 25 boulevard Malesherbes. His father, Eugène Roussel, was a wealthy stockbroker; his mother, née Marguerite Moreau-Chaslon, came from a bourgeois family of some prominence. There were two elder children—Georges, who died of tuberculosis in 1901 at the age of thirty, and Germaine, who later married into the nobility, becoming Comtesse de Breteuil, later Duchesse d'Elchingen.

We may imagine for Roussel a Proustian childhood, dominated by his possessive and eccentric mother: the Roussels were, in fact, near neighbors of the Prousts, who lived at 9 boulevard Malesherbes; they had common friends, including the painter

Madeleine Lemaire, in whose salon Proust made his debut in society and who painted a portrait of Roussel as a child, and later illustrated his poem "Le concert" in *Le gaulois du dimanche*, as she had illustrated Proust's *Les plaisirs et les jours*. Proust and Roussel knew each other—how well, we do not know. There is a reference to a Madame Roussel in Proust's correspondence with his mother; and a passage in a letter from Proust to Roussel, containing polite praise of Roussel's *La doublure*, included in the publicity brochures which accompanied Roussel's books. The curious similarity between the temperament and work of the two men (Roussel seeming a kind of dark and distorted reflection of Proust) has often been noted: Cocteau, for instance, called Roussel "the Proust of dreams."

The Roussels' wealth increased and during the late eighties they moved from the boulevard Malesherbes to a large *hôtel particulier* off the Champs-Élysées at 50 rue de Chaillot (now 20 rue Quentin-Bauchart). When Roussel was thirteen, his mother persuaded his father to let him leave the lycée and continue his studies at the Paris Conservatory, where he studied piano with Louis Diémer and won a second and then a first honorable mention. He began to compose songs at the age of sixteen, but gave these up for poetry a year later because he found that "the words came easier than the music."

In 1897, when he was twenty, his first book, a "novel" in verse entitled *La doublure* (which can mean either "The Understudy" or "The Lining"), was published at his own expense by the firm of Lemerre, known especially for its editions of the Parnassian poets. While he was writing *La doublure*, Roussel had experienced for several months "a sensation of universal glory of an extraordinary intensity." The complete failure of the book plunged him into a state of violent despair from which he never fully recovered. Later he was treated by the famous psychiatrist Pierre Janet, who describes him under the name of Martial in his book *De l'angoisse à l'extase*. Here is Janet on Roussel:

> He lives alone, cut off from the world, in a way which seems sad but which suffices to fill him with joy, for he works almost constantly. . . . He will not accept the least bit of advice; he has an absolute faith in the destiny reserved for him. "I shall

reach the heights; I was born for dazzling glory. It may be long in coming, but I shall have a glory greater than that of Victor Hugo or Napoleon. . . . This glory will reflect on all my works without exception; it will cast itself on all the events of my life: people will look up the facts of my childhood and will admire the way I played prisoner's base. . . . No author has been or can be superior to me. . . . As the poet said, you feel a burning sensation at your brow. I felt once that there was a star on my brow and I shall never forget it." These affirmations concerning works which do not seem destined to conquer a large public and which have attracted so little attention seem to indicate weakness of judgement or exalted pride—yet Martial merits neither criticism. His judgment on other subjects is quite sound, and he is very modest and even timid in his other conduct.

Embittered by the failure of *La doublure* and the works which followed it, and perhaps also by the derision that greeted his rare appearances in Paris society, Roussel began to lead the retired, hermetic existence which Janet mentions. He installed himself in the Second-Empire mansion which the family owned in Neuilly at 25 boulevard Richard Wallace—an elegant, secluded avenue bordering the Bois de Boulogne. Here he worked constantly behind the closed shutters of his villa, which was set among several acres of beautifully kept lawns and flower beds, like the villa Locus Solus in his novel of that name, the property of a Jules Verne inventor-hero named Martial Canterel, who is of course Roussel himself.

After the First World War, during which he held a relatively safe and simple post, Roussel began to travel widely, sometimes using the luxurious *roulotte* (a kind of prototype of today's "camper") which he had had specially constructed. But he did little sightseeing as a rule, preferring to remain in his cabin or hotel room working. He visited Tahiti because he admired Pierre Loti; from Persia he wrote to his friend Madame Dufrène that Baghdad reminded him of Lecocq's operetta *Ali-Baba:* "The people wear costumes more extraordinary than those of the chorus at the Gaîté." As Michel Leiris points out, "Roussel never really traveled. It seems likely that the outside world never broke through into the universe he carried within him, and that, in all the countries he visited, he saw only what he had put there in advance, elements which corresponded absolutely with that universe that was peculiar to him. . . . Placing the imaginary above all else, he seems to have experienced a much stronger attraction for everything that was theatrical, trompe-l'oeil, illusion, than for reality."

In the 1920s, Roussel began to write for the theater. He had already produced a theatrical version of his 1910 novel *Impressions d'Afrique*, which had run for a month in 1912. It seems that he approached the theater because the public had failed to "understand" the work in its form as a novel. Roussel apparently believed that there was a concrete, hidden meaning to the work which the spectators might grasp if they could see it acted out before them. Produced in May 1912 at the Théâtre Antoine, with some of the leading actors of the day, including Dorival and Duard, *Impressions d'Afrique* struck the Parisian public as an enormous joke, though it did attract spectators like Apollinaire, Duchamp, and Picabia. But Roussel's later plays were fated to receive even harsher treatment.

Imagining that the failure of *Impressions* was due to his lack of experience in writing for the stage, Roussel commissioned Pierre Frondaie, a popular pulp-fiction writer of the Maurice Dekobra variety, to turn his novel *Locus Solus* into a play. But neither the adaptation, the fashionable Caligariesque sets, the expensive costumes by Paul Poiret nor the "Ballet de la gloire" and the "Ballet sous-marin" which filled up most of the second act could save the play from the guffaws of the public and the spleen of the critics. Roussel and his strangely titled work became the butt of jokes overnight, and everyone waited with impatient malice for his next play.

This was *L'étoile au front*, which opened on May 5, 1924, at the Théâtre du Vaudeville. Still undaunted, Roussel had hoped to attain success at last by writing an original play, rather than by adapting his novels. But the uproar at the opening went beyond anything seen previously. The text was drowned out by the jeers of the public, who threw coins at the actors; the latter (who included Jean Yonnel, later *doyen* of the Comédie Française) moved up to the footlights and began to argue vehemently with the spectators. But this time Roussel had his partisans: the Surrealists, including Breton, Aragon, Leiris, Éluard, Desnos, and Masson, who applauded wildly and fought with those who had come to attack the play.

Paul Éluard, reviewing the play in *La révolution Surréaliste,* wrote:

> The characters are all marked with the same sign; each is a prey of the same imagination, which carries earth and heaven on its head. All the stories in the world are woven out of their words; all the stars in the world are at their foreheads, mysterious mirrors of the magic of dreams and of the strangest and most miraculous events. Will they succeed in distracting these insects, who make a monotonous music with their thinking and eating, who hardly listen to them and cannot fathom the grandeur of their delirium? Conjurers, they transform pure and simple words into a crowd of characters overwhelmed by the objects of their passion. What they hold in their hands is a golden ray, the blossoming of truth and dignity, of felicity and love. May Raymond Roussel continue to show us everything which has not been. We are a small group for whom this reality alone matters.

And Aragon called Roussel a "president of the republic of dreams."

Such tributes, though gratifying, were far from the universal public adoration for which Roussel believed himself destined. He never mingled much with the Surrealists, though they tried in vain to establish friendly relations with him. Sometimes he would receive them politely, but he seems not to have appreciated their work: once when asked his opinion of it, he replied that he found it "un peu obscur." His last play, *La poussière de soleils,* was produced in 1926. This time the reviews were as hostile as ever, but a note of fatigue had crept into them: the joke was beginning to wear thin. Discouraged, Roussel decided to abandon the theater. He completed and published a long poem, *Nouvelles impressions d'Afrique,* on which he had been working since 1915, and began a final novel which was published in its unfinished state in the posthumous collection, *Comment j'ai écrit certains de mes livres* (1935). In the spring of 1933, determined to leave Paris for good, he traveled to Sicily with his companion Madame Dufrène, the only person with whom he ever was at all intimate (though their relationship appears to have been completely platonic). For several years he had been drugging himself in a vain attempt to recapture *la gloire,* and he had spent some time at the clinic in St.-Cloud where Cocteau was undergoing the treatment he describes in *Opium.* At the Grande Albergo delle Palme in Palermo, Roussel grew increasingly weaker; on one occasion he cut his wrists in the bathtub, and expressed pleasant surprise afterward at "how easy it was to die." On the morning of July 14, 1933, his body was found on a mattress on the floor, close to the door that connected his room with Madame Dufrène's; the causes and circumstances of his death have never been satisfactorily explained.

Roussel's work can be divided with almost ludicrous facility into four periods, each quite different from the others. The first two books consist entirely of rhymed quasi-photographic descriptions of people and objects; the next two are novels in which description again dominates, but here the things described are fantastic scenes or inventions; the two plays which follow are merely collections of anecdotes which the characters recount to each other. The last work published in his lifetime is the intricate poem *Nouvelles impressions d'Afrique,* whose complex arrangements of parenthetical thoughts prefigure the stories-within-stories of the last, incomplete novel, entitled *Documents pour servir de canevas.*

Though the failure of *La doublure* apparently ruined Roussel's life, we can be thankful that the book did not have the success he had hoped for. Janet says that Roussel considered it his greatest work, and continued writing only to call the attention of the public to this first masterpiece. Actually it is the least interesting of his books, though it is evident from the first line that we are in the presence of a writer who cannot be judged by ordinary literary standards. In *La doublure* he starts out to tell a sordid Zolaesque story of a romance between a fifth-rate actor, Gaspard, and a demimondaine, Roberte; their lovemaking is recounted in a way that suggests how François Coppée might have written if he had been influenced by Alain Robbe-Grillet:

Sur sa poitrine à la peau blanche des dessins
Compliqués sont formés d'un côté par des veines;
Son corset par devant a ses agrafes pleines
De reflets sur leur cuivre étincelant, plat.

On the left side of her bosom, complicated designs
are formed on the white skin by veins; the flat,
sparkling copper of the hooks at the front of her
corset is full of reflections.

Roberte and Gaspard decide to leave Paris for Nice on Roberte's money; at Nice they mingle in the carnival and thereafter the book is given over to a description of the parade: Roussel insists on the trumpery character of the papier-mâché floats, and lavishes his scorn on the falseness of the whole spectacle. It is not surprising, of course, that a young, hypersensitive poet would settle on this ready-made symbol of the vanity of appearances. But Roussel's real interest is in the physical aspects of the carnival— its symbolic value is merely a pretext for mathematically precise description. Just as his exaltation while writing the book and his subsequent despair are the normal reactions of a young poet magnified to an extent where they no longer make sense in terms of ordinary human behavior, so the conventional literary elements in *La doublure* are distorted past all recognition.

La vue (1904) is made up of three long poems: *La vue, Le concert,* and *La source.* In the first, the narrator describes in incredible detail a tiny picture set in a penholder: the view is of a beach resembling that of Biarritz, where Roussel spent his summers. The second poem is a description of an engraved illustration of a band concert on the letterhead of a sheet of hotel stationery. In the third, the narrator is seated at lunch in a restaurant:

Tout est tranquille dans la salle où je déjeune.
Occupant une place en angle, un couple jeune
Chuchote avec finesse et gaieté; l'entretien
Plein de sous-entendus, de rires, marche bien.

All is calm in the dining room where I am having lunch.
A young couple at a corner table are whispering gaily
and wittily together. Their conversation, full of
private jokes and laughter, is going well.

The next fifty pages describe a spa pictured on the label of a bottle of mineral water on the narrator's table. Only at the end of the poem do we return to the dining room; the couple "chuchote toujours des choses qu'on n'entend pas" (are still whispering things which can't be overheard). Love is even farther out of the picture than it was in *La doublure;* the poet, like a prisoner fascinated by the appearance of the wall of his cell, remains transfixed by the spectacle before his eyes, which is not even a real scene but a vulgar reproduction. The other poems in the volume end on a similar note of despair for the unattainable world of human relationships; at the end of *La vue* the objective tone is suddenly dropped as the author evokes "le souvenir vivace et latent d'un été / Déjà mort, déjà loin de moi, vite emporté" (the hidden, undying memory of a summer / already dead, already far from me, borne swiftly away). One sees how much the "new novelists," especially Alain Robbe-Grillet, whose title *Le voyeur* is an intentional allusion to *La vue,* have learned from Roussel. Their exasperatingly complete descriptions of uninteresting objects originated with Roussel, and so did the idea of a universe in which people are merely objects and objects are endowed with an almost human hostility.

Reality, so very unsatisfactory, has made its last appearance for some time in Roussel's work. In the novel *Impressions d'Afrique* (1910) he turns his attention to "what has not been." Here again the plot of the novel is merely a pretext for description. A group of Europeans has been shipwrecked off the coast of Africa. Talou, a tribal king, is holding them for ransom. In order to distract themselves until the ransom money arrives, the travelers plan a "gala" for the day of their liberation. Each contributes a number utilizing his or her particular talents, and the first half of the book is an account of the gala, punctuated by a number of executions which Talou has ordained for certain of his subjects who have incurred his wrath. The second half is a logical explanation of the preposterous and fantastic scenes which have gone before.

Locus Solus (1914) recounts a similar chain of events. A prominent scientist and inventor, Martial Canterel, has invited a group of colleagues to visit the park of his country estate, Locus Solus (Solitary Place). As the group tours the estate, Canterel shows them inventions of ever-increasing complexity and strangeness. Again, exposition is invariably followed by explanation, the cold hysteria of the former giving way to the innumerable ramifications of the latter. After an airborne pile driver which is constructing a mosaic of teeth and a gigantic glass diamond filled with water in which float a dancing girl, a hairless cat, and the preserved head of Danton, we come to the central and longest passage: a description of eight curious *tableaux vivants* taking place inside an enormous glass enclosure. We learn that the actors are actually dead people whom Canterel has revived with "resurrectine," a fluid of his invention which if injected into a fresh corpse causes it continually to act out the most important moment of its life. This passage, one of the most unforgettable in Roussel's work and one of many which are haunted by the idea of death, was written around the time his mother died, after a long series of family deaths. (Giacometti, who read *Locus Solus* a number of times, told me once that Roussel's inventions, and this one in particular, had directly inspired much of his early work, including the sculpture *The Palace at 4 A.M.*)

After completing their tour of Locus Solus, the guests follow Canterel to the villa for a "joyous dinner," and this very full day comes to a close.

In *Locus Solus* and *Impressions d'Afrique,* Roussel used a method of writing which he describes in *Comment j'ai écrit certains de mes livres.* Sometimes he would take a phrase containing two words, each of which had a double meaning, and use the least likely meanings as the nucleus of a story. Thus the phrase "maison à espagnolettes" (house with window latches) served as the nucleus for an episode in *Impressions d'Afrique* about a house (a royal family or house) descended from a pair of Spanish twin girls. Elsewhere, he would transform a common phrase, a book title, or a line of poetry into a series of words with similar sounds. A line of Victor Hugo, "Un vase tout rempli du vin de l'espérance," was denatured by Roussel into "sept houx rampe lit Vesper," which he developed into a tale of Handel using seven bunches of holly tied with different colored ribbons to compose, on a banister, the principal theme of his oratorio *Vesper.*

Just as the mechanical task of finding a rhyme sometimes inspires a poet to write a great line, Roussel's "rimes de faits" (rhymes for events) helped him to utilize his unconscious mind.

Michel Leiris says, "Roussel here rediscovered one of the most ancient and widely used patterns of the human mind: the formation of myths starting from words. That is (as though he had decided to illustrate Max Müller's theory that myths were born out of a sort of 'disease of language'), transposition of what was at first a simple fact of language into a dramatic action." Elsewhere he suggests that these childish devices led Roussel back to a common source of mythology or collective unconscious.

Both of the published plays, *L'étoile au front* and *La poussière de soleils,* are collections of anecdotes. In the former, the pretexts are provided by the various curios in a collection; in the latter, by the clues in a treasure hunt which eventually lead to the discovery of a will. The thread of narration is passed from one character to another, resulting in a lilting and oddly dramatic language.

There is, of course, no more attempt at plot or characterization than in the novels. And yet, the plays are theatrical in a curious way. The anecdotes cast on the characters who tell them an unearthly glimmer that is like a new kind of characterization. And these stories, cut up and distributed among the speakers, somehow propel us breathlessly forward. The plays are among the strangest and most exciting in modern literature.

Nouvelles impressions d'Afrique (1932) is Roussel's masterpiece. It is a long poem in four cantos which bear the names of African curiosities. Each canto starts off innocently to describe the scene in question, but the description is immediately interrupted by a parenthetical thought. New words suggest new digressions; sometimes as many as five pairs of parentheses ((((()))))) isolate one idea buried in the surrounding verbiage like the central sphere in a Chinese puzzle. In order to finish the first sentence, one must turn ahead to the last line of the canto, and by working backward and forward one can at last piece the poem together. The odd appearance which the bristling parentheses give the text is complemented by the militant banality of the fifty-nine illustrations which Roussel commissioned of a hack painter through the intermediary of a private detective agency.

It adds up to a tumultuous impression of reality which keeps swiping at one like the sails of a windmill. The hiccoughing parenthetical passages that accumulate at the beginning and end of each canto tend to subside in the middle, giving way to endless catalogues or lists: for example, lists of gratuitous gifts; idle suppositions; objects that have the form of a cross; or others that are similar in appearance but not in size, and which one must be careful not to confuse, such as a pile of red eggs under falling snow on a windless day and a heap of strawberries being sprinkled with sugar. Just as the hazards of language resulted in the strange "rhyming events," here other trivial mechanisms create juxtapositions that are equally convincing. The logic of the strange positions of its elements is what makes the poem so beautiful. It has what Marianne Moore calls "mysteries of construction."

Michel Leiris says of the poem, "We find here, transposed onto the level of poetry, the technique of the stories with multiple episodes [*tiroirs*] so frequent in Roussel's work, but here the episodes appear in the sentences themselves and not in the story, as though Roussel had decided to use these parentheses to speed the disintegration of language, in a way comparable to that in which Mallarmé used blanks to produce those 'prismatic subdivisions of the idea' which he mentions in the preface to the *Coup de dés*." Roussel is the only modern French poet whose experiments with language can be likened to those of Mallarmé. And there is, in fact, a feeling of disintegration in *Nouvelles impressions* which has been building up ever since the dangerous accumulations of adjectives in *La doublure*, the perilously conserved corpses of *Locus Solus*, and the pitiless chains of anecdotes in the plays (which resulted in a "theater of cruelty" that outdid anything Artaud ever dreamed of, turning a civilized bourgeois audience into a horde of wild beasts). In *Nouvelles impressions* the unconscious seems to have broken through the myths in which Roussel had carefully encased it: it is no longer the imaginary world but the real one, and it is exploding around us like a fireworks factory, in one last dazzling orgy of light and sound.

Many writers, including André Breton and Jean Ferry (whose *Étude sur Raymond Roussel* is invaluable as a key to *Nouvelles impressions*), have felt that Roussel hid some secret meaning or message in his work. Breton (in his preface to Ferry's book) makes a convincing case for Roussel as an alchemist whose books are coded messages concealing the Grand Oeuvre—the Philosopher's Stone. According to Breton, the various clues in the treasure hunt in *La poussière de soleils* form a decipherable message, while Michel Leiris sees an autobiographical "chain" in the illustrations for *Nouvelles impressions:* "Voluntary death: wall of snow and fire, organ point, ultimate ecstasy, unique way of savoring—in an instant—'*la gloire.*'" But if it seems possible that Roussel did bury a secret message in his writings, it seems equally likely that no one will ever succeed in finding out what it is. What he leaves us with is a work that is like the perfectly preserved temple of a cult which has disappeared without a trace, or a complicated set of tools whose use cannot be discovered. But even though we may never be able to "use" his work in the way he hoped, we can still admire its inhuman beauty, and be stirred by a language that seems always on the point of revealing its secret, of pointing the way back to the "republic of dreams" whose insignia blazed on his forehead.

Postscript

The above essay was written in 1961 and published in *Portfolio and ARTnews Annual* in 1962. Much of the information came from my own research in France at a time when very few people there or elsewhere took Roussel seriously as a writer. (I even gained a brief notoriety in Paris as "that crazy American who's interested in Raymond Roussel.") Since then, Roussel has been rediscovered and is now considered an ancestor of much experimental writing being done today both in Europe and America. Volumes have been devoted to him, notably Michel Foucault's study and a biography by François Caradec, *Vie de Raymond Roussel* (Paris: Pauvert, 1972; a much expanded version was published in 1997—*Raymond Roussel*, Paris: Fayard). The novels *Impressions of Africa* and *Locus Solus* have been published in English translation by the University of California Press; and a collection of posthumous fragments (*Flio*) has appeared in France. In addition to the foregoing essay, I published an article on Roussel's plays in an all-Roussel number of the French review *Bizarre* and a short introduction to an unpublished chapter from his final unfinished novel, *Documents pour servir de canevas*, in the review *L'Arc* in 1962. At that time the chapter, which I found in Paris, was the first unpublished work of Roussel's to come to light in the thirty years since his death.*

In view of the attention Roussel has received in the last decade or so, my introductory essay reprinted here, written before Foucault's book appeared, seems rudimentary. Since then, the field of Roussel studies has been vastly enlarged, mainly due to the accidental discovery of a trunk of Roussel's manuscripts and other documents in 1989. See Mark Ford's authoritative *Raymond Roussel and the Republic of Dreams* (London: Faber and Faber, 2000; Ithaca: Cornell University Press, 2001).

From Michel Foucault's *Death and the Labyrinth: The World of Raymond Roussel*, translated by Charles Ruas (New York: Doubleday and Co., 1986). Written in 1961. First published as "Re-establishing Raymond Roussel," in *Portfolio and ARTnews Annual* 6 (Autumn 1962). Reprinted as "On Raymond Roussel," in Raymond Roussel's *How I Wrote Certain of My Books*, translated and annotated by Trevor Winkfield (New York: Sun, 1977). Reprinted as the introduction to *How I Wrote Certain of My Books and Other Writings by Raymond Roussel*, edited by Trevor Winkfield (Exact Change, 1995).

*This introduction is the next piece in the current collection.

Introduction to Raymond Roussel's "In Havana"

The text which follows is apparently the first unpublished work of Raymond Roussel to be discovered up to now.[1] It was intended to be the first chapter of Roussel's last, unfinished novel, which was published minus this opening chapter in his posthumous collection, *How I Wrote Certain of My Books*, under the title *Documents to Serve as an Outline*. In addition to its purely literary attractiveness, the fragment presents a number of peculiarities.

The first is that it survived at all. The published *Documents* was preceded by a note from Roussel dated January 15, 1932:

> If I die before having completed this work and in case someone wishes to publish it even in its unfinished state, I desire that the beginning be suppressed, and that it begin with the First Document, which follows, and that the initials be replaced by names which will fill in the blanks, and that it be given a general title: *Documents to Serve as an Outline.*

Nonetheless the publisher Lemerre had begun by printing the beginning Roussel later wanted to suppress: the proofs for most of it are extant, and for the last few lines, a handwritten note has turned up among papers of Roussel discovered since his death. The fact that at the time he wrote the note in January 1932 he had finished only six of the thirty "documents" which were to make up the novel leads one to believe that at his death in July 1933 he had still not made a definitive decision to keep or suppress the first chapter: perhaps he had it printed so early on in order to give himself time to reflect on the matter.

For several reasons I have decided not to observe Roussel's stated desire that the chapter not be published. First and most important, it seems to me that any text by Roussel deserves to be known. In addition it appears obvious that it was not doubts about the quality of the work that prompted Roussel to write the note quoted above, but a simple desire for symmetry: shorn of their introduction, the six documents form an easily publishable whole.

The personality of the writer furnishes an additional justification: it is well known that he was haunted by the idea of posthumous glory. "This glory will shine on all my works without exception; it will reflect on all the events of my life; people will look up the details of my childhood and admire the way I played prisoner's base," he confided to Dr. Pierre Janet, who treated him. Since the glory that was to come was the great consolation of his unhappy life, we might conclude that the publication of this text would not have displeased him.

The first chapter sheds new light on the documents it was meant to precede and which are, in my opinion, one of Roussel's most remarkable works.[2] We now see that the novel was to take place in Cuba, but that it was interrupted almost at the beginning by a series of digressions (as in *Impressions of Africa* and *Locus Solus*). Each of the chapters is made up in turn of dozens of very short narratives, adroitly dovetailed, which form the actual fabric of the novel. Each document, we now see, is an illustration of the superiority of Europe over America and is the result of patient research by a member of the club of which M . . . is the female president.

However, the mysterious aspects of the work, those surrounding the coded meanings in which it seems so rich, those resulting from Roussel's method of composition and the very nature of his writing (of which he left only a brief explanation in his essay "How I Wrote Some of My Books"), cannot be explained merely by his known techniques of composition. On the single galley proof which comprises the text, proper names are left blank and replaced by initials, while dates are omitted.[3] No doubt this will provide those who believe Roussel's work to be one vast and theoretically decipherable riddle with a persuasive argument. The presence of the initials and the absence of any name or date strongly suggest the use of a code. This hypothesis is all the more plausible given Roussel's well-known passion for mystery and mystifications, cryptograms, ciphers and other tools of secrecy.

Thus, to start with commonplace phrases, deform them, obtain phrases that are very close phonetically and use the latter as elements of a narrative, is to use a code. Moreover, references to ciphers and clues abound in his work: the "grille" or cipher-stencil that figures in the story of the Zouave in *Impressions of Africa* reappears in the Fifth Document, where the soldier Armand Vage inherits from a wealthy sister "a piece of cardboard pierced with two holes, which could only be a stencil meant to lead to the discovery of a treasure." (More of him later.)

As regards style, the text has the same radical concision and the peculiar transparency of *Documents*. After the acrobatics of *New Impressions of Africa,* with its interlaced parenthetical passages inserted willy-nilly in the procrustean bed of the alexandrine, Roussel's prose reaffirms its rigor, even more marked here than in *Locus Solus*. He submits his sentences to processes of condensation that result in amazing verbal crystallizations. Furthermore he imposes a new discipline on himself by forcing each of the episodes of his book to fulfill a narrative function: A . . . 's "measure of authority" serves the same story-spinning purpose in this preparatory chapter as does the superiority of Europe in the documents themselves. Incidentally the procedure recalls the "lists of examples" in *New Impressions of Africa*.

In the course of these few pages we come upon a number of motifs and words dear to Roussel. Among the former are the passionate friendship of two siblings (recalling Séil-Kor and Nina in *Impressions of Africa,* Fermoir and Tige in "The Coils of the Great Serpent," and perhaps Roussel's deep affection for his own sister when they were children); the theme of twins (the "Espagnolettes" of *Impressions of Africa*) of unequal growth (the rubber tree and the palm in the same book); the *catin* (harlot, strumpet), who appears in *New Impressions* and throughout Roussel's work, with a past described as *houleux* (turbulent, checkered): Jean Ferry correctly cites the latter as one of Roussel's favorite adjectives. Moreover the setting of the book, Havana, Cuba, hints at a coarse play on words. Concerning the scatological element in *New Impressions,* Ferry wrote in his book-length essay on the poem: "I shall limit myself to pointing out Roussel's extraordinary prudery with regard to this sort of subject matter in his earlier works. I should very much like to know, once others have studied and resolved the problem, what sluices burst in him on this occasion, causing these malodorous streams to run together." But it seems to me that these references had already appeared, in hidden form, in previous works. Among the objects ornamenting the Square of Trophies in *Impressions of Africa* is a small privy-like building whose gently sloping roof is made of *feuillets* ("leaves" but also "sheets of toilet paper") taken from the book *The Fair Maid of Perth* (the French pronunciation of Perth is the same as that of *pertes,* a type of vaginal discharge); several portraits of the Electors of Brandenbourg ("Brandebourg," the gallicized version of the place-name, might be a pun on *bran de bourg:* "shit of the town"); and a watercolor depicting the "immoral" Flore training her lorgnette (the phrase is "braquer sa lorgnette," transformable into a spoonerism, *lorgner sa braguette:* "ogle his codpiece") on an actor performing on a stage. One could cite other examples that seem to suggest that the solemn façade of Roussel's prose style is in fact riddled with puns, spoonerisms and other *jeux de mots* which are often of an obscene nature.[4]

But "Cuba"; the "Club" with its thirty members, each charged with the mission of "providing the handsomest stone for the edifice"; as well as the fact that, of a total of thirty documents, only six were completed, bring us once again to that "cube" that occurs throughout Roussel's work, and whose possible meaning is suggested by André Breton in his preface to Ferry's *Essay on Raymond Roussel:* "The cube . . . represents one of Roussel's chief preoccupations and one of the main clues in his play [*The Dust of Suns*], and is also one of the capital stages in the production of the philosopher's stone . . . Fulcanelli, in his work on alchemy, reproduces the image of a cubical stone secured by ropes that is part of a bas-relief decoration of the St. Martin fountain, a few steps from the theatre where *The Dust of Suns* was performed." And a similar stone makes a striking appearance in the Fifth Document: "On his twenty-first try, struck by the words 'cube' and 'mesmerize' [*méduser*], perfectly framed by the two holes in the stencil, Armand Vage abstained from further meditative reading: '*A cube would mesmerize him.*' Having lifted a remarkably cubical mossy stone at the edge of a brook that ran through his sister's garden, he discovered a substantial hoard."[5]

One hesitates before a number of possible interpretations. The puns suggested by this "Cuba" where the novel is situated make one wonder whether Roussel hasn't proceeded "alchemically" on several levels: that of the psychological unconscious (sublimation of shameful material by the work of the artist); that of language—Cuba for *cul bas* (posterior), *Havane* (the French word for a shade of tan like that of a cigar) for the color of excrement; and finally that of alchemy itself in Breton's sense.

The text presents a further singularity. At the end of the chapter, M . . . , looking for a costume befitting her role as president of a club founded to publicize the glory of Europe, has a sudden inspiration: "Among some Dresden porcelains displayed from time immemorial in a vitrine in her parlor was one that depicted the Rape of Europa. A graceful garment, closely modeled after that of the statuette—and completed by a flesh-colored leotard—became her presidential uniform."[6] Curiously,

The Rape of Europa. Photography by David Lee.

a Dresden figurine representing the Rape of Europa figured in the important art collection of Mme. Roussel, the writer's mother. A photograph of it is reproduced in the lavish catalogue printed for the sale of the collection, which was organized by Roussel and his sister in 1912, shortly after their mother's death. This porcelain was then an object that Roussel himself had seen "from time immemorial" in his mother's salon (it is perhaps worth pointing out that her name, Marguerite, begins with an M), and is not a figment of his imagination. Yet we know that Roussel made it a rule to exclude all reality from his work;

Africa and America. Photography by David Lee.

Janet writes: "Martial [Roussel] has a very interesting conception of beauty in literature: the work of art must contain nothing real, no observation of the real or spiritual world, only totally imaginary arrangements." For a reason we cannot know, Roussel here uses an existing object, a porcelain statuette sold at auction twenty years earlier. One could hardly deduce the presence of an autobiographical element in his work from the circumstance, but it is nonetheless interesting since it suggests that the relationship between the life and work of this most secretive of French writers may be less disjunct than was previously supposed. The details we possess concerning that life are, unfortunately, minimal, but it is always possible that new facts will be revealed which will shed further light on an oeuvre so carefully concealed behind enigmas of all kinds.

Will the cipher be decoded? Will the secret—philosopher's stone or "hoard"—which those familiar with the work (Leiris, Breton, Ferry) agree that it conceals ever be discovered? It's unlikely, despite the new clues that "In Havana" seems to contain. Doubtless the beauty of a work like this is directly linked to the obscurity of its author's intentions; its charm is partly that of some antique mechanism constructed for a use that escapes us today. Perhaps the message Roussel wanted to leave with us comes down to this: the impossibility of knowing all; the possibility of a superior knowledge to which we will not attain.

NOTES

The preceding article was published in the French review *L'arc* in 1962. I wrote it in English and it was translated into French by a friend, the late Michel Thurlotte. My original text seems to have disappeared, so that for the purposes of this publication [Atlas Anthology 4 (1987)] I have had to translate it from French back into English.

1. 1962.

2. Not everyone agrees: Rayner Heppenstall, in his *Raymond Roussel: A Critical Study,* sees in them signs of "deterioration of mind."

3. This was not a new practice for him: the names of characters were also left blank in the published version of "The Place of the Red Buttons," one of the *Texts of Early Youth.* In the manuscript of *Documents,* which I saw once at the home of some distant cousins of Roussel, dates

were left blank and names indicated by an initial and a blank. But since the proofs have apparently not survived, it is impossible to know whether the names and dates were eventually supplied by Roussel or (as he had requested in his note) by another hand. The names *sound* Rousselian.

Speaking of proofs, when I was beginning research on Roussel in about 1959 I went to the offices of Lemerre, which was then moribund but still extant, asking to see any papers they might have relating to Roussel. I was told that there were indeed files but that I would need the permission of a member of the family in order to examine them. I received this permission from Michel Ney, Roussel's nephew and heir, who accompanied me to the Lemerre offices, whereupon the same official I had spoken to previously told us that they had no Roussel papers! A few months later Lemerre shut down for good and its archives were, I believe, destroyed.

4. I am indebted to Pierre Martory for suggesting these possible plays on words, and also for discovering a copy of the catalogue of Mme. Roussel's art collection (see note 6) at a Paris flea market, at a time when no one knew of its existence.

5. Strangely, Palermo, the city that Roussel seems to have chosen as his place of death, numbers among its curiosities a cubical castle of the Norman period known as "La Cuba."

6. The French phrase "L'Enlèvement d'Europe" could mean both "The Rape of Europa" and "Europe's Carrying Off the Prize."

Mme. Roussel owned more than eighty Dresden figurines (as well as paintings by Gainsborough, Lawrence, Fragonard, Nattier, Greuze, Corot and others), including, in addition to "Europa," two allegorical figures representing America and Africa (see pp. 51, 52). In my copy of the sale catalogue, someone jotted down both the estimates and the actual prices attained by the various lots at the auction: there, at least, America seems to have triumphed with a price of 12,500 francs, as against 1,500 fetched by "The Rape of Europa."

From *Atlas Anthology* 4 (1987). First published in French as a preface to "Un inédit de Raymond Roussel," in *L'arc* 19 (Summer 1962), the first publication in the original French of "In Havana." Reprinted in *How I Wrote Certain of My Books and Other Writings by Raymond Roussel,* edited by Trevor Winkfield (Exact Change, 1995).

A Conversation with Kenneth Koch

K. K.: John, do you think we both might be too much concerned with matters of taste? Or don't you think it's possible to be too much concerned with it?

J. A.: What else is there besides matters of taste?

K. K.: How would you change that statement if you wanted to put it in a poem? I think that statement would seem too pompous to you to put into a poem. Or too obvious.

J. A.: I would not put a statement in a poem. I feel that poetry must reflect on already existing statements.

K. K.: Why?

J. A.: Poetry does not have subject matter, because it is the subject. We are the subject matter of poetry, not vice versa.

K. K.: Could you distinguish your statement from the ordinary idea, which it resembles in every particular, that poems are about people?

J. A.: Yes. Poems are about people and things.

K. K.: Then when you said "we" you were including the other objects in this room?

J. A.: Of course.

K. K.: What has this to do with putting a statement in a poem?

J. A.: When statements occur in poetry they are merely a part of the combined refractions of everything else.

K. K.: What I mean is, how is the fact that poetry is about us connected to the use of statements in poetry?

J. A.: It isn't.

K. K.: But you said before—

J. A.: I said nothing of the kind. Now stop asking me all these questions.

K. K.: I'm sorry.

J. A.: Now I'll ask you a few questions. Why are you always putting things in Paris in all of your poems? I live there but it seems to me I've never written anything about it.

K. K.: Isn't "Europe" mainly set there?

J. A.: No. Reread that poem. It all takes place in England.

K. K.: What about the gray city and the snow valentines and so on—even though the main part of the narrative obviously takes place on the flying fields of England, the real psychological locale of the poem always seemed to me to be in Paris. No? Where were you when you wrote it?

J. A.: In Paris. But there is only one reference to Paris in the entire poem.

K. K.: Well, I wrote *Ko* in Florence.

J. A.: I wish you would answer my question and also explain—

K. K.: And there is only one reference to Florence in it, but the way things come together and take place always seemed to me very dependent on the fact that it was written in Florence. What did you want me to answer?

J. A.: Let's ignore for the moment at least your enigmatic statement that the way things come together reminds you of Florence—

K. K.: I did not say that.

J. A.: Anyway I wish you would explain for me and our readers—

K. K.: Listeners.

J. A.: —why we seem to omit references to the cities in which we are living, in our work. This is not true of most modern American poetry. Shudder.

K. K.: Hmm. I guess we do. I did write one poem about New York while I was in New York, but the rest of the poems about America I wrote in Europe.

J. A.: I repeat, why we seem to omit ALMOST all references—?

K. K.: I find it gets to be too difficult to get through my everyday associations with things familiar to me for me to be able to use them effectively in poetry.

J. A.: Snore.

K. K.: I myself am bored by my attempts to make abstract statements and wish I could do it facilely as you do. I'm going to cut out my previous statement. What made you snore?

J. A.: Well, if you're cutting out your statement, then my snore naturally goes with it, I suppose.

K. K.: Maybe I won't cut it out. Or I might just keep the snore.

J. A.: It sounded too much like the way all artists talk when asked to explain their art.

K. K.: Yes, I agree. I dislike my statement. Why do you suppose we are so bothered by such things?

J. A.: It's rather hard to be a good artist and also be able to explain intelligently what your art is about. In fact, the worse your art is the easier it is to talk about it. At least, I'd like to think so.

к. к.: Could you give an example of a very bad artist who explains his work very well?

j. a.: (Silence)

к. к.: I guess you don't want to mention any names. Why don't you want to mention any names, by the way? Especially since I once heard you say that names are more expressive words than any others.

j. a.: Some people might get offended. I don't see the point of that.

к. к.: Do you mean you're afraid?

j. a.: No. Just bored in advance by the idea of having to defend myself.

к. к.: Have you ever been physically attacked because of your art criticism?

j. a.: No, because I always say I like everything.

к. к.: Would you say that that is the main function of criticism?

j. a.: If it isn't it should be.

к. к.: How can one talk about what should be the function of something?

j. a.: Our problem seems to be to avoid it.

к. к.: To avoid what?

j. a.: Talking about what you said.

к. к.: Let me go back a little.

j. a.: That's always a mistake.

к. к.: All right, I'll take you at your word. But we were getting on to something interesting—but it went by so quickly.

j. a.: This is true of much great poetry.

к. к.: And even truer of the rest of it. I was thinking today as I drove over here what my poetry could possibly do for me or for anyone who reads it. I thought it might make people happy temporarily.

j. a.: That's a pretty tall order.

к. к.: I know. I was just going to change the word from happy to something else.

j. a.: I'd be interested to know what you were going to change it to.

к. к.: Maybe to pleasantly surprised.

J. A.: Now you're talking!

K. K.: I was thinking about that and about what seemed the uselessness of it all. In fact I think about that a lot.

J. A.: Is Joseph Dah* your ideal?

K. K.: In which phase? As an action poet or as a regular poet, which he becomes after the death of Andrews?

J. A.: As an action poet.

K. K.: I was thinking about that in the car today, though I didn't think about Joseph Dah. I was wondering if there was some way to make one's actions as varied and interesting as poetry; I then thought probably not, since I would get too tired, and also there is the problem of getting older and weaker. This made me think about whether it really was possible to retain some degree of strength and youth in one's poetry even though one's body were getting weak and old. Then I wondered if there were any point in doing this. I thought that if I was wondering if there was any point in remaining young and strong and in being great and happy then I must be bothered or depressed about something else, since in what I have usually considered my normal states I am very interested in these things. Thinking thus, I drew into the Hazans' driveway and we began this interview.

J. A.: Do you have any idea about how you could make your actions more varied than they are?

K. K.: Absolutely none.

J. A.: Your witness, Mr. Defense Attorney.

K. K.: You're a wit and I see that you are obviously going to win this interview.

J. A.: I don't like to think that I might have wit. It's the one chink in my nonexistent armor.

K. K.: Your last remark would indicate you don't have to worry too much about it.

J. A.: I'll pass over your use of the subjunctive and return to the "problem." What is the nature of our poetry? I mean, first, is it poetry? And second, does it have a nature?

K. K.: A third question might be whether your poetry and mine are sufficiently similar to be discussable as "our poetry." Let's

---

*A character in Koch's *Ko, or a Season on Earth.*

just say that they are; otherwise we'd have to make too many distinctions as we went along.

J. A.: Can you think of an example of poetry?

K. K.: Yes. Though it depends on what you mean by the word. There is, after all, a certain well-deserved opprobrium attached to it.

J. A.: Mmmm. But just what is this opprobrium and who deserved it? I was reading recently in a book by Jean Paulhan that ever since the nineteenth century poets have been contemptuous of poetry and novelists of novels. In fact, somebody—I believe it was Sainte-Beuve—once criticized somebody else—Balzac, I think—by saying, "Ça tombe dans le roman"; and Victor Hugo prided himself on not being "just a poet." On the other hand, you hear a lot of painters these days say that the only thing that interests them is painting. Since I brought up the subject of painters, I would like to mention that the spaces between things seem to be getting bigger and more important.

K. K.: Do you mean in painting or in life?

J. A.: We'll work this out later. Meanwhile, I once read that as music becomes less primitive and more advanced the intervals between the notes get bigger. Compare the "Volga Boatmen" with the Love-Death from *Tristan und Isolde*. A lot of our good painters seem to rub out most of the picture these days. It gets harder to make the connections between things. Now I'd like to quote a line of your poetry in order to prove this. (Long silence.)

K. K.: Why don't we use some of your lines instead?

J. A.: Okay. Toss me my book.

K. K.: Do you mean you couldn't find any examples in my poetry?

J. A.: Mmmm. You cut out all of your incomprehensible poems.

K. K.: No, I didn't. What about "January 19th?"

J. A.: "Lorna Doone fizzled the dazzling icicle pencil by sheer blue shirts."

K. K.: What are the spaces in it?

J. A.: The words that would explain the relationships between these various things.

K. K.: You mean that would explain how one could fizzle a pencil by shirts?

J. A.: That's right.

K. K.: Could you please give me an example from your own poetry, to make it clearer?

J. A.: I think it's already clear enough but I will if you insist.

K. K.: It is quite brilliant.

J. A.: Nonsense. "Night hunger / of berry . . . stick." This isn't such a good example as a matter of fact.

K. K.: Why?

J. A.: What with the prevailing climate in poetry, these lines seem perfectly crystalline to me and should to any reader with a normal I.Q.

K. K.: When you say "crystalline," do you mean that the lines mean only one definite thing?

J. A.: Well, not more than about four at the most.

K. K.: It does seem obvious. A man is hungry for berries at night and goes out to get them with a stick. Or else he goes out to get them and he is touched on the face by a stick (part of a branch). Or the berry itself is hungry at night and looks to the stick for refreshment, which it does not get from it. Or the berry is so hungry at night that it dies, its whole branch dies and later becomes a stick. Or a man is hungry for berries at night, goes out to get one and it sticks to him. Or the berry gets so hungry at night that in its hunger it attaches itself to something else and gets stuck to it. These seem to me just a very few of the meanings related to all the possible meanings as our galaxy is to the sum total of all galaxies.

J. A.: Since none of these meanings is very interesting, what was the poet's point in making it all so ambiguous, assuming that this itself was not the point? I mean making it ambiguous so as to conceal the apparent lack of interest in the various ideas expressed.

K. K.: Well, if you are following the poem and if you come to a place where you don't know if you're a man or a berry and you keep going along anyway, then you're having a mystical experience. Lines like these enable the reader to escape from his ordinary consciousness of himself. Aside from which, it's very enjoyable to feel like a berry or a stick or a person you know nothing about.

J. A.: I don't know as I'd care to feel like a berry, let alone a stick, and I too often feel like a person I know nothing about.

K. K.: What's his name?

J. A.: If I knew his name I'd know something about him.

K. K.: Go on with what you were saying about your line. What's your answer to your question?

J. A.: No, I was just wondering if ambiguity is really what everybody is after, but if it is the case, why?

K. K.: People seem to be after it in different ways. Actually one tries to avoid the Cleanth Brooks kind, no? It seems an essential part of true ambiguity that it not seem ambiguous in any obvious way. Do you agree?

J. A.: I don't know. I'm wondering why all these people want that ambiguity so much.

K. K.: Have your speculations about ambiguity produced any results as yet?

J. A.: Only this: that ambiguity seems to be the same thing as happiness—or pleasant surprise, as you put it. (I am assuming that from the moment that life cannot be one continual orgasm, real happiness is impossible and pleasant surprise is promoted to the front rank of the emotions.) Everybody wants the biggest possible assortment of all available things. Happy endings are nice and tragedy is good for the soul, etc., etc.

K. K.: You speak after my own heart but you speak more as an aesthetician than as a man. Perhaps there is really no distinction between the two, but some pleasures do free one from desiring others.

J. A.: Name one.

K. K.: The pleasure of relief from pain frees one temporarily from the desire to suffer.

J. A.: So the desire to suffer is a pleasure?

K. K.: No desire is a pleasure. But suffering is accounted a pleasure by many. Let me put it another way. Relief from pain frees one momentarily from the desire to take great risks involving pain but which might lead to some small pleasure.

J. A.: I think that ambiguity includes all these things.

K. K.: An obviously evasive answer, but I'm afraid we're off the subject anyway. A better example is that if one is passionately in love one does not desire a lot of other people. In fact love sometimes makes people indifferent to pain and even death. I know this is true both from books and from experience.

J. A.: I won't embarrass you by calling attention to the obvious flaws in your argument. Getting back to my favorite theme, the idea of relief from the pain has something to do with ambiguity. Ambiguity supposes an eventual resolution of itself, whereas certitude implies further ambiguity. I guess that's why so much "depressing" modern art makes me feel so cheerful.

K. K.: Could you go back now and explain what you felt when you wrote those lines about the berry?

J. A.: Afraid not. I had even forgotten the lines, let alone having written them. And this has some bearing on our topic of discussion.

K. K.: Many poets don't ever forget what they've written. I can see our forgetting our lines either as good or as bad. Do you forget any place in which you've lived or anyone you've liked very much? I mean within the last five years.

J. A.: I don't quite see what the point of that is. I mean writing a line of poetry isn't the same as living someplace.

K. K.: I was just thinking of how your forgetfulness might be criticized—that is, from the point of view that what you write doesn't mean enough to you for you to remember it. I don't agree with this criticism at all. I just thought my remark might stir you into explaining why you don't necessarily remember your poems.

J. A.: If you don't agree with this criticism, then perhaps you'd be kind enough to explain why, since I fear it's a very telling one.

K. K.: I don't believe that you do. If you did you'd memorize your poems.

J. A.: It seems to me that forgetting plays a bigger role in our poems than either of us is willing to own up to. Not only do we forget the place where we live, as I pointed out earlier—

K. K.: You did not say that. You said we didn't write about the place in which we live.

J. A.: Well, we might just as well have forgotten it, for all the difference it makes. Also what about sex, which seems to make no appearance in either of our works—that I can think of at the moment.

K. K.: Do you mean the details of sexual intercourse? Practically every poem either of us has written seems to me to be about love in some form or another.

J. A.: Well, so what happened to those details?

K. K.: I hope they are still there.

J. A.: Look again.

K. K.: Yes, I've just gotten word that they are still there. On the other hand, there are a number of things that would not be there at all if we didn't write about them.

J. A.: Does this mean that you think these things are important?

K. K.: What things?

J. A.: Whatever it is that's there.

K. K.: Do you mean the things we write about or the details of physical love?

J. A.: The things that wouldn't be there unless we wrote about them, blockhead.

K. K.: It is you who are the blockhead for not making your questions clearer.

J. A.: Maybe this has some bearing on the topic of our discussion.

K. K.: In what way?

J. A.: I can't remember what it was that we were talking about.

K. K.: You seemed to be talking about ambiguity; and then you seemed to think that being a blockhead had something to do with it.

J. A.: I think we should clear up the question as to whether the ambiguity in our work is the result of modern life's having made us ashamed of our experiences that we cannot write about them in any other way, or whether we feel that if we turn quickly around we'll discover something that wouldn't have happened otherwise.

K. K.: The first possibility you mention I don't understand—how can "modern life" make us ashamed?—but the second is very appealing. I don't feel, by the way, that what I am after in my work is ambiguity.

J. A.: What do you feel that you are after?

K. K.: Guess.

J. A.: I give up.

K. K.: Do you mean to say that you have been reading my poems all these years thinking ah there he's succeeded in getting that ambiguity he's after, and oh there he hasn't? I mean you don't really think that a main aim in my poetry is to be ambiguous, do you?

J. A.: Well, it would help if you would consent to give a straight answer to my last question.

K. K.: I think the difficulty of my doing so has considerable bearing on the topic under discussion.

J. A.: Since you refuse to reply unambiguously, I must conclude that ambiguity is the central thing in our work.

K. K.: I have always liked your poetry, but your command of logic leaves me speechless with admiration.

J. A.: Perhaps this has some bearing on the topic of our discussion.

K. K.: I don't see how.

J. A.: I assume that you were being ironic when you said my command of logic left you speechless with admiration. Therefore poetry is not logical or is not necessarily so.

K. K.: What you say is very unclear, but I suppose you mean that since I find one of your remarks illogical and since I like your poems, that therefore I must like poems which are illogical. But I don't find your poems either logical or illogical. If you want this interview to have the logic of a poem and not ordinary logic we will have to start over again.

J. A.: If you don't find them logical or illogical, then what do you find them?

K. K.: Your question doesn't make any sense.

J. A.: Neither does your poetry.

K. K.: Do you think there's only one way of making sense? (We seem to be trying to trap each other into making pompous statements.)

J. A.: Yes, we seem to be determined both to discuss poetry and not to discuss anything at all. This is probably what we do in our poetry. I only wish I knew why we feel it to be necessary.

K. K.: I should think if we really wanted to know why we felt it to be necessary that we could probably find out. I don't think we really care.

J. A.: You're right.

K. K.: Perhaps there's an element in our poetry of not wanting to be too definite, not wanting to name things too clearly, in order that nobody else can possess any one of them independently of the whole poem. But the statement I have just made, although it seemed rational to me when I made it, now seems to me to make no sense.

J. A.: Does this ever happen to you when you write poetry?

K. K.: Constantly. It's very exciting when it does; if one writes fast enough when this is happening one can catch the movement of the mind, which is I think something I care about very much, more than ambiguity for example. Of course it's true that the mind perceives everything ambiguously. I think we may be close now to an answer to our problem.

J. A.: Why does catching the movement of the mind seem important to you?

K. K.: I knew you'd pick up on that bit of critical gibberish. But I rather think you know what I mean and that you are stalling for time.

J. A.: Whenever I read a sentence, including a line of my own poetry, I am beset by the idea that it could have been written any other way. When you are conscious of this while writing, it can often be very exciting. I respond to works of art which express this idea, such as the music of Busoni, the main element of whose style is that it didn't necessarily have to sound this way.

K. K.: Do you think the kind of art that you and I like and create might be called "evasive"? Do you think we like the feeling of ambiguity and multiple possibilities partly or wholly because we don't want to be pinned down to anything we've done or are about to do?

J. A.: Possibly. But I think that if we like things that are evasive it's because there's no point in pursuing something that is standing still. Anything that is standing still might as well be dead.

K. K.: What about overtaking something that's moving clearly in one direction or meeting something head on? I mean, why this passion for two things at once? Obviously it corresponds to reality. One sleeps and is in bed at the same time. But why is this so important to us and other artists?

J. A.: I don't understand what you mean about sleeping and being in bed at the same time.

K. K.: Oh. That was just an example of how simultaneous actions or states in reality correspond to those in art. I mean, all aesthetic attitudes or ideas correspond to the real state of things. We could just as easily be so warmly interested in the concreteness of everything, or in its human or divine qualities, as we are in its ambiguity and multiplicity.

J. A.: But all these things you mention do constitute multiplicity. It seems necessary to illustrate this fact by examples.

K. K.: Would you say that's why you write poetry?

J. A.: Yes.

K. K.: For whom do you do this illustration?

J. A.: For the average reader.

K. K.: Do you expect to help him in this way?

J. A.: No, I expect him to help me.

K. K.: How?

J. A.: By drawing attention to the fallacies in my approach.

K. K.: Has any average reader ever done this for you?

J. A.: No, but I'm still hoping that he will. That's what keeps me going.

K. K.: You would say that you write then chiefly in the hope of being corrected?

J. A.: I think I've made myself sufficiently clear and would welcome a few statements from you. How about criticizing some of my poetry, for instance?

K. K.: Which one?

J. A.: Well—"The Suspended Life" for instance. I rather like this poem but I don't like the first part so much; as often happens it was necessary to write it in order to get to the more interesting part, but by that time the uninteresting part had gotten thoroughly enmeshed with the rest and could not be removed without causing its collapse.

K. K.: What part do you mean by the first part? I think the whole poem is terrific.

J. A.: The part up to the first space.

K. K.: Why do you like the first part less?

J. A.: The lack of connection between the sentences doesn't refresh me. Also there are too many things like your work. Such as the "tooth weather information clinic" and "the buttons' pill." I am more interested in the conversation in the middle and I only really like the landscapes at the end.

K. K.: I think "And sudden day unbuttoned her blouse" is one of the prettiest lines in the world. I'd like to talk about "Europe" for a moment; it seems to me to present a whole new way of relating words to experiences and to each other. Since many people find it very hard to read, could you give them any suggestions for making it less so?

J. A.: No.

K. K.: Were you consciously trying to be ambiguous in "Europe"? Were you conscious of having big spaces between things?

J. A.: I guess so. I was trying to conceal the plot of a book I picked up on the quais, *Beryl of the Biplane*. At the same time I heard a piece on the radio by an Italian composer who had taken a recording of a poem by Joyce* and transformed the words until they were incomprehensible but still gave an idea of the original. I got the title from the name of a subway station in Paris. It seemed to me that I was at last permitting myself to allude to Europe, which had been my center of activity for several years, but by merely listing a lot of things and situations that could be found in most other places as well and by keeping the ceramic title of the subway station firmly in mind it seemed to me that I could convey the impression that Europe was just another subject, no more important than a lot of others. I suggest that you not ask me why I was doing these things.

K. K.: It seems clear enough why. You didn't use any cut-ups in writing "Europe," did you?

J. A.: Yes. I used some passages from *Beryl*. I think I might also have put in a few words from an article in *Esquire* as well as a mistranslation of something I saw written by an automatic toy in the toy museum at Neuchâtel (*des mécanismes précis nous animent*, which I misread as *nous aiment*).

K. K.: There's no key to understanding the poem, of course, no hidden meaning?

J. A.: No, it's just a bunch of impressions.

K. K.: Why is the idea of keys and hidden meanings not appealing to you?

J. A.: Because someone might find them out and then the poem would no longer be mysterious.

K. K.: I feel the same way. Do you use any deliberate methods to make your poems mysterious?

J. A.: I don't know, but it just occurred to me that detectives and detective work crop up quite often in our poems. As for example, your sheriff searching for a walnut, a poem which I have always found beautiful without knowing why. Perhaps it's because

---

*Luciano Berio, "Omaggio a Joyce."

the idea of someone searching scientifically for something is beautiful, even though I have no desire to imitate that person.

K. K.: I think what I was feeling when I wrote those lines was that the frenziedness of the search for the walnut was like the emotion I felt for the woman the poem is about. I wasn't thinking of a scientific search, actually. Could you tell me why the figure of the janitor occurs so often in your recent work?

J. A.: Possibly because of "The Janitor's Boy" by Nathalia Crane. He's a love-death symbol. On page 93 of *Ko* is the memorable line, "Some towns of course are famous for two things." This seems to be typical of your habit of making an absurd abstract statement as though there was no point in trying to make any other kind. I find this typical of the defeatist attitude which pervades your work and which I greatly admire.

K. K.: Such statements seem to me not so much defeatist as affirmative. I feel that we need a lot of new things to think about.

J. A.: I'll accept that. It seems to me a reasonable place to end this interview.

This conversation was commissioned by Interview Press, in Tucson, Arizona, and published in 1965. Reprinted in *The World* 30 (July 1976), a special "Reviews, Commentary, Interviews" issue of the magazine of the Poetry Project at St. Mark's Church in-the-Bowery in New York City, edited by Anne Waldman. Copyright © 1965, 1976, 2004 by John Ashbery and the literary estate of Kenneth Koch. Reprinted with the permission of Karen Koch for the Kenneth Koch Literary Estate.

Brooms and Prisms: Jasper Johns

Jasper Johns's latest show at the Castelli Gallery consisted of four very large paintings on which he had been at work for some time, in one case (*According to What*) since the summer of '64. Big in scope, radical in their compelling synthesis of styles, they are perhaps Johns's finest works to date and among his most astonishing productions in this present phase of history, when astonishment has become obsolete and practically inconceivable.

Though these paintings develop from his previous work, they have a new freedom and breadth. Whatever was locked up in his former hieratic emblems—targets, flags, numbers, monochrome surfaces—has been let out, sweeping these elements out of the picture or rearranging their debris into what Wallace Stevens calls "a completely new set of objects." The force of Johns's early work was in its highly concentrated, enigmatic, ambiguous quality: the flag's stripes were turned in on each other; the viewer was firmly excluded, and he had the feeling of watching a battery being charged. The new paintings show to what uses Johns is able to put the energy accumulated. They transcend the limits of the gnomic and of unstated satire.

Johns is one of the few young painters of today whose work seems to defy critical analysis, and this is precisely a sign of its power—it can't be explained in any other terms than its own, and is therefore necessary. Speaking of the articles that have been written about him, he said recently that he liked several of them very much although they were not actually about the work, but rather "made things lively around the work." This is in fact what the work does for itself: it produces a charged atmosphere of conflicting invitations and exclusions, but this is a kind of by-product of the paintings, a buffer state which makes them seem even more difficult and remote. Yet despite their aloofness, their refusal either to satisfy or disappoint our notion of what paintings ought to be, their existence as paintings is never in question.

The largest and most complex painting of the four is *According to What* (a title which accurately characterizes it as a sort of equation with insufficient conditions for determining the unknown). It is among other things a major restatement of themes and materials from Johns's work of the last few years: assemblage (a coathanger, a kitchen chair with a plastic leg glued to it); collage (a torn band of newspaper which is not newspaper but a silk-screen reproduction); redundant written indications (the word "stretchers" accompanied by directional arrows pointing to same); a panel hinged to the bottom of the frame; wooden letters, also hinged, which spell out names of colors and are sometimes painted other colors; thoughtfully staged messiness (such as white dripping over dark, as in Pollock's *The Deep*); and careless neatness (the shaded gradations of the central panel, and a multicolored column of circles in squares, like stoplights). The whole gives an impression of organized chaos or arbitrary order. The canvas is divided down the center by the band of colored discs that successfully prevents any communication between the two halves, marching over the horizontal band of newsprint that might otherwise perform this function. Elsewhere the "red-yellow-blue" letters set up an additional vertical barrier, and further confuse the already hectic brushwork in this section, as much with their occasionally readable message as with their rainbow colors and "sloppy" painting. On the right, a blocked-off area of Action Painting seems to be trying for monumentality, but is impeded by the incongruous presence of a bent coathanger and spoon, and by the band of newsprint that fizzles out on the left.

What is it all about? Precisely these conflicts, these conflicting conflicts, between different kinds of things and between individual things within these kinds, which project a powerful impression of the simultaneity of events as they happen around us, and of the texture of reality. And so it fulfills Johns's intentions as stated in a 1964 *ARTnews* interview: "I am concerned with a thing's not being what it was, with its becoming something other than what it is, with any moment in which one identifies a thing precisely and with the slipping away of that moment, with any moment seeing or saying and letting it go at that."

We cannot "understand" the record of changes Johns has kept, but we can appreciate the amplitude of the means with which he orchestrates his untranslatable statement. One notable feature is his use of materials from the recent past with telling disregard for their present degree of fashionableness. Others are the inevitably affecting bigness, the surges of color, the monumentality and formal clashes, all curiously at variance with the cold and static final effect, but which must be included in any inventory of the painting's contents.

The three remaining pictures are relatively bold and simple, though they seem to be saying that simplicity and boldness are no more (and no less) what was meant than clutter and baroque dissonance. *Studio* is mostly big rectangular shapes including an impression of a door which projects below the bottom edge of the picture. It adjoins an oblong resting on squares, vaguely suggestive of a canvas on an easel, striated with a kind of rudimentary sunburst. Also included are an impression of a ruler (Johns rarely lets us forget how useful he finds this implement) and a string of empty beer cans like a mocking signature, but perhaps also to represent all the things ordinarily found in a studio which the painter chose to leave out, and thus to indicate this omission as well as to add a mournful plastic note.

Much of the force of the picture comes from its being organized around a thin diagonal line that crosses the whole canvas, mounting from left to right like a slow crescendo, past the ineffectual chorus of the beer cans at far right and on into outer space. It marks the top of the "canvas" within the picture and is roughly parallel to the tilting horizontals of the "door." One is not immediately aware of this axis, only of the force it generates among the squarish forms whose stability opposes it, and which nevertheless are pushed into line with it. Hence a feeling of massed, pitted forces lacking in the looser, more ambiguous *According to What*, where a similar diagonal, the band of newsprint, is denied a major structural role through being overlaid by a stronger vertical and by patches of overpainting.

The tilting horizontal axis reappears in *Eddingsville*. Again the various compositional elements either do or do not adhere to its ruthlessly simple program, and their choices again create an impression of immobilized conflict.

This picture is interesting for its allusions to current modes, from Op stripes and discs, given a "painterly" fillip here and there, to Action Painting, to assemblage—this time in the form of cans and miscellaneous kitchen equipment clamped to a ruler, ending in an artificial hand. This might be viewed as a deliberate rebuttal of recent critical attempts to limit painters to one kind of painting; Johns would no doubt consider this a legitimate subject for a picture, since the critics involved are part of the New York art world in which he lives, just as the easel and beer cans are part of the studio in which he also lives. Reality begins at home. And it would be in line with his 1964 statement: "I don't put any value on a kind of thinking that puts limits on things. I prefer that the artist does what he does, rather than that, after he's done it, someone says he shouldn't have done it. I would encourage everybody to do more rather than less. I think one has to assume the artist is free to do what he pleases so that whatever he does is his own business, that he had choices, that he could do something else."

But if Johns did begin by intending to spoof certain current notions of what art should be, he certainly went much further than that. *Eddingsville* is a big, disturbing picture that asks questions about the value of doing different things and proposes few answers, setting up a climate of tension that is further put across by the relentless upward drift of its composition.

The most striking of the four canvases to my mind is the large untitled one of 1964–65 which completes the show. It is one of Johns's finest, strangest creations. Unlike the other three it has no upward movement, but an intermittent horizontal one that keeps to the bottom of the canvas and is sparsely punctuated with discs, oblongs, hand-prints and even an impression of the artist's face, ending with a battered broom which seems to have served to sweep all extraneous material out of this composition. After the density of the others it surprises by its emptiness, emphasized by the rainbow "arches" at the top, produced by smearing pigment with a ruler which was then fastened to the canvas next to this evidence of its use. (The smeared rainbows appear in a still uncompleted painting, not in the show—a diptych whose two halves are reverse images of each other; that is, a rainbow oblong on a gray ground is reflected as a gray oblong on a rainbow ground, with the two lathes used for smearing appended to the frame, like stagehands taking a bow with the actors in a play.)

Is it these arches that give an almost classical repose and spaciousness to this picture? For despite appearances (including the quirky face-print), it has classical breadth, if by classical we mean clarity, tautness of argument, things filling their space accurately and a dramatic trajectory whose every point is visible. All these figure in the makeup of the painting.

Except for *The Studio,* the new paintings are remarkable for their violent chromatics: Johns has never before laid color on so lavishly, one might say "with a vengeance," for there is something vengeful and violating (but cold) in the way it is dished out. The fields of heavy red, yellow, purple and blue in *Untitled* (with some of the letters used to spell these words seeping into them, barely visible, as though there were no longer any point in insisting on names) approach some decibel threshold. There is a feeling of intensity at its peak, of imminent disintegration.

This violence does not contradict the neo-classical spirit of *Untitled;* it is part of it. Perhaps this spirit is best defined, once again, by Johns when he says: "I think one might just as well pretend that he is the center of what he's doing and what his experience is and that it's only he who can do it." This is what distinguishes Johns's bizarre classicism from romanticism. Unlike the romantic, who imagines he is at the center of things, Johns takes up this position consciously: he thinks that he might as well pretend to be there. And this implied distance between the artist and his work gives the latter its fascination and autonomous power.

Review of a Castelli Gallery show. From *ARTnews* 65, no. 3 (March 1966). Copyright © 1966 *ARTnews* LLC, reprinted courtesy of the publisher.

Tradition and Talent: Philip Booth, Stanley Moss, and Adrienne Rich

Style is only a means, even though it is the means, as Henry James said, by which "we shall be saved." Therefore a modernist style in poetry ought to be neither better nor worse than a traditional one, since the final impact of the poem is what counts and it ought to be possible to say things that are equally true and important in any language. In practice, however, this does not work out. While it is true that some of the best twentieth-century poets (F. T. Prince, Robert Fitzgerald, Denis Devlin, among others) write the English language very much as the nineteenth century handed it over to them, they are exceptions.

Too often the traditionalists of today fall prey to the built-in curbs to the mind and the imagination which a traditional style imposes. For many young poets, these limitations actually seem to constitute an attraction. They have chosen an academic stance, one feels, because of a deep-rooted disinclination to experiment, to take risks, to believe that there can be other values than established ones.

Philip Booth is the archetype of the conservative younger poet. Matter and manner are derived from Robert Frost, and he has successfully reproduced Frost's wry music. "Choosing a Homesite," the first poem in *Weathers and Edges,* shows him at his best. Here he evokes the creeping industrialization of the American landscape in lines whose graceful, over-and-under movement keeps dipping in and out of commercial jargon.

> . . . you could do worse
> in truth, than finance a lot
> in some strategically optioned, still-
> to-be-paved development; a last
> choice, yes, but zoned, green,
> and *No Cash Down*
> for paraplegic veterans.

Unfortunately, the very next poem, "Incident in Santo Domingo," is a little anthology of Booth's commonest faults, such as trying to enliven a dully reportorial passage with a few calculating vulgarities ("Marine to the butt, he'd / screwed their women blue") and unnecessary coinages ("and signed his bitching home / with the wife-word, 'Love'"). His irony is often heavy-handed, as when he pretends to excuse his trigger-happy protagonist on the grounds that "The heat / was bad, and he hadn't had leave / for a week." Yet all this might be acceptable if we could feel the necessity behind the poem. It remains a set-piece, battening on the day's headlines and everybody's hatred of war. In short, what Auden has called "a poem written merely for the sake of writing some poem."

We hear a lot about people and places we do not know, such as Condon's Rock, the Sedgwick Boulder, Port Clyde, and a friend named Don Dike, who owns a farm "twenty-nine miles from nowhere." Booth is here flouting one of the primordial rules of social conduct by discoursing at length on topics with which his hearers are not familiar. Most of us, unfortunately, cannot gauge the rightness of "white as / Machias after / the hayrake rain," and after a while our attention begins to wander.

It wanders too when Mr. Booth begins talking about the weather or his beloved Maine islands merely to lure us down familiar metaphysical paths. Rare is the grain of sand in which he can't spot the world; seagulls, dories, and schools of herring are likewise windows giving on eternity, until we begin to suspect that he is in direct, hot-line communication with it. At Don Dike's place he steps outside to "take a leak" and feels that "my water / was part of the ground: I ran downstream / past Don Dike's dark barn / dark where the trout swam light." This final line is felicitous, but one would prefer it in a context less burdened with cosmic meaning.

Adrienne Rich is also a traditional poet, but not a conventional one. She has made progress since those schoolgirlish days when she would come home from a Bach concert worried that "A too-compassionate art is half an art." Such unpressing issues are now left behind. She speaks in dense, short lines that suggest the laconic exchanges of a couple who have outlived more elaborate forms of communication, and she emerges as a kind of Emily Dickinson of the suburbs, bleakly eyeing the pullulation and pollution around her, sometimes being shocked into passionate speech, as here:

> Whatever you are that weeps
> over the blistered riverbeds
> and the cracked skin of cities
> you are not on our side

or, in this beginning:

> Ailanthus, goldenrod, scrapiron,
>   what makes you flower?
> What burns in the dump today?

In lines like these, where inner and outer reality fuse into a kind of living fabric, Miss Rich is what Mr. Booth only seems to be: a metaphysical poet.

Sometimes she does succumb to the mania for over-interpretation that plagues Mr. Booth. (The technical term for this ailment is *objective correlativitis*. It attacks poets in their late thirties and is especially prevalent in New England; elms are thought to be carriers.) In "Breakfast in a Bowling Alley in Utica, New York," Miss Rich, appalled by the crumminess of her surroundings, chews a defrosted steak sandwich "thinking of wheatfields—a gold-beige ceinture—," trying to forget about TV aerials and mobile homes, until she remembers that in one of the latter there is "perhaps, a man / alone with his girl / for the first time." Everybody's hell is different, but a reader conversant with those of Burroughs, Ginsberg, and Ed Sanders, for instance, is not likely to be shaken up by Miss Rich's bowling alley, or reassured by the couple in the trailer.

But it is not often her way to present to us problems which we have to make an effort to take seriously, followed by their imaginary solutions. In this hard and sinewy new poetry she has mastered the art of tacking between alternative resolutions of the poem's tension and of leaving the reader at the right moment, just as meaning is dawning. She does this beautifully in "Mourning Picture," based on Edwin Romanzo Elmer's primitive painting of parents on a New England lawn watching the spirit of their dead child:

> I tell you, the thread that bound us lies
> faint as a web in dew.
> Should I make you, world, again,
> could I give back the leaf its skeleton, the air
> its early-summer presence, shadowless,
> and leave *this* out? I am Effie, you were my dream.

Like the work of Prince, Fitzgerald, and Devlin, the best of the poems in Stanley Moss's *The Wrong Angel* (his first book, though he has published widely in magazines since the late forties) elude the temporal classifications of traditional and avant-garde. The poems collected here are of two kinds: short, meditative lyrics that quickly rise to dramatic climaxes; and more ambitious travel and costume pieces, sometimes in groups, that are less convincing.

In the latter, the poet often turns his back on the reader in order to take a color snapshot ("snow is on the mountain top / Above Granada and hot almond trees below / Blossom pink and white for miles into the valley") or to meditate on the vicissitudes of history, ancient and modern, which can lead to lines as resoundingly empty as: "Through sand a dead child rains flesh on the earth." In the *Lot* and *Antony and Cleopatra* cycles, he sets himself ambitious philosophical and pictorial programs, but seems to lose interest before the end. *Antony* in particular harks back to such misguided experiments as MacLeish's *The Hamlet of A. MacLeish.*

This is too bad, because the shorter pieces are very fine indeed. Once Moss abandons Shakespearian props, once he forgets his European travels and starts remembering those other, inward, ones, he becomes a highly original poet. For the lyrics are travel poems in the true sense: Moss is aware that "Now we are familiar / With ourselves as unfamiliar things," but he also knows that "Who breathes / Comes to nothing: absence, a world"; and in the poem "Sailing from the United States," he announces:

> I leave this crockery heaped on a shelf
> For an old regime, to work myself
> As a mine, subject to explosions and cave-in.

He was wise to do so; the rickety, abandoned mine shaft turns out to be studded with gold. Passages like:

> Dare I lead your love here to sleep,
> To oversleep, the awakening of the world?
> I exchange day for a room, the room for night,
> And briefest thoughts of people still asleep
> Common among these city rooms as sleep.

have the mysterious urgency of Hart Crane at his quietest and most persuasive. A seemingly ordinary phrase like "these city rooms" turns out to have unexpected resonances, like Crane's "uneven valley graves": no matter how often we return to it, it keeps its secret.

In this poem, and in others such as "Pastoral," "Scroll," "The Gift," "Winter," and a cycle about a Long Island summer, Moss explores the velleities of "the impossible sunken soul" in language whose hard permanence coexists with a slow, tender music. "Squall," the last of the Long Island series, is a fine example of Moss's mingled humor and bleakness, of his verbal and visual oddities, and of the compelling lightness of his rhythm. It deserves to be quoted in full:

> I have not used my darkness well.
> Not the Baroque arm that hangs from my shoulder,
> Nor the Baroque arm of my chair.
> The rain moves out in a dark schedule.
> Let the wind marry. I know the Creation
> Continues through love. The rain's a wife.
> I can not sleep or lie awake. Looking
> At the dead I turn back, fling
> My hat into their grandstands for relief.
> How goes a life? Something like the ocean
> Building dead coral.

Review of Philip Booth's *Weathers and Edges* (New York: Viking, 1966); Adrienne Rich's *Necessities of Life: Poems 1962–65* (New York: Norton, 1966); and Stanley Moss's *The Wrong Angel* (New York: Macmillan, 1966). From *Book Week* 3, no. 52 (September 4, 1966). "Squall" by Stanley Moss, from *The Wrong Angel*, copyright © 1966 by Stanley Moss. Reprinted by permission of the author.

Frank O'Hara, 1926–1966

For a large segment of the art world and for a whole generation of young American poets, the accidental death of Frank O'Hara on July 25, 1966, at the age of forty, had some of the incredibility and numbing after-effects of President Kennedy's. It seemed, and seems, impossible that someone so involved with life, who in a sense reinvented it and translated it into a language which we could for once understand, could be abandoned by it. The fact that he was hit by a vehicle on Fire Island, where roads and traffic do not exist, added to our incredulity until we remembered that such violent anomalies are the stuff of Frank's poetry, and that they are rules, not exceptions.

Frank was the first of a group of poets who for one reason or another found themselves almost as involved with contemporary art as with poetry. Other modern poets, of course, have drawn inspiration from painting; but this example of give-and-take between poetry and art is unique in America. There were several reasons for it in Frank's case, starting with the personal one of his close friendship with a number of painters (one might almost say susceptibility to their friendship): Larry Rivers, Mike Goldberg, Grace Hartigan (all of whom illustrated editions of his poetry), Jane Freilicher, Joan Mitchell, Helen Frankenthaler, Norman Bluhm—the list could be extended indefinitely. As Larry Rivers remarked at Frank's funeral, "I am one of about sixty people in New York who believed that Frank was my best friend."

But this affinity with artists was no doubt a symptom rather than a reason for Frank's deep involvement with art. The real reason is probably that when Frank began writing poetry in the late 1940s, the poem was a moribund form. The poetry explosion happened a decade later; meanwhile the "action" was in Action Painting and the other phenomena of what is now called the "heroic" period of postwar American painting. No one with a sense of adventure was going to be drawn to the academic poetry that flourished at the time; nor, with a few exceptions, did poets make suitable companions: they were too preoccupied with what Kenneth Koch calls "the myth / And the Missus and the midterms"* and with the politics of getting into never-to-be-heard-of anthologies.

Thus Frank's dual personality as a poet and art critic was actually a single one, and it is likely that his brilliant art criticism may one day be discovered by those who today know only his poetry; and perhaps the public familiar with his contribution to modern art will eventually read his poetry. Although much of the poetry is available in the six volumes he published, his art writings are at the present time lamentably scattered. Some of his best criticism is in the short reviews he wrote while a regular

---

* From "Fresh Air," by Kenneth Koch.

ARTnews critic from 1953 to 1955, and in his longer *ARTnews* pieces on individual artists, including Fairfield Porter, Giorgio Cavallon, George Spaventa, and David Smith. Elsewhere he published a book on Jackson Pollock; a little-known, brilliant article on young American painters in the review *Folder;* and a number of catalogue texts—most recently those for the exhibitions of Robert Motherwell and Reuben Nakian, which he organized at the Museum of Modern Art in his capacity as curator. (At the time of his death he had begun arranging a large Pollock retrospective at the museum.)

Frank's achievement, both as poet and art critic, is a matter of written record. But in addition to this there was his immense importance as an *animateur.* Few people were so aware of what was going on, not merely in the "art world" but in the life around us; few knew so well what to do about it, how to get people to act in their own and in art's best interests. His loss is deeply felt even by casual acquaintances; its consequences will, unfortunately, be felt by people who never knew him at all.

Obituary. From *ARTnews* 65, no. 5 (September 1966). Copyright 1966 *ARTnews* LLC, reprinted courtesy of the publisher.

Writers and Issues:
Frank O'Hara's Question

Frank O'Hara's bizarre accidental death on July 25 (he was hit by a car on Fire Island, where traffic presumably does not exist) was the biggest secret loss to American poetry since John Wheelwright was killed by a car in Boston in 1940. The extent of Wheelwright's loss has yet to be gauged: had he lived into the poetry-hungry forties he probably would have had a determining influence on today's younger poets. As it is, he remains undiscovered except for ritual inclusion in a few of the more comprehensive anthologies.

That a sophisticated, aristocratic Marxist writing way-out poetry in Boston in the thirties was not going to make much of a dent in the minds of his contemporaries was perhaps decreed from the start. Frank O'Hara's relative neglect is a more complex phenomenon. First of all, neglect in today's acceptance world has been practically abolished: every poet is assured of "a certain" success, and Boileau's remark that an oaf is always sure of finding a bigger oaf to admire him is truer than ever. Given this situation, O'Hara was perhaps more fortunate than Wheelwright. At least his books were published by leading publishers of poetry (Grove and City Lights), and there were invitations to read at universities, an all-O'Hara number of a little magazine (*Audit*) and best of all, friendships and correspondence with a whole school of young poets who claim him as their chief influence. At certain moments he could probably imagine that his poetry was receiving the acclaim it deserved.

Yet it all fell somehow short. Like most truly original artists today, when tradition menaces the individual talent in ways undreamed of by T. S. Eliot, O'Hara and his achievement are caught between opposing power blocs. "Too hip for the squares and too square for the hips" is a category of oblivion which increasingly threatens any artist who dares to take his own way, regardless of mass public and journalistic approval. And how could it be otherwise in a supremely tribal civilization like ours, where even artists feel compelled to band together in marauding packs, where the loyalty-oath mentality has pervaded outer Bohemia, and where Grove Press subway posters invite the lumpenproletariat to "join the Underground Generation," as though this were as simple a matter as joining the Pepsi Generation, which it probably is. Whatever it is, join it; you can examine it later and neutralize it, if necessary, from within.

Frank O'Hara's poetry has no program and therefore cannot be joined. It does not advocate sex and dope as a panacea for the ills of modern society; it does not speak out against the war in Vietnam or in favor of civil rights; it does not paint gothic vignettes of the post-Atomic age: in a word, it does not attack the establishment. It merely ignores its right to exist, and is thus a source of annoyance for partisans of every stripe.

Furthermore, it ignores the rules of poetry. Without demonstrating awareness of even the basic etiquette of prosody, O'Hara grabs for the end product—the delight—and hands it over, raw and palpitating, to the reader, without excuses—for how could there be any? It is not surprising that critics have found him self-indulgent: his *culte du moi* is overpowering; the poems are all about him and the people and images who wheel through his consciousness, and they seek no further justification. "This is me and I'm poetry—baby," seems to be their message, and unlike the "message" of committed poetry it incites one to all the programs of commitment as well as to every other form of self-realization—interpersonal, Dionysian, occult, or abstract.

Such a program is absolutely new in poetry: Surrealism was after all limited to the unconscious and O'Hara throws in the conscious as well—doesn't it exist too? Why should our unconscious thoughts be more meaningful than our conscious ones since both are a part of poetry, and "poetry is in the grass," as Pasternak magnificently put it? Here everything "belongs": unrefined autobiographical fragments, names of movie stars and operas, obscene interjections, quotations from letters—the élan of the poem is such that for the poet merely to mention something creates a place for it, ennobles it, makes us realize how important it has always been for us. A passage which he deliberately tries to purge of all meaning in any accepted sense by dumping in everything in his mind at a given moment, such as:

> what sky
> out there is between the ailanthuses
> a 17th century prison an aardvark
> a photograph of Mussolini and
> a personal letter from Isak Dinesen
> written after eating

can be succeeded by a calm evaluation of the "intense inane" that surrounds him:

> it is cool
> I am high
> and happy
> as it turns
> on the earth
> tangles me
> in the air

and between these two passages (from the long poem *Biotherm*) occurs a mediating line which might stand to characterize all of Mr. O'Hara's art:

I am guarding it from mess and measure.

Despite its distant origins in French Surrealist poetry, O'Hara's work is closest not to another poetry but to certain modern painting, particularly that of Jackson Pollock whose career was so strangely linked to his. (Frank wrote a book on Pollock and was arranging a show of his work for the Museum of Modern Art at the time of his death, almost exactly ten years after Pollock's, which also resulted from a car crash on Long Island; both men are buried in the little country cemetery at Springs, Long Island.) Like Pollock, O'Hara demonstrates that the act of creation and the finished creation are the same, that art is human willpower deploying every means at its disposal to break through to a truer state than the present one. The work of both is in the form of a heroic question: can art do this? Is this really happening? But the fact that the question is at last being asked is itself an affirmation of our power to act on the vagueness that is always "A Step Away From Them," to quote one of O'Hara's title. Frank O'Hara was the first modern poet to realize that the question was there, waiting to be asked, and he formulated it in terms of the highest beauty.

From *Book Week* 4, no. 3 (September 25, 1966).

Jerboas, Pelicans, and Peewee Reese: Marianne Moore

Marianne Moore is, with the possible exception of Pound and Auden, the greatest living poet in English. A new book by her automatically has the status of a literary event, and this faintly abusive term begins to take on real meaning when the book turns out to be her longest and best collection since the 1935 *Selected Poems*.

In his preface to that book, T. S. Eliot accurately placed Miss Moore's work in "that small body of durable poetry written in our time." He also provided a valuable negative definition of poetry: "The choruses of Sophocles, as well as the songs of Shakespeare, have another concern besides the human action of which they are spectators, and without this other concern there is no poetry. And, on the other hand, if you aim only at the poetry in poetry, there is no poetry either." Miss Moore says this in another way in her essay "Humility, Concentration and Gusto": "Originality is in any case a by-product of sincerity"; and again in her essay on William Carlos Williams (both are in her collection *Predilections*): "The poem is often about nothing we wish to give our attention to, but if it is something [Williams] wishes our attention for, what is urgent for him becomes urgent for us."

So with Miss Moore: perhaps the urgency of jerboas, frigate pelicans, or the Dodgers never dawned on you, but as soon as she turns to them they become *the* subject, just as the sentiments expressed in the choruses of Sophocles (slightly dull, like all expressed sentiments) are the spools onto which poetry is wound. The subject of poetry for Miss Moore is any subject in which she is interested and in which we might conceivably be interested. No more is necessary to establish a neutral ground where reader and writer may meet and the latter begin operations. This means remaining apparently intent on her animal or vegetable subject and the deductions to be made from it, and only incidentally producing those blinding flashes of poetry that are the reward for our attentiveness.

In some poems of recent years the distinction of "apparently intent" has become blurred; Miss Moore can sometimes get so engrossed in a subject that she forgets about the poetry. I find "Carnegie Hall: Rescued" her least good published poem:

> Paderewski's "palladian
> majesty" made it a fane;
>   Tschaikovsky, of course,
>   on the opening
>   night, 1891;
>   and Gilels, a master, playing.

What is the matter with this poem is not its fustian quality, which Miss Moore has transformed before (in her ode to Walter Alston and Peewee Reese, for instance), but the fact that she has become dangerously entranced with the purpose at hand. Save

Carnegie Hall! A good idea, but one's total accord with the program is the extent to which one can participate in this poem, as well as in a couple of others, such as "W. S. Landor" and "Rescue with Yul Brynner."

Still, *Tell Me, Tell Me* is a magnificent book. There have been fine poems in her three collections since *Collected Poems,* but most of them have seemed like sequels to "The Monkeys," "The Jerboa," "Marriage," "Novices" and others. The best of the new poems, however, are in a new style whose late, queer clarity resolves the fragmented brilliance of the early work. We no longer have that dazzling obscurity unlike any other since it is not a romantic affair, as in early Auden and Dylan Thomas, nor a question of arcane scholarly reference, as in Eliot and Pound, but rather the result of too many clarities superimposed—the obscurity of an algebraic formula for a slow student. Now she proceeds directly to the core of strangeness, isolating it in a few words, as in the abrupt ending of "To a Giraffe":

> After all
> consolations of the metaphysical
> can be profound. In Homer, existence
>
> is flawed; transcendence, conditional;
> "the journey from sin to redemption, perpetual."

Or the ending of "Charity Overcoming Envy":

> Deliverance accounts for what sounds like an axiom.
>
> The Gordian knot need not be cut.

At times like these one imagines Miss Moore as impatient of the glittering ramifications that accompany statements in her early work—"the swarming madness of excellence," as she beautifully says of Pound's *Cantos.* She seems to be implying that there is a short cut to truth which does not necessitate anything so melodramatic as cutting the Gordian knot—an expedient which she in fact tried earlier in "public" poems like "What Are Years?" and "In Distrust of Merits." These poems are highly esteemed, but I for one did not need to be told that Miss Moore distrusted merits, nor could I accept from her a Millay-ism like

"dust" for "transitory things" in the lines "Beauty is everlasting /
and dust is for a time." Her new, tough simplicity is not a development from these poems, but it might be a result of the discipline imposed by her La Fontaine translations. Closer to the
originals than the originals themselves, these are among the
truly miraculous works of our time, and ought to be required
reading for every beginning poet. Forced to avoid digressions
and to keep syntax and verbal texture severely uncluttered, Miss
Moore created a style whose tense, electric clarity is unlike anything in poetry except perhaps La Fontaine, and even this is de-
batable. It is not surprising that this discipline should now be
bearing fruit in her new poetry.

Some of us will regret the kaleidoscopic collage effects of the
early poems, and with reason, for they were also a necessary lesson in how to live in our world of "media," how to deal with the
unwanted information that constantly accumulates around us.
What can we do about those stacks of *National Geographics,* leaf-
lets from the Bell Telephone Company, the *Illustrated London
News,* the *New York Times Magazine,* business letters, overheard remarks, and also the habits of jungle flora and fauna, which we
shall probably never see and which in any case can never concern us? Well, live with them is Miss Moore's answer, recognizing
them as part of the rhythm of growth, as details of life possibly
helpful in deducing the whole, in any case important as details.

But the rewards of proceeding around the Gordian knot are
also great. Few of her poems make such a quick effect of wholeness as "Old Amusement Park" in the present volume, with its
evocation of the place:

> where crowds flock to the tramcar,
> rattling greenish caterpillar
>   as bowling-ball thunder
>   quivers the air. The park's elephant
>   slowly lies down aslant . . .

immediately succeeded by its imprint in the mind:

> It's the old park in a nutshell,
> like its tame-wild carrousel—
>   the exhilarating peak

when the triumph is reflective
and confusion, retroactive.

An ending as sudden and surprising as the moment when the rider leans out into space.

Again and again Miss Moore tells us in the fewest possible words something we never consciously knew, as for instance that all triumphs are not reflective, that indeed few are; that "consolations of the metaphysical" are *after all* profound; that "Envy" (an allegorical figure in a tapestry in "Charity Overcoming Envy") is obsessed by greed "since of things owned by others he can only take some": further insight into greed comes in the casual phrase "man's uncompunctious greed" in the poem "Granite and Steel." At the end of her beautiful poem around Leonardo da Vinci (who, like the author, "saw as treachery / the all-in-one-mold") she gives startling formulation to the alternatives that face an artist once he has created:

> . . . Could not Leonardo
> have said, "I agree; proof refutes me.
> If all is mobility,
> mathematics won't do":
> instead of, "Tell me if anything
> at all has been done?"

Through these many-colored webs of words Miss Moore constantly pushes the shuttle of inquiry. She is already certain of much: hatred (she would, more correctly, call it "dislike") of hypocrisy, pretentiousness, revenge, self-seeking; belief in moral precepts as simple as the Golden Rule and in the positive value of humility ("humility is an armor"), deference ("deference may be my defense") and restraint ("'The deepest feeling always shows itself in silence; / not in silence, but restraint'"), or, to give all these things a generic name, in continuity:

> Tell me, tell me
>
> where might there be a refuge for me
> from egocentricity
> and its propensity to bisect,
> mis-state, misunderstand
> and obliterate continuity?

Why continuity? Because the way things happen naturally is, if we can find it, our best grace. Poetry is perhaps the most exact model for "happening," as seen in the poem "Saint Valentine":

> Verse—unabashedly bold—is appropriate;
>   and always it should be as neat
> as the most careful writer's "8."
>   Any valentine that is *written*
> Is as the *vendange* to the vine.
>   Might verse not best confuse itself with fate?

If Marianne Moore's poetry confuses itself with anything it is with fate, taken in the sense of Auden's "a way of happening." More than any other modern poet, she gives us the feeling that life is softly exploding around us, within easy reach. Reading her, one has the illusion that one could somehow manage without the other great modern poets if one had to. Suddenly Eliot seems heavy after all, Stevens unprofitably moony, Auden too close to the issues, Pound rhetorical, William Carlos Williams's grasp of modern idiom and life somehow superfluous. These illusions are, to be sure, always dispelled by one's next reading of these poets. But no poet ever lets us feel that we could do without Marianne Moore. Her poetry exists beyond all attempts to draw a qualifying noose around it, in that magical, near distance where verse and fate are best confused.

Review of Marianne Moore's *Tell Me, Tell Me: Granite, Steel, and Other Topics* (New York: Viking Press, 1964). From *Book Week* 4, no. 8 (October 30, 1966).

The Decline of the Verbs:
Giorgio de Chirico

Surrealism has probably been the most powerful single influence on the twentieth-century novel, yet it has produced few notable Surrealist novels. André Breton's *Nadja,* the official masterpiece, has aged badly and reads intermittently like a solemn put-on. Far better is *The Magnetic Fields,* his early collaboration with Philippe Soupault, and the collection of short prose narratives called *The Immaculate Conception,* which he wrote with Paul Éluard. With this work and a few of Aragon's pre-Communist novels, such as *The Peasant of Paris* and *The Adventures of Telemachus,* the list of major works of Surrealist fiction is almost complete. The finest of them, however, is probably *Hebdomeros,* written by Giorgio de Chirico in 1929 and now finally available in English. It scarcely matters that de Chirico, both as a painter and a writer, was "not really" a Surrealist. If this is true, then the term ought to be refined to include him and also to exclude a great deal of drivel that can qualify as Surrealism under the famous "automatic writing" clause in Breton's manifesto.

Everything about *Hebdomeros* is mysterious. De Chirico wrote it a decade after his genius as a painter had mysteriously evaporated. He wrote it in French, a language not his own, and he invented for the occasion a new style and a new kind of novel which he was not to use again, but which could be of great interest to writers today who are trying to extend the novel form. Yet except for a few short fragments, de Chirico wrote nothing else which can be called literature, and apparently he set little store by *Hebdomeros.* It remained unobtainable and all but unknown until 1964, when it was reissued in France.

The novel has no story, though it reads as if it did. Its sole character is Hebdomeros, a kind of "metaphysician" who evolves through various landscapes and situations, alone or accompanied by a shadowy band of young disciples. His ancestry can be traced back to Maldoror, Manfred, and Melmoth, via Nietzsche, whom de Chirico always passionately admired and with whom he shared an enthusiasm for the city of Turin—its arcades, towers, public statuary, and agoraphobia-inducing piazzas are common themes in his early painting, as James Thrall Soby has pointed out.* Like Nietzsche and de Chirico, Hebdomeros is sometimes forced to speak in "a language that on any other occasion would have brought upon his shoulders not only the sarcasm of the crowd, which often is necessary to far-reaching minds, but also the sarcasm of the elite, that same elite to which he boasted, with every right, of belonging, but which, to his great regret, he was

---

*Giorgio de Chirico (New York: The Museum of Modern Art, 1955).

obliged to renounce, as the prophet renounces his mother. This happened each time that a creation of a special character obliged him to isolate himself completely and place himself beyond good and evil, but especially beyond the good."

But if Hebdomeros shares the epical moodiness of other romantic supermen of the nineteenth century, he also has a Socratic strain which sets him apart. Unlike the hero of Lautréamont's *Les chants de Maldoror,* who is committed to evil, he is uncommitted: "His theories of life varied according to the sum of his experiences." His actions and pronouncements, and the movement of the book as a whole, are always unexpected and so take on a power of persuasion which Lautréamont's novel, for all its insane beauty, lacks.

The hypnotic quality of *Hebdomeros* proceeds from de Chirico's incredible prose style. His long run-on sentences, stitched together with semicolons, allow a cinematic freedom of narration; the setting and the cast of characters frequently change in mid-clause. In this fluid medium, trivial images or details can suddenly congeal and take on a greater specific gravity, much as a banal object in a de Chirico painting—a rubber glove or an artichoke—can rivet our attention merely through being present. His language, like his painting, is invisible: a transparent but dense medium containing objects that are more dense than reality.

What gives *Hebdomeros* a semblance of plot and structure is the masterful way in which leitmotifs are introduced, dropped and reintroduced where one least expects them; the work has an almost Mahlerian, or Proustian, texture. Revolutions and assassinations; vast emigrations; comets, earthquakes, and tidal waves; visions of the Arctic, of Africa, and of Greece; bourgeois salons in which the hero feels strangely at home—these form a backdrop against which he moves, "both Dante and Virgil," as one critic has said. But they unfold in such a way that one is seldom conscious of a repetition, only of a shifting, deftly orchestrated texture.

Gradually the novel builds up to a long central episode. We are in a thriving seaport town where Hebdomeros and his friends are living in a castle. A ship flying unknown colors has arrived in port; one of the passengers is a certain Thomas Lecourt who is known locally as "the prodigal son"; Hebdomeros and his friends watch his weary progress along the road to his father's villa, which lies in a park of eucalyptus trees. A joyous parade of citizens cheers him on, but they suddenly fall silent at the sight of the mute, shuttered villa.

The noises died down; the wind held its breath, the curtains which had billowed out romantically in the open windows sank back again like flags when the wind drops. Men in shirt-sleeves who had been playing billiards suddenly stopped play-ing as though they had become immensely weary, weary of their past life and of their present life and of the years that still awaited them, with their long procession of hours, sad or sunny, or simply neutral, neither sad nor sunny, just hours!

A few days later the prodigal's father, whose sufferings "the recent return of his son had undoubtedly alleviated though un-fortunately not dispelled," gives a reception in his honor, which is marred by an unfortunate quarrel between two guests who are acting in a pantomime. Hebdomeros soon leaves this region for new adventures and, after telling his friends a long tale of his own father, he is again alone, a prey to new and deeper doubts of his superiority, his penetration. Suddenly he finds himself with a woman who has "the eyes of his father; and he *understood.* She spoke of immortality in the great starless night. 'O Heb-domeros,' she said, 'I am Immortality. Nouns have their gender, or rather their sex, as you once said with much finesse, and the verbs, alas, decline. Have you ever thought of my death? Have you ever thought of the death of my death? Have you *thought of my life?* One day, O brother . . .'"

And the book ends with a view of "green islands, marvelous islands," where "a long sacred procession of celestial birds, of an immaculate whiteness, flew by singing." The not entirely satis-factory enactment of the return of the prodigal has found a perfected form; immortality is a female noun with the eyes of the father: she exists beyond the "declining verbs" of living, dying, and being born again, a hard-to-define deity, rather like the one Nietzsche seems always to be implying, and one in whom the fantastic fluctuation of Hebdomeros's super-mind may finally be contained and resolved.

De Chirico himself has long since vanished inside this im-mortality. His deliberate rejection of the work for which the world remembers him seems curiously prefigured and perhaps even justified by a number of passages in *Hebdomeros,* of which this is perhaps the most unforgettable: "Though autumn had stripped bare the century-old trees, this whole vast horizon spoke of everlasting life."

Review of Giorgio de Chirico's *Hebdomeros* (New York: Four Seasons Book Society, 1966). From *Book Week* 4, no. 15 (December 18, 1966). Reprinted as a preface to *Hebdomeros* (New York: PAJ Publications, 1988). Reprinted as an introduction to *Hebdomeros* (Cambridge, MA: Exact Change, 1992).

Introduction to a Reading by Robert Duncan

Robert Duncan, as I'm sure most of you know, is one of our finest contemporary poets. He was born in Oakland, California, January 7, 1919, under the sign of Capricorn which is characterized by the medieval book of Arcandam as "one who reaches the heights while keeping his eyes on the ground." According to Mr. Duncan's publisher he was a college dropout in the late thirties; during the Second World War he lived in New York, where he edited the *Experimental Review* with Sanders Russell, publishing such writers as Anaïs Nin, Henry Miller, Lawrence Durrell, and Kenneth Patchen. He returned to California where he has mostly lived since, except for a period in the mid-fifties when he taught at Black Mountain College, and with his friends Charles Olson and Robert Creeley established a revolutionary kind of poetry, which we now know as "Black Mountain."

His most recent books of poetry are *Roots and Branches* and *Bending the Bow;* his early poems, dating from the days in New York, were recently republished in a book called *The Years as Catches,* and reading them for the first time I was struck by their tone, a peculiar, resonant blend of metaphysical poetry and Surrealism which was typical of much of the advanced poetry written in America in the late thirties and forties—a fine and touching moment in our poetry that has so far been little noticed by subsequent critics, and which combined elements of French and English Surrealism with American plain directness—we find it in poets like Delmore Schwartz, Paul Goodman, Jean Garrigue, the Auden of that period, Randall Jarrell, George Barker and others—a brief Renaissance flourishing in the shadow of the war, eventually to be disrupted by it as the poets became war poets and other kinds of poets. It seems from this distance a kind of golden age, when our poets who counted as poets spoke different dialects of a common poetic language.

Robert Duncan, more than any other poet, is a bridge between that world and today's. Formed by the forties Surreal or at any rate "experimental" poetry, as it was called then, he has continually pushed on toward a kind of poetry that is more truly experimental. He is the alchemist of modern poets, and his work is an endless series of experiments, each changing the nature of the last (he has written that each poem is a revision of what has gone before). Alchemy exists beyond a universal doubt that it can realize its object, just as Duncan's quest can never be fulfilled precisely because it is an ideal one. Yet in the course of it he enlarges his preoccupations so that their original goal is lost in revelations. Reading him, we feel we are living into the body, down toward the soul which is below rather than above, until one day we emerge on the heights, like Capricorn, without realizing that was where we were heading all along. This arrival is not an isolated moment in Duncan's progress but the total of all his explorations of mind, body, religion, love, sex, politics, each of which has changed the others as breaths modify the life that precedes them, and whose essence is their continuing. But he has said it better in his poem called "Structure of Rime XXIV," which begins: "In the joy of the new work he raises horns of sublime sound into the heat surrounding the sheets of crystalline water to make walls in the music. // And in every repeat majestic sequences of avenues branch into halls where lovers and workers, fathers, mothers and children gather, in a life, a life-work, the grand opus of their humanity, the old alchemists' dream."

And which ends: "And we have made a station of the way to the hidden city in the rooms where we are."

From a reading given at the YMHA, New York City (1967).

Up from the Underground:
Jane Bowles

Few surface literary reputations are as glamorous as the underground one Jane Bowles has enjoyed since her novel *Two Serious Ladies* was published in 1943. The extreme rarity of the book, once it went out of print, has augmented its legend. When a London publisher wanted to reprint it three years ago, even Mrs. Bowles was unable to supply him with a copy.

With the present publication of her "collected works," which comes with an introduction by Truman Capote and blurbs by Tennessee Williams ("my favorite book"), Alan Sillitoe ("a landmark in twentieth-century American literature") and others, Jane Bowles has at last surfaced. It is to be hoped that she will now be recognized for what she is: one of our best modern writers of fiction. At the same time it should be pointed out that she is not quite the sort of writer that her imposing list of Establishment admirers seems to suggest. Her work is unrelated to theirs, and in fact it stands alone in contemporary literature, though if one can imagine George Ade and Kafka collaborating on a modern version of Bunyan's "Pilgrim's Progress" one will have a faint idea of the qualities of *Two Serious Ladies*.

Her collected works are comprised of the novel, the play *In the Summer House* and seven shorter pieces. Each deals in some way with the conflict between the weak and the strong, a conflict which in Mrs. Bowles's work usually results in a draw. Her strong characters are nervous, domineering women given to ruthless but inaccurate self-analysis. They believe themselves to be idealists, and are in search of some fixed, but vague, goal. In the end they collapse, undone by their failure to take "the terrible strength of the weak" into account. The weak scarcely fare any better. They have developed organs for surviving the attacks of the strong, but, hopelessly in love with them, they rarely survive their immolation.

Sometimes a final glimmer of hope comes to them, in the form of endless vistas of despair. Mrs. Constable, alcoholic and bereft of her daughter at the end of *In the Summer House,* achieves this negative fulfillment and emerges as the only character in the play to command our negative respect: "They say that people can't live unless they fill their lives with petty details. That's people's way of avoiding the black pit. I'm just a weak, ordinary, very ordinary woman in her middle years, but I've been able to wipe all the petty details from my life . . . all of them. I never rush or get excited about anything. I've dumped my entire life out the window."

Two Serious Ladies tells the separate odysseys of two very different women: Christina Goering and Frieda Copperfield. Miss Goering, a "strong" character, decides she can achieve salvation only through divesting herself of her family mansion and living on less than a tenth of her income. She rents a small, uncomfortable house on what appears to be Staten Island and surrounds herself with a nondescript circle of friends, whom she regularly deserts to make mysterious night forays into a nearby town, where she takes up with Andy, a despondent barfly. Mrs. Copperfield reluctantly accompanies her husband on a trip to Panama, and finds herself perversely happy with Pacifica, a prostitute, in the seamy Hotel de las Palmas.

Only twice do the paths of the two heroines cross: at the beginning of the book and at the end, when they meet in a restaurant. Miss Goering now believes herself to be well on the way to the curious self-realization she has in mind. Mrs. Copperfield has taken a drunken "downward path to wisdom" like Mrs. Constable's in *In the Summer House;* she is now in love with Pacifica, who is about to marry a young man. "I can't live without her, not for a minute. I'd go completely to pieces," Mrs. Copperfield confides to Miss Goering, who replies without irony: "But you have gone to pieces, or do I misjudge you dreadfully?"

> "True enough," said Mrs. Copperfield, bringing her fist down on the table and looking very mean. "I have gone to pieces, which is a thing I've wanted to do for years. I know I am as guilty as can be, but I have my happiness, which I guard like a wolf, and I have authority now and a certain amount of daring, which, if you remember correctly, I never had before."

But the real tragedy is Miss Goering's. Mrs. Copperfield can gauge the depths to which she has sunk, but Christina in her quest for sainthood remains oblivious of the disastrous effect she has on other people, including Andy, who apparently committed suicide after she left him. With her probing but limited insight into herself she manages to perceive at the end of the novel that "hope had discarded a childish form forever," but this perception comes meshed with a further and graver delusion:

> "Certainly I am nearer to becoming a saint," reflected Miss Goering, "but is it possible that a part of me hidden from my sight is piling sin upon sin as fast as Mrs. Copperfield?" This latter possibility Miss Goering thought to be of considerable interest but of no great importance.

Mrs. Bowles's seemingly casual, colloquial prose is a constant miracle; every line rings as true as a line of poetry, though there is certainly nothing "poetic" about it, except insofar as the awkwardness of our everyday attempts at communication is poetic. This awkwardness can rise to comic heights, and in doing so evoke visions of a nutty America that we have to recognize as ours. An old man whom Christina questions about a certain cabaret in a place called Pig Snout's Hook replies:

> "Yes . . . certain people do like that type of music and there are people who live together and eat at table together stark naked all the year long and there are others who we both know about"—he looked very mysterious—"but," he continued, "in my day money was worth a pound of sugar or butter or lard any time. When we went out we got what we paid for plus a dog jumpin' through burning hoops, and steaks you could rest your chin on."

In her later stories Mrs. Bowles has played down the picaresque local color she used to such effect in the novel. Especially in "A Stick of Green Candy," the story which ends the book and is apparently her most recent, she achieves a new austerity that is as impressive as anything she has done. As in all her work, it is impossible to deduce the end of a sentence from its beginning, or a paragraph from the one that preceded it, or how one of the characters will reply to another. And yet the whole flows marvelously and inexorably to its cruel, lucid end;

it becomes itself as we watch it. No other contemporary writer can consistently produce surprise of this quality, the surprise that is the one essential ingredient of great art. Jane Bowles deals almost exclusively in this rare commodity.

Review of *The Collected Works of Jane Bowles,* introduction by Truman Capote (New York: Farrar, Straus and Giroux, 1966). From the *New York Times Book Review* (January 29, 1967).

Alfred Chester's Sweet Freaks

Throwing the book—almost any book will do—at humanity for having made a mess of itself has become a kind of compulsory athletic credit for the budding novelist. Recently, William Burroughs and Hubert Selby Jr. have proved not only that the "modern world" is a singularly horrible place, but also that it is a lot more horrible than Céline and Genet thought it was. The journey to the end of night has been rerouted via the last exit to Brooklyn, where, as anyone who has never been there knows, human existence is ghastly beyond belief. And the implication is always that the reader is somehow to blame for this. "*You* made the world this way, you faceless *hypocrite lecteur!* Do you think I enjoy writing like this? You make me do it and I hate you for it!" So that it is increasingly difficult to approach a new work of fiction without feeling guilty about not feeling that collective guilt which is supposed to be as inherent in us as magnanimity was in the Noble Savage.

"Ah, the human estate, the human estate," sighs a character in *The Exquisite Corpse* who could be a spokesman for the author, and there are indeed signs that Alfred Chester was intending to sum up once more the prosecution's case against John Doe (the name, alas, of another of the characters in this novel). He has assembled a large cast of freaks and ghouls to act in a Grand Guignol morality play intended to eclipse all other recent efforts in the genre. Fortunately the enthusiasm he brings to this task has carried him over into a world of make-believe that for all its horror is somehow companionable. At the very moment when he is piling the Pelion of perversion on the Ossa of scatology, Chester breaks into a schoolboy giggle and the whole edifice comes clattering down in multicolored fragments, some of them lovely. The novel is not an indictment nor a scream, but a lively macabre diversion, recommended to readers with strong stomachs—but is there still anybody who hasn't one?

The characters are introduced in a rapid series of vignettes. Xavier's curiosity about his dying father's body leads him to finger the exposed intestine, spraying the sickroom with liquid excrement. Mary Poorpoor has a lesbian "husband": the fairies steal her baby and leave a monstrous changeling in its place. Baby Poorpoor himself, a pudgy, unlovable fruit, metamorphoses into James Madison who in turn becomes the nymphomaniac Madame Madison. T. S. Ferguson, a happily married commuter, doubles as the sadistic John Doe who keeps James Madison as a sex-slave in a city apartment. Tommy, whose handsome face turned hideous after an operation, is in love with a Puerto Rican named Ismael who writes letters signed "Isobel" to Dr. Rose Franzblau. The outlines of the characters merge freely. Is Tomtom Jim, the Negro "exterminating angel," a combination of Tommy and of James Madison? It is hard to say for sure, but the novel is so loosely constructed—like the Surrealist parlor game from which it takes its name—that this scarcely matters.

The looseness could have been exploited to better effect if Chester—as he sometimes seems about to do—had in the end drawn all the far-flung destinies of his characters into a Gordian knot, the way Dickens did in *Bleak House* for instance. Instead he has settled for an all-over, pointillist field that is otherwise effective. He has used the materials of a novel to make something like a poem—a hybrid thing, but a thing still very much worth doing, as the poisoned eloquence of his writing proves on almost every other page.

The endlessly varied theme of the novel, which in the end does associate the various limbs of the *cadavre exquis* into a kind of whole, is the familiar one of masks and identities. John Anthony, apparently yet another of Baby Poorpoor's alter egos, lives in a kind of Salvation Army warehouse of discarded costumes, where he fashions lifelike masks for himself and for disfigured Tommy. Mary Poorpoor's baby can be seen by others but not by herself (just as Chester's first novel dealt with a corpse who was visible to everyone but the narrator). Baby's name changes merely because he happens to be wearing a windbreaker marked "James Madison High School." And Ismael, disfigured himself at the end of the book, is delighted that terrified passersby think the new face is "really him."

These shifting Pirandellian transformations eventually take on tragic urgency through sheer repetition, and when a series of long-anticipated deaths finally arrives, it is as though a miniature world were crumbling. (The death of James Madison, which happens in a carnivorous forest connected by phone booth to the outside world, is one of the most haunting passages in the book.) Characters we have resisted believing in suddenly become larger than life as they appear for the curtain call.

In general, *The Exquisite Corpse* is a far more satisfying book than *Jamie Is My Heart's Desire*, Chester's first novel. That work was highly praised, but in my opinion was aimless and carelessly written, its deliberate ugliness both gratuitous and half-hearted. Here, on the contrary, it is *meant;* and though rats scamper under the Brooklyn El and razor-wielding maniacs lurk under arc-lamps oftener in this novel than they do in real life, Chester can often rise to powerful evocations of metropolitan grandeur and misery and weave them into a disturbing metaphysical worldview, for example: "Here was the everlasting tree-lined street with its soothing shadows, its tremendous yellow moon, its smell of cut grass and of drenched lilac. Here, change and death were gay masks worn by the eternal past so as not to bare its grotesque constancy."

One is left feeling impatient with Chester for his occasionally slapdash handling of some marvelous raw materials; for loose ends; for his teenager's fascination with the gothic and grotesque; and for things that look, smell, taste, and sound bad. And sometimes for his writing, which can pass from heights of incandescent evil to the homespun thirties surrealism of Saroyan's *The Man on the Flying Trapeze*. His next novel could be the major statement that has been awaited from him. Yet meanwhile, one still emerges from the acid bath of this one feeling singularly toned up. It's as though Chester were confronting us with the sadistic leer of his John Doe after the latter has succeeded in bringing tears to James Madison's eyes: "Does that story make you feel bad?" he asked. "Does it make you feel human?"

Review of Alfred Chester's *The Exquisite Corpse* (New York: Simon and Schuster, 1967). From *Book Week* 4, no. 27 (March 12, 1967).

A Game with Shifting Mirrors: Jorge Luis Borges

In the six years since he won the International Publishers Prize, Jorge Luis Borges has been belatedly recognized in this country as the greatest living Spanish-language writer. *A Personal Anthology,* first published in Buenos Aires in 1961, is the fifth of his books to appear in English in as many years. It is the author's own choice of his favorite works, arranged without regard for chronology but according to "sympathies and differences."

Speaking of his choice in a prologue, Borges announces: "I should like to be judged by it, justified or reproved because of it, and not by certain exercises in excessive and apocryphal local color which keep cropping up in anthologies and which I can not recall without a blush." It would seem that he is referring to some of the very pieces on which his reputation rests, such as "The Garden of Forking Paths," "The Immortal," "The Babylon Lottery," "Tlön, Uqbar, Orbis Tertius," "Pierre Ménard, Author of Don Quixote" and "The Approach to Al-Mu'tasim." To describe these masterpieces as exercises in local color is either some elaborate Borgesian jest or else the sign of an urge toward auto-da-fé as obscure to us as Kafka's deathbed injunction to destroy his works.

Indeed, a reader coming to Borges's books for the first time would do better to begin with *Ficciones* or *Labyrinths,* for not only does the present collection omit the works mentioned earlier, but it also overemphasizes the somewhat less satisfactory poetry and the brief, rather fragile parables which were collected in *Dreamtigers*. Nevertheless, *A Personal Anthology* does include "The Aleph," a magnificent and celebrated story not hitherto available in English, as well as a number of other well-known pieces: "Death and the Compass," "Funes, the Memorious," "A New Refutation of Time."

Of course, there is no reason to believe that this book is intended for the "general reader," nor even to take Borges's own statement of its purpose too seriously, in view of the examples of literary duplicity that abound in his work. And then there is the curious fact that this book partially duplicates his other books available in English, which in turn partially duplicate each other, so that the very form of his English-language oeuvre is, in his own phrase, "a game with shifting mirrors." Could the author in fact have planned it this way? His Pierre Ménard is a minor twentieth-century French writer who succeeds so well in totally identifying himself with Cervantes that he is actually able to write a couple of chapters of *Don Quixote* exactly as Cervantes wrote them. Borges quotes two identical passages from the Cervantes and Ménard versions, praising the latter as more remarkable given the circumstances and time of its creation. And he concludes: "Would not the attributing of 'The Imitation of Christ' to Louis-Ferdinand Céline or James Joyce be a sufficient renovation of its tenuous spiritual counsels?"

Perhaps a similar if contrary idea presided over the selection of *A Personal Anthology*. Mightn't as strange and marvelous a writer as Jorge Luis Borges appear even more so when stripped of his finest creations, or rather with just enough of them put together with enough lesser pieces to persuade the reader that Borges is someone else: perhaps that "other" Borges in his parable "Borges and I"—not the one who "contrives his literature" but the one who likes "hourglasses, maps, eighteenth-century typography, the taste of coffee and Robert Louis Stevenson's prose"?

Borges's prologue also contains what I believe to be another red herring. He writes: "Croce held that art is expression; to this exigency, or to a deformation of this exigency, we owe the worst literature of our time . . . Sometimes I, too, sought expression. I know now that my gods grant me no more than allusion or mention." This might in fact be true of some of the more schematic tales in this volume, such as "The End" or "The Captive"—bony allegories with some of the aridity of Unamuno's fiction, or, at worst, suggestive of O. Henry, Richard Harding Davis or Lord Dunsany. But elsewhere Borges is revealed as a master of "expression," which he defines as the ability to "reproduce a mental process with precision." Sometimes he even carries it to the point of expressionism in phrases like "from the dusty garden arose the useless cry of a bird"; but oftener it is fantastic accuracy—or accurate fantasy—that overpowers us, as in this description of the Emperor of China's vast palace: "It seemed impossible that the earth should be anything other than gardens, watercourses, architectural and other forms of splendor. Each hundred steps a tower cut the air; to the eye their color was identical, though the first one was yellow and the last scarlet, so delicate were the gradations and so long the series."

In fact, the danger with Borges is that the reader may overlook texture and content for the implacable outline that contains them. In her book *Borges: the Labyrinth Maker,* Ana Maria Barrenechea calls him "an admirable writer pledged to destroy reality and convert Man into a shadow." But she immediately adds, "Nonetheless, a purely negative and false idea of Borges's work should not result . . . Borges's creativity is characterized by the richness and complexity of his art." Nor are the catalogues of minutiae and trivial events which he translates into desolate visions of eternity as discouraging as their infiniteness at first suggests.

True, Funes the Memorious can remember everything he has ever experienced, and the sum total of these memories is chaos. "He remembered the shapes of the clouds in the south at dawn on the 30th of April 1882, and he could compare them in his recollection with the marbled grain in the design of the leather-bound book which he had seen only once, and with the lines in the spray which an oar raised in the Rio Negro on the eve of the battle of the Quebracho"; at the same time he is "almost incapable of general, platonic ideas. It was not only difficult for him to understand that the generic term *dog* embraced so many unlike specimens of different sizes and different forms; he was disturbed by the fact that a dog at three-fourteen (seen in profile) should have the same name as the dog at three-fifteen (seen from the front)."

Similarly, the narrator in "The Aleph" has a sudden vision of everything in the universe: "I saw the delicate bone structure of a hand; I saw the survivors of a battle sending out post cards . . . I saw the oblique shadow of some ferns on the floor of a hot-house; I saw tigers, emboli, bison, ground swells and armies; I saw all the ants in the world." It is a numbing message, like that intoned in E. M. Forster's Marabar Caves: "Everything exists, nothing has value"; but with the slight difference that every-thing has value—an equal value, but a value nonetheless. This is implied by the colossal scale and also the intricacy which have gone into the staging of the fraudulent tableau of eternity. And though it is truc, as Borges wrote in "The Immortal," that we know nothing of the gods "except that they do not resemble man," someone evidently cares enough to clothe the dream with an air of truth. Borges is at times close to affirming this, as when he says in "The Wall and the Books," "Music, states of hap-piness, mythology, faces scored by time, certain twilights, certain places, all want to tell us something, or told us something we should not have missed, or are about to tell us something. This imminence of a revelation that does not take place is, perhaps, the aesthetic fact."

One always ends up comparing Borges to Kafka, and it is true that each is obsessed by the same enigma: the fabulous complexity of the universe confronting man's ridiculously in-adequate attempts at unraveling it. Occasionally both writers use the same symbols to project this enigma: bureaucracy, the Great Wall of China, Don Quixote and Sancho Panza. Each adds a reluctant codicil: Kafka's is the lighted window that is Joseph K.'s last vision before his execution; Borges's is the "im-minence of a revelation that does not take place." But Ana Maria Barrenechea warns us: "Kafka's anguish derives from being excluded from participation in an order in which he exists; Borges is indifferent because he does not believe in that order." And belief or its opposite determines a different kind of art in both cases: in Kafka's an "open form," self-propelling, open to modification, not unlike Charles Olson's "projective verse"; in Borges's a closed one, self-contained, pre-determined, the work of a metaphysical Fabergé.

A similar opposition underlies much of the art of our time, and it determines opposite responses: we read Kafka from something like necessity; we read Borges for enjoyment, our own indifference taking pleasure in the frightful but robust spectacle of a disinherited cosmos. Each, like the northern and southern hemispheres of Borges's Tlön, is a different aspect of the same aggressive, enigmatic planet.

Review of Jorge Luis Borges's *A Personal Anthology*, translated by Anthony Kerrigan (New York: Grove Press, 1967). From the *New York Times Book Review* (April 16, 1967).

Ecrivain Maudit: Witold Gombrowicz

A Polish writer, Witold Gombrowicz has spent much of his life as an exile in Argentina. During the last decade his novels have been published and highly admired in France, where he now lives. His theater has also had a certain success there, possibly because of its reassuring resemblance to Ionesco's. A runner-up and now a winner (with his novel *Cosmos*) in the prestigious International Literary Prize competition, his fame has fanned out through Europe along familiar publishing circuits, and now arrives in America. These two novels are the first volumes in a uniform series of his works projected by Grove (though *Ferdydurke* was originally published here in 1961 by another publisher).

Banned successively by the Nazis, the Stalinists and the present Polish regime, Gombrowicz has been until now an authentic *écrivain maudit*. Whether this is enough to justify the complete works treatment is another matter. Curious case that he is, one can think without trying of twenty European writers who deserve extensive translation into English more than he. In France alone, and starting at the beginning of the alphabet, one comes up with Antonin Artaud, André Breton, René Crevel, not to mention a host of younger writers like Jean Cayrol, Daniel Boulanger and Georges Perec.

Ferdydurke was first published in 1937 in Poland, where it is said to have caused a sensation among the avant-garde. Its random construction and the curious differences in tone from section to section suggest that it might have been a stringing together of several short stories. John Wain, who considers it "a masterpiece," says of it that "Gombrowicz proceeds to expose— and annihilate—the frauds and shams of traditional conduct and society." Alas, he does no such thing. Tacking unsteadily between Caligariesque fantasy and Zolaesque naturalism, he never succeeds in making "traditional conduct and society" real enough to demolish. The novel refuses to let itself be taken seriously, and it must ultimately face the consequences.

After a promising beginning in which Johnnie, the narrator, dreams of himself as an adolescent mocking his present thirty-year-old self and being mocked by it in turn, he is interrupted while writing by the arrival of Professor Pimko, "the distinguished Cracow philologist, small, puny, bald and bespectacled, in striped pants and tailcoat, his yellowish nails projecting under his light-yellow gloves." With the appearance of this caricatural personage, who proceeds to behave like Emil Jannings in one of his more trying roles, the author abruptly lessens his grip on the reader and never quite succeeds in regaining it.

Pimko hustles Johnnie off to his school, where the principal activity seems to be developing the students' "backsides"—an ominous-sounding curriculum that is never fully explained. Johnnie takes a room with a family called the Youthfuls—a pair of wildly progressive parents and their ice-cold daughter Zutka, who ignores their superfluous encouragements toward "free-love." This passage, together with a couple of Sternian digressions, is the best part of the book.

Johnnie sets out for the country with a classmate, the bully Mientus, on an unlikely and ambiguous whim of the latter's to shake off the sophistication of the city and live with a noble savage in the form of a "stable-lad." Here begins a series of misadventures not only for the protagonists but for the novel. The boys end up at the estate of Johnnie's uncle and aunt, where, beneath a façade of gentility, a cannibalistic spirit prevails—the uncle is fond of beating the servants to a pulp on the pretext that "they like it," which apparently they do. Yet the author seems uncertain whether to present the situation as an expressionist metaphor or a slice of Polish life—in the end neither interpretation is affecting. By the time the book ends, one's interest in Johnnie and his quest for maturity has cooled, especially after the revelation that he may not be an incarnation of Schopenhauer's "will" after all, but a rather decent guy under the existentialist veneer.

Pornografia, a more recent novel, is also set on a Polish country estate, this time during the Nazi occupation. Witold, the middle-aged narrator, is invited to the country by his friend Hippolytus (or "Hippo") to discuss an unspecified business deal. He takes along his companion Frederick, also middle-aged, and characterized by "an obvious but hidden indecency." Immediately Witold is curiously attracted by two adolescents on the estate: Henia, his host's daughter, and Karol, the administrator's son. "For me it was fantastic, almost inconceivable that they would both behave as though they were not seducing each other. I waited for them in vain to betray themselves. Their indifference seemed incredible."

The remainder of the novel is given over to this wait. The frightening innocence of youth, its beauty, its unreflecting indifference are a sort of acid bath from which the two men hope to emerge rejuvenated or at least realized. Frederick writes a note to Witold: "We need courage and determination to proceed with our venture even if it should look like a licentious obscenity. Obscenity ceases being obscene if we persevere! We must push on because if we give way the obscenity will crush us."

This appears to be a major theme in Gombrowicz's work: Johnnie in *Ferdydurke* has to destroy Zutka's adolescent calm in order to go on living, and Gombrowicz himself says in the preface to *Pornografia*: "Youth seemed to me the highest value of life . . . but this 'value' has a particularity undoubtedly invented by the devil himself: being youth it is below the level of all values . . . I believe the formula 'Man wants to be God' expresses very well the nostalgia of existentialism, while I set up another immeasurable formula against it: 'Man wants to be young.'"

This raw credo is somehow moving, and it takes on additional force in the novel because of Witold's gnawing doubt as to whether anything at all is happening outside his mind: the apparent indifference of the two children toward each other is a wall against which he has no choice but to beat his head. At the end, after Karol and Henia have helped assassinate a Resistance agent who was on the verge of collaborating with the Germans, a mutual smile on the faces of the four protagonists—Henia, Karol, Witold and Frederick—is the closest thing to a concrete realization of the fantasies of the two old men that they are to achieve.

Pornografia is an unsuccessful novel. Once its theme is stated it is never really developed, merely prolonged. Meanwhile the author promenades his characters endlessly around the estate, filling in with weighted description of scenery and people: in *Ferdydurke* the sun was a "super-bum," and here the river "lay there like a corpse"; frogs hop with "revolting, fat splashes"; Hippolytus is constantly described as "bloated" and an old washerwoman is "a broad-bottomed slut with sagging breasts, hideous, rancid and foully decrepit, with evil little eyes." Clearly a pretty unhealthy situation already prevailed on the estate before the arrival of the two reprobates, so that their practices seem less remarkable for these extenuating circumstances. One cannot help comparing *Pornografia* unfavorably to James's *The Sacred Fount,* an infinitely more subtle and finally horrifying account of people living their lives in and through the lives of others.

Nevertheless, one waits to see more of Gombrowicz; if he is not on the present evidence a very satisfying novelist, he is at least not an easy one. On the basis of the digressions in *Ferdydurke* and extracts from Gombrowicz's diaries in the preface to *Pornografia,* one has the impression that speculative rather than narrative prose is his province, and the diaries, when they appear, ought to be worth reading.

Alastair Hamilton's translation of *Pornografia* (from the French) reads flawlessly. Eric Mosbacher's of *Ferdydurke,* from an unspecified language—perhaps the French also?—is less good: forced to find an equivalent for Polish peasant *patois,* he comes up with something that I take to be North Country cockney, as: "Afterwards 'e gave 'un a zloty to keep 'is mouth shut, and told 'un that if he didn't keep 'is mouth shut, 'e'd get the sack!" There must have been other alternatives.

Review of Witold Gombrowicz's *Ferdydurke,* translated by Eric Mosbacher (New York: Grove Press, 1967), and *Pornografia,* translated by Alastair Hamilton (New York: Grove Press, 1966). From the *New York Times Book Review* (July 9, 1967).

Straight Lines over Rough Terrain: Marianne Moore

It is more than thirty years since Marianne Moore published her *Selected Poems;* fifteen years ago she gave us her *Collected Poems,* and now, in the month of her eightieth birthday, *Complete Poems* appears. If this sounds inexorable, one should note that Miss Moore shows no sign of abandoning poetry: the new book has new poems and new versions of old ones (notably a reworking of "The Steeple-Jack" which not only restores the drastic cuts made in the *Collected Poems* version, but actually adds to and improves on the seemingly unbeatable 1935 text of this masterpiece). There seems no reason not to look forward to *More Complete Poems;* as long as we can ask, like the student in her poem of that title, "When will your experiment be finished?" we may expect the reply, "Science is never finished."

In reviewing her last collection a year ago, I wrote that "Marianne Moore is, with the possible exception of Pound and Auden, the greatest living poet in English." After rereading her in this magnificent volume (which reprints all her books of poetry starting with *Selected Poems* as well as a handful of uncollected poems and selections from the La Fontaine translations), I am tempted simply to call her our greatest modern poet. This despite the obvious grandeur of her chief competitors, including Wallace Stevens and William Carlos Williams. It seems we can never remind ourselves too often that universality and depth are not the same thing. Marianne Moore has no *Arma virumque cano* prefacing her work: she even avoids formal beginnings altogether by running the first line in as a continuation of the title. But her work will, I think, continue to be read as poetry when much of the major poetry of our time has become part of the history of literature.

Yet it seems to me that we underestimate Miss Moore. True, Eliot placed her work in "that small body of durable poetry written in our time," and others have concurred; but there is a point at which her importance gets lost in the welter of minutiae that people her poems, and in the unassuming but also rather unglamorous wisdom that flashes out between descriptions of bizarre fauna and rare artifacts. Is she not a sort of Mary Poppins of poetry, or, to state the case against her as quickly as possible, an American La Fontaine, who, great poet that he is, always seems on the verge of becoming a tiresome moralist like Chamfort or even Poor Richard? Prudence and good judgment are not virtues we associate with the highest poetry, and here is Miss Moore telling us that she distrusts "merits" (so do we); that "A mirror-of-steel uninsistence should countenance / continence"; that "Truth is no Apollo / Belvedere, no formal thing"; that "the deepest feeling always shows itself in silence; / not in silence, but restraint."

Caution, healthy disrespect, restraint: is this the way of poetry? She is the opposite of a mystic, and it is hard to believe that there can be poetry without a grain of mysticism, a dark corner somewhere. But Miss Moore is explicit:

> . . . complexity is not a crime, but carry
> it to the point of murkiness and nothing is plain. Complexity,
> moreover, that has been committed to darkness, instead of
>
> granting itself to be the pestilence that it is, moves all a-
> bout as if to bewilder us with the dismal
> fallacy that insistence
> is the measure of achievement and that all
> truth must be dark.

And again:

> The opaque allusion, the simulated flight
> upward, accomplishes nothing.

This is strong language, but strong not exactly in the way we expect from great poetry, which has never, including Milton, been overly concerned with setting the record straight and sending the reader about his business. Without, however, suggesting that there is in Miss Moore's work a strain counter to the sentiments she *seems* to be expressing here (and of course, we should not assume that they are hers merely because she uses the form of direct address), that the swarming details, each one crystal clear, often add up not merely to complexity but to a "darkness" which gives contours to her "truth"—without going this far, one can still note that all here is not so modest, cheerful and brightly lit as the lines I have quoted seem to imply. She is not a moralist or an antiquarian, but a poet writing on many levels at once to produce work of an irreducible symphonic texture. If "restraint" is really an animating force in her poetry, then it is a strange kind of restraint indeed.

When we examine any of the poems that comprise the Moore canon—poems like "The Steeple-Jack," "The Fish," "Novices," "Marriage," "The Monkeys," "Bowls," "In the Days of Prismatic Color"—we are brought up against a mastery which defies attempts to analyze it, an intelligence which plays just beyond our reach. They start smoothly and calmly enough ("The monkeys winked too much and were afraid of snakes"), like a ride on a roller coaster, and in no time at all one is clutching the bar with both hands, excited and dismayed at the prospect of "ending up in the décor," as the French say of a car that drives off the road. And, not infrequently, this happens. I will never be entirely certain of what "it" is in "The Fish."

> Repeated
>   evidence has proved that it can live
>   on what can not revive
>   its youth. The sea grows old in it.

And there are other cases in which I become aware before the end of a poem that Miss Moore and I have parted company somewhat further back. Sometimes, as in "The Jerboa," the author has her say and retires, leaving you in the company of some curious little rodent. And her mode of direct address can be misleading: toward the end of "To Statecraft Embalmed" you become aware that she is no longer addressing an ibis, or even you, the reader; for the last minute she has been gazing absently at something terribly important just over your left ear.

These are not the manners of a governess, whether endowed with magic powers or not. "There is something attractive about a mind that moves in a straight line," and though Marianne Moore's mind moves in a straight line, it does so over a terrain that is far from level. Only something like alchemy could account for the miracle of some of these poems, such as "An Octopus," which is for me perhaps the greatest of all of them. We start with an octopus, evoked with the customary precision ("dots of cyclamen-red and maroon on its clearly defined pseudo-podia"), but the creature seems to be a glacier or else the two are superimposed, for now we are in a landscape of sierras and fir trees, while the author continues tacking imperturbably among excerpts from Ruskin, the *Illustrated London News*, the *London Graphic*, *The National Parks Portfolio* and a remark overheard at the circus, switching landscapes, language and levels with breathtaking abruptness, rising from botanical note-taking to pinpoint emblems of supernatural clarity that could be out of Shelley:

> the white volcano with no weather side;
> the lightning flashing at its base,
> rain falling in the valleys, and snow falling on the peak—

We can now appreciate the full extent of her disdain for "the simulated flight / upward."

Perhaps it is in her translations of La Fontaine, which I confess I prefer to the originals, that one sees most clearly her gift for language-making, for creating something where nothing was before. This sounds like a paradox since the poems are after all translations, but in trying to find an equivalent tone for La Fontaine's, she happened on a new language—new to poetry and new to her, since she had to abandon her glittering, allusive style to hoe the straight row of the original. And yet her speech, strict as it is, resounds with allusions and untapped possibilities. At the same time she has laid the hard-hearted, bourgeois ghost that hovers over the *Fables* even at their happiest—Miss Moore's verses are snug but not smug. And the earlier poems tell us why: it is not La Fontaine who would have appended this moral to a poem: "The passion for setting people right is in itself an afflictive disease / Distaste which takes no credit to itself is best." Nor would he have written: "one is not rich but poor / when one can always seem so right."

In short one can never be sure precisely what she is up to; like the unidentified protagonist of "In This Age of Hard Trying, Nonchalance Is Good and" whose "by- / play was more terrible in its effectiveness / than the fiercest frontal attack," she has set about poetry with all the tools at her disposal. Common sense is just one; so are intelligence and integrity that dazzle, an eye and ear that are almost magical in their power to re-create reality for us, and a mastery of form that outpaces the most devoted reader. All of these are brought to bear, as through a prism, on the amorphous "world" that surrounds us; the result is poetry in the almost-satisfactory definition of Théodore de Banville, which Gide quotes in the preface to his *Anthology of French Poetry:* "That magic which consists in awakening sensations with the help of a combination of sounds . . . that sorcery by which ideas are necessarily communicated to us, in a definite way, by words which nevertheless do not express them." Or, as Miss Moore says more succinctly: "Ecstasy affords the occasion and expediency determines the form."

Review of *The Complete Poems of Marianne Moore* (New York: Macmillan, 1967). From the *New York Times Book Review* (November 26, 1967).

The New York School of Poets

I have been invited here to represent something called the New York School of Poets. People invent these labels and later they tell you it applies to you and what does it mean. In my case, it is especially puzzling because the term "New York School of Poets" was thought up by someone, I don't know who, at some point during a ten-year period I spent in Europe. When I returned to live in America, I was told about the New York School and that I was in it, although most of my creative years had been spent in France. Of course, I am aware of the poets who are counted as belonging to the New York School, but I am not sure exactly what the name designates; I'm not even sure whether it's good or bad to belong to the New York School. I think on the whole I dislike the name because it seems to be trying to pin me down to something. That's the trouble with all these labels like Beat, San Francisco School, Deep Image, Objectivist, Concrete and so on. Their implication seems to be that poetry ought to be just one thing and stick to it. If you start out writing haikus, man, then it's haikus from here on in sort of thing. One thing that I am certain of as regards poetry is that I feel it should be anything it wants to be; that the poet should be free to sit down to his desk and write as he pleases without feeling that someone is standing behind him telling him to brush up on his objective correlatives or that he's just dropped an iambic foot. If the poem is no good when he's finished, he will then have no one to blame but himself, and can go on to the next poem in a cheerful frame of mind. This might be one definable characteristic of the New York School—its avoidance of anything like a program. Of course, this is not just a characteristic of the New York School, but of poetry in general, if by poetry you mean Keats or Spenser or Chaucer or Whitman or Rimbaud and the Surrealists. They wrote what they believed to be poetry without worrying too much about anything else, and it turned out to be poetry, and that is why we remember them and still read them. When we are looking for poetry, we know where to go.

However, much as I hate labels, I realize that they are necessary in this day and age. If a critic wishes to allude briefly to a poetic movement in passing, he obviously must use this label without going into all the reasons it is unsatisfactory, and maybe he is right; maybe it is wrong for things to get so complex that a label can't do them some sort of justice. So I will try again to explain about the New York School of Poets. It began with Kenneth Koch, Frank O'Hara, and myself, who met each other in college. We were all writing poetry when we met; none of us was much like the others but we shared common enthusiasms about modern French poetry, modern music, and painting, which seemed much more congenial to us than the American and English poetry we knew. Eventually we all wound up in New York studying or looking for jobs—which reminds me of a point I would like to make about New York, namely, that if you live in most other places, like San Francisco, Paris, or Bloomington, you are, almost against your will, taking a stand of some kind, and the stand is that you are not living in New York. If you live in New York, however, you are probably not doing so because you like it or you feel it expresses you, but because it's the most convenient place: there are people, jobs, concerts and so on, but it doesn't add up to a place: one has no feeling of living *somewhere*. That is another reason I dislike the New York School term—because it seems to designate a place, whereas New York is really an anti-place, an abstract climate, and I am not prepared to take up the cudgels to defend such a place, especially when I would much rather be living in San Francisco. At any rate, when we got to New York, we met other poets such as James Schuyler, Barbara Guest, Kenward Elmslie, and others; their poetry was not very similar either but it all eventually got tagged as New York School because we happened to be friends. We also got to know some artists and a few of us began to write about art in *ARTnews,* because poets are always broke and the editor is a nice man who happens to like poets. It was about this time that I went to France as a Fulbright student and stayed on and on and on.

When I got back, I found that the New York School thing had grown to be a kind of movement. In fact, after a recent article about it in the *Times Book Review* a lady wrote Kenneth Koch asking for the address of the New York School of Poets because she wanted to enroll in it. In trying to piece together what happened while I was away, I come up with the following. First there was a big poetry explosion about 1957, set off by Allen Ginsberg and Gregory Corso but gradually extending all over the nation until it has reached a point where every night in New York and some other cities you have your choice of several poetry readings to go to. This was completely unknown a few years before, when the only poetry readings were given at the YMHA by distinguished poets and nobody cared about poetry, even one's closest friends. Now everyone cared because they found it could be a way of life, and for this, as I say, I think Allen is responsible. Regarding the New York School, there was at the time a New York School of Painting, and since we had all continued to write for *ARTnews* and hang around with the artists—not entirely because we wanted to be influenced by painting, as has been incorrectly stated, but because the artists liked us and bought us drinks and we, on the other hand, felt that they—and I am speaking of artists like de Kooning, Franz Kline, Motherwell, Pollock—were free to be free in their painting in a way that most people felt was impossible for poetry. So I think we learned a lot from them at that time, and also from composers like John Cage and Morton Feldman, but the lessons were merely an abstract truth—something like "Be yourself"—rather than a practical one—in other words nobody ever thought of scattering words over a page the way Pollock scattered his drips, but the reason for doing so might have been the same in both cases. But the reason, as I see it, why the term New York School took hold, is because of the famous New York School of Painting and our fringe involvement with it.

I guess I have told you a number of things that the New York School isn't, and I would like to say a few things that it is, but this is very hard because our program is the absence of any program. I guess it amounts to not planning the poem in advance but letting it take its own way; of living in a state of alert and being ready to change your mind if the occasion seems to require it. I hate to repeat Henry James's corny advice to a writer, "Be one of those people on whom nothing is lost," but it is eminently practical and I see no other way to be. And this really is what the Surrealists were doing—not letting anything be lost on them—and our poetry is descended from Surrealism in the sense that it is open. I do not think of myself as a surrealist, but

I feel akin to it in the same way that the poet Henri Michaux does—he once said that he wasn't a Surrealist, but that Surrealism for him was *la grande permission*—the big permission. The big permission is, I think, as good a definition as any of poetry, of the kind that interests me at any rate.

Statement at the National Book Awards symposium "Poetry Now," at the St. Regis Hotel, New York (March 5, 1968).

Comment on Lee Harwood's
The White Room

Lee Harwood's poetry lies open to the reader, like a meadow. It moves slowly toward an unknown goal, like a river. It is carelessly wise, that is, wise without knowing or caring what wisdom is. In these things it seems more like recent American poetry than English poetry. The English language is constantly trying to stave off invasion by the American language; it lives in a state of alert which is reflected to some degree in English poetry. The American language does not know it is invading the English language and would not understand about this, since it considers all worlds desirable and is always borrowing or inventing new, not always necessary ones. Lee Harwood's English is like American English in that it lacks a strong sense of possession. At the same time, it has a pearly, soft-focus quality one rarely sees in American poetry, and which I associate with poets like William Wordsworth and Matthew Arnold. The "great" poetry I like best has this self-effacing, translucent quality. Self-effacing not from modesty but because it is going somewhere and has no time to consider itself.

From the dust jacket of Lee Harwood's *The White Room* (London: Fulcrum Press, 1968). Excerpts reprinted on the dust jacket of Harwood's *Landscapes* (London: Fulcrum Press, 1969). Full text reprinted on the insert accompanying Harwood's recording of his own poems on the record *Landscapes* (Steam P1202).

Review of Ted Berrigan's *The Sonnets*

Life has changed, and so has the slice-of-life. Katherine Mansfield would have difficulty recognizing her genre in the grainy, talky, casually obscene films of Andy Warhol, and she would probably make even less of the slices of poetry that Ted Berrigan has hacked off from a seemingly endless loaf and served up under the *caveat emptor* title *The Sonnets*. Yet the link is there. Miss Mansfield was ahead of her time in revealing a contemporary "scene" that shocked people even as they recognized it. And the meandering journals of Warhol and Berrigan, though they don't yet speak for everyone, emanate from an area of the sixties psyche that is disturbingly familiar. They feel like what tomorrow is going to be like.

Mr. Berrigan is a bearded East Village poetry magus, founder of an influential underground magazine called *C* (for no reason) which has, incidentally, featured covers and other contributions from Mr. Warhol. Berrigan is an adept of what it has been agreed to call the New York School of Poets, a label generally used with either disparaging or commendatory intent and, like most labels, not very useful, since it includes writers who have little in common with one another. What it does seem to connote, beyond a vaguely accurate geographical locus for the poets involved, is a poetry that experiments with form, that is, with words.

The theory that poetry is made of words rather than ideas has been with us, waning and waxing, since Mallarmé. It seems a curious conceit, at least until one starts to examine poetry closely; and yet even a presumably "idea" poet like W. H. Auden once said that poems are written not by intellectuals but by "the man who likes to hang around words, trying to figure out what they mean." The American who did this oftenest was Gertrude Stein, though she is seldom mentioned by younger poets as an influence nor indeed given more than lip service by anybody else. Sherwood Anderson wrote in his 1922 preface to her *Geography and Plays* that she had foregone the privilege of "wearing the bays of the great poets to go live among the little housekeeping words, the swaggering bullying street-corner words, the

honest working, money saving words, and all the other forgotten and neglected citizens of the sacred and half-forgotten city,"
adding: "Would it not be a lovely and charmingly ironic gesture
of the gods if, in the end, the work of this artist were to prove
the most lasting and important of all the word slingers of our
generation!"

Yet the Battle of the Words shows no sign of ending at the
conference table. Poet Jim Harrison wrote in these pages a few
weeks ago (January 28, 1968) that "among bad poets there is a
sort of 'let's roll up our sleeves and get down to brass language'
attitude"; by "bad poets," he may have meant Mr. Berrigan and
his New York School ilk. (That same Sunday, the *Times Magazine*
section published an article on Lévi-Strauss which mentioned
that a "structuralist" critic, Michel Foucault, recently published
a book demonstrating that thought originates with words rather
than vice versa.) The *New York Review of Books* has characterized
New York School poetry as "the Instant Mix, alchemic spontaneity, mud into mosaics, a form as popular right now with the
New York avant garde as Sara Teasdale's posies must have been
in her day." In less principled quarters, however, it has been
greeted as a sign of healthy revolt against the academic stuffi-
ness that periodically infests American poetry, and the counterpart of advanced movements in the other arts which somehow
achieved tolerance more readily than related experiments in
poetry.

Surely poetry is ideas? Yes, but aren't ideas words? Maybe and
maybe not, but it is clear that insofar as they conjugate ideas,
words, other than the basic English in which any idea may be expressed, enter into their fabric. And an idea, to mean anything
to anybody, must be conjugated, made kinetic, be on its way to
some other place. Mr. Berrigan's words seem often to be taking
his ideas on a very brisk outing, from which they return with
flushed cheeks and euphoria in their lungs.

> Into the closed air of the slow
> Now she guards her chalice in a temple of fear
> Each tree stands alone in stillness
> To gentle, pleasant strains
> Dear Marge, hello. It is 5:15 a.m.

Poor Sara Teasdale! The last line, incidentally, is one of many similar ones which recur in poems throughout the volume, producing a spliced audiotape effect that is a feature of the Instant Mix. One can never be sure whether it is the author speaking, or somebody he overheard in the street, or a newspaper or a letter or another poem.

Discouraging as this sounds, I think it is one of the real achievements of the New York School. The polyphonic style in Berrigan's poetry, and in that of Kenneth Koch, David Shapiro, and others, results from breaking up the traditional structure of poems. We are no longer listening to the poet's voice, but to many voices, in harmony or totally out of touch with one another, relaying garbled or clear or conflicting messages. The effect occasionally resembles a passage of Webern's music, where a simple musical phrase is distributed among a variety of instruments. And the meaning, more often than not, stems not from the meaning of the words but from the relation among them that their forced contiguity sets up. They impinge on and seep into one another to produce new shades of meaning and eventually new ideas.

More, perhaps, than any of his colleagues, Berrigan has converted poetry into an environment, possibly because "we love / Ourselves / Music, salve, pills, kleenex, lunch." Like so much recent art, it renders criticism obsolete, except insofar as the critic feels called upon to express approval or disapproval. There are no apologies to be made for ugly lines and no prizes to be handed out for good ones: that would be like smashing your window or pinning a blue ribbon on it because you like or dislike the view. It is the aesthetic of "It's what's happening, baby," and as we all slide mindlessly toward total media mix, there is still time to notice, in reading Mr. Berrigan, that the poetry is there.

Unpublished review, written in early 1968, of Ted Berrigan's *The Sonnets* (New York: Grove Press, 1967). Commissioned and set in type by the *New York Times Book Review* but not printed.

Throughout Is This Quality of Thingness: Elizabeth Bishop

One hopes that the title of Elizabeth Bishop's new book is an error and that there will be more poems and at least another *Complete Poems*. The present volume runs to a little more than two hundred pages, and although the proportion of pure poetry in it outweighs that of many a chunky collected volume from our established poets (Miss Bishop is somehow an establishment poet herself, and the establishment ought to give thanks: she is proof that it can't be all bad), it is still not enough for an addict of her work. For, like other addicting substances, this work creates a hunger for itself: the more one tastes it, the less of it there seems to be.

From the moment Miss Bishop appeared on the scene it was apparent to everybody that she was a poet of strange, even mysterious, but undeniable and great gifts. Her first volume, *North and South* (1946), was the unanimous choice of the judges in a publisher's contest to which eight hundred manuscripts were submitted. Her second won the Pulitzer Prize. One of her poems is enough to convince you that you are in expert hands and can relax and enjoy the ride: in the words of Marianne Moore reviewing *North and South,* "At last we have someone who knows and is not didactic." Few contemporary poets can claim both virtues.

Her concerns at first glance seem special. The life of dreams, always regarded with suspicion as too "French" in American poetry; the little mysteries of falling asleep and the oddness of waking up in the morning; the sea, especially its edge, and the look of the creatures who live in it; then diversions and reflections on French clocks and mechanical toys that recall Marianne Moore (though the two poets couldn't be more different: Miss Moore's synthesizing, collector's approach is far from Miss Bishop's linear, exploring one).

And yet, what more natural, more universal experiences are there than sleep, dreaming and waking; waking as she says in one of her most beautiful poems, "Anaphora," to: "The fiery event /

of every day in endless / endless assent." And her preoccupation with wildlife and civilized artifacts comes through as an exemplar of the way we as subjects feel about the objects, living or inert, that encircle us. We live in a quandary, but it is not a dualistic conflict between inner and outer reality; it is rather a question of deciding how much the outer reality is our reality, how far we can advance into it and still keep a toe-hold on the inner, private one. "For neither is clearer / nor a different color / than the other," as Miss Bishop says.

This strange divided singleness of our experience is a theme that is echoed and alluded to throughout Miss Bishop's work, but never more beautifully than in a short prose poem called "Rainy Season; Sub-Tropics," here collected for the first time. It consists of three monologues spoken by a giant toad, a crab and a giant snail, respectively, somewhat along the lines of Jules Renard's "Histoires Naturelles," yet Miss Bishop's poems are actually brief, mordant essays on the nature of being. Conceivably these are thoughts that could occur to the creatures in question, yet at the same time they are types, and not metaphors, of thoughts that occur to an intellectually curious person. "I live, I breathe by swallowing," confides the toad, who also mentions "the almost unused poison that I bear, my burden and my great responsibility." And the snail, frank but bemused, observes: "I give the impression of mysterious ease, but it is only with the greatest effort of my will that I can rise above the smallest stones and sticks."

One can smile at the way these creatures imperfectly perceive their habitat, but their dilemma is ours too, for we too confusedly feel ourselves to be part thing and part thought. And "We'd rather have the iceberg than the ship, / although it meant the end of travel." Our inert thingness pleases us, and though we would prefer not to give up "travel" or intellectual voyaging, in a showdown we would doubtless choose the iceberg, or object, because it mysteriously includes the soul: "Icebergs behoove the soul / (both being self-made from elements least visible) / to see them; fleshed, fair, erected indivisible."

This quality which one can only call "thingness" is with her throughout, sometimes shaping a whole poem, sometimes disappearing right after the beginning, sometimes appearing only at the end to add a decisive fillip. In "Over 2,000 Illustrations and a Complete Concordance," which is possibly her master-piece, she plies continually between the steel-engraved vignettes of a gazetteer and the distressingly unclassifiable events of a real voyage. A nightmarish little prose tale called "The Hanging of the Mouse" concludes with a description so fantastically accurate that it shoots currents of meaning backward into the enigmatic story: "His whiskers rowed hopelessly round and round in the air a few times and his feet flew up and curled into little balls like young fern-plants."

As one who read, reread, studied and absorbed Miss Bishop's first book and waited impatiently for her second one, I felt slightly disappointed when it finally did arrive nine years later. *A Cold Spring* (1955) contained only sixteen new poems, and the publishers had seen fit to augment it by reprinting *North and South* in the same volume. Moreover some of the new poems were not, for me, up to the perhaps impossibly high standard set by the first book. Several seemed content with picture-making; they made marvelous pictures, it is true, but not like those in *North and South,* which managed to create a *trompe-l'oeil* that conquered not just the eye and the ear but the mind as well. And in several the poet's life threatened to intrude on the poetry in a way that didn't suit it. One accepted without question the neutral "we" in earlier poems as the necessary plural of "I," but a couple of the new ones veered dangerously close to the sentimental ballad of the Millay-Teasdale-Wylie school, to one's considerable surprise, notably "Varick Street" with its refrain: "And I shall sell you sell you / sell you of course, my dear, and you'll sell me."

A Cold Spring does however contain the marvelous "Over 2,000 Illustrations" which epitomizes Miss Bishop's work at its best: it is itself "an undisturbed, unbreathing flame," which is a line of the poem. Description and meaning, text and ornament, subject and object, the visible world and the poet's consciousness fuse together to form a substance that is indescribable and a continuing joy, and one returns to it again and again, ravished and unsatisfied. After twenty years (the poem first appeared in *Partisan Review* in 1948) I am unable to exhaust the meaning and mysteries of its concluding line: "and looked and looked our infant sight away," and I suspect that its secret has very much to do with the nature of Miss Bishop's poetry. Looking, or attention, will absorb the object with its meaning. Henry James advises us to "be one of those on whom nothing is lost," without specifying how this is to be accomplished. Miss Bishop, at the end of her poem "The Monument," which describes a curious and apparently insignificant monument made of wooden boxes, is a little more specific: "Watch it closely," she tells us. The power of vision, "our infant sight," is both our torment and our salvation.

Her next book, *Questions of Travel* (1965), completely erased the doubts that *A Cold Spring* had aroused in one reader. The distance between Varick Street and Brazil may account for the difference not just in thematic material but in tone as well. We are introduced to the country in the opening poem, "Arrival at Santos," with its engaging casual rhymes ("seen" rhymes with "Miss Breen," a fellow passenger) and rhythms; its prosy, travel-diary style, its form so perfectly adapted to its content that there isn't a bulge or a wrinkle. After telling us about the ocean voyage and the port where it has ended, she terminates as only she can with a brief statement of fact that seems momentous: "We leave Santos at once; / we are driving to the interior."

Her years in the *là-bas* of Brazil brought Miss Bishop's gifts to maturity. Both more relaxed and more ambitious, she now can do anything she pleases, from a rhymed passage "From Trollope's Journal" to a Walker Evansish study of a "Filling Station"; and from a funny snapshot of a bakery in Rio at night ("The gooey tarts are red and sore") to "The Burglar of Babylon," a ballad about the death of a Brazilian bandit in which emotionally charged ellipses build up a tragic grandeur as in Godard's *Pierrot le fou.*

Perhaps some of the urgency of the *North and South* poems has gone, but this is more than compensated by the calm control she now commands. Where she sometimes seemed nervous (as anyone engaged in a task of such precision has a right to be) and (in *A Cold Spring*) even querulous, she now is easy in a way that increased knowledge and stature allow. Her mirror-image "Gentleman of Shalott" in *North and South* was perhaps echoing her sentiments when he said, "Half is enough." But the classical richness of her last poems proves that frugality need not exclude totality; the resulting feast is, for once, even better than enough.

Review of Elizabeth Bishop's *The Complete Poems* (New York: Farrar, Straus and Giroux, 1969). From the *New York Times Book Review* (June 1, 1969).

Further Adventures of Qfwfq, et al.: Italo Calvino

It was natural that Italo Calvino, born into a family of scientists and himself a student of folklore (he has made a comprehensive compilation of Italian folk tales), with a penchant for social allegory (his earlier novel, *The Baron in the Trees*, may be read as a reflection of his experiences as a Partisan), would develop a literary form uniquely suited to his interests: the science-fiction parable. In *Cosmicomics*, which was published here last year, and now in *t zero*, he has mined this rather unpromising vein extensively and at times with brilliant results.

Cosmicomics was a collection of tales with a common narrator, Qfwfq, a protean being, capable of evolving unscathed if nonplussed along with the universe from its beginnings. Each tale bore a short preface discussing some particular phenomenon of evolution, which Qfwfq would then meticulously elaborate into fiction. Some of the stories were remarkable (particularly the first, "The Distance of the Moon," which among other things offered a convincing scientific argument for the moon's being made of cheese), but finally the form wore a little thin. One grew accustomed to Qfwfq's beginning life as a protozoon and ending up behind the wheel of a Ferrari in pursuit of The Only Girl, who had different names like Ayl or Ursula H'x but who, whether mollusc or movie star, was always the same fascinating, unattainable substance. Calvino has been likened to Chesterton and David Garnett and, alas, he does occasionally wander into the tepid never-never land, halfway between whimsy and surrealism, of *The Man Who Was Thursday* and *Lady into Fox*.

Though *t zero* continues for a while to chronicle the adventures of Qfwfq, there are indications that Calvino has tried to break the snug mold in which the earlier stories were cast. As a result, the new book is both more uneven and more interesting. It is composed of three rather arbitrarily juxtaposed sections, each made up of several stories. The first group, in which we meet Qfwfq as a commuter in a moon-menaced New Jersey of the future and on the Italian Riviera of today, is a rerun of *Cosmicomics*. The second group, "Priscilla," is a mad and dazzling scientific dissertation on the nature of love and death. The third, despite its echoes of Borges, Kafka and the *nouveau roman*, does have one story, "The Count of Monte Cristo," which juggles these influences so skillfully as to re-create them.

Calvino's prose is by no means easy or congenial. (The translation, incidentally, is by William Weaver, who won a National Book Award for his translation of *Cosmicomics* and who has surpassed himself in this far more difficult text.) He has abandoned the elegant *trompe-l'oeil* style of *The Baron in the Trees*, a kind of literary equivalent of Visconti's flawlessly detailed costume epics. Perhaps he abandoned it because the extended metaphor which served that novel as a plot (a young eighteenth-century nobleman decides to live in the trees and never comes down to earth again) did not quite fill out the book's dimensions.

Today, on the contrary, Calvino has a horror of vacuums: he has trimmed these stories to the bone, using long run-on sentences that keep skidding out from under one as idea engenders idea. He is a master of the false summation (introduced by connective devices like "in sort," "in other words," "or rather," "I would almost say," etc.) which does not sum up at all but develops the embryo of a thought through stages the reader could not have imagined. This organic, growing prose, reflecting the movement of the universe as it passes from gas to liquid to sponges to crystals to cosmic jelly, is marvelously right and also very taxing to read. But "Priscilla" is worth it. One has to live the density of Calvino's style to live the density of the experience he is describing, which is the experience of wanting the opposed, complementary, outside substance that is the object of love:

> The pain of having to bear the fact that the potentially mine is also potentially another's, or, for all I know, actually another's; this greedy jealous pain is a state of such fullness that it makes you believe being in love consists entirely and only in pain, that the greedy impatience is nothing but jealous desperation, and the emotion of impatience is only the emotion of despair that twists within itself, becoming more and more desperate, with the capacity that each particle of despair has for redoubling and arranging itself symmetrically by the analogous particle and for tending to move from its own state to enter another, perhaps worse state which rends and lacerates the former.

It is everybody's story. Calvino may well be the Proust of 2001.

In "Priscilla" (the heroine, by the way, scarcely appears at all in human form, only as a principle; she is apparently an *Anglosaxonne* living in Paris) Calvino shows signs of doing what one kept hoping he would do in *Cosmicomics:* breaking open the Fabergé puzzles he is so expert at and getting into something less ordered, less clear, the real guts of the universe whose vagaries he plots so well from the outside. If he could explode one of his epigrammatic tales into a long messy novel, one feels, he would emerge as a truly amazing writer. There are hints in "Priscilla" that the primal lover in him, shut up in cells as effectively as in a cell but still able to protest this state of affairs in language that is like a long, lucid scream, may yet prevail over the ironies of the aristocratic amateur scientist.

One might hope this a little more strongly if Calvino had not succeeded so well, on his own terms, in the final tale of *t zero:* "The Count of Monte Cristo," a flawlessly constructed philosophical palace of mirrors on the order of Borges's "Pierre Ménard, the Author of Don Quixote" or Kafka's "The Burrow." Starting with the cast of characters of Dumas's novel, he develops a metaphor of the human condition of ever-increasing complexity.

While the prisoner Edmond Dantès lies in his cell, the Abbé Faria is endlessly tunneling in the walls of the fortress: "The walls and vaults have been pierced in every direction by the Abbé's pick, but his itineraries continue to wind around themselves like a ball of yarn." Dantès's plan for escape is the opposite: reflection rather than action, creating a reliable mental image of the fortress using the evidence of the Abbé's soundings; yet both methods are entwined, interdependent: "The only way to reinforce the imagined fortress is to put the real one continuously to the test."

After the odds against escaping have been multiplied even further by the introduction of new elements such as the probability of Napoleon's escape from St. Helena and the velleities of Dumas, the author, as he gums together the story, the prisoner reaches his unexpectedly happy conclusion:

> If I succeed in mentally constructing a fortress from which it is impossible to escape, this conceived fortress either will be the same as the real one—and in this case it is certain we shall never escape from here, but at least we will achieve the serenity of one who knows he is here because he could be nowhere else—or it will be a fortress from which escape is even more impossible than from here—and this, then, is a sign that here an opportunity of escape exists: we have only to identify the point when the imagined fortress does not coincide with the real one and then find it.

Calvino is now saying something that could be said in no other way (and, perhaps significantly, he has here abandoned the science-fiction genre); thanks to the stock characters and plot the point in question is almost visible. Whether he now chooses to dig deeper into the soul of matter, as in "Priscilla," or to throw up constructions that mirror its metaphysical implications, as in "The Count of Monte Cristo," his next book is certain to be worth waiting for.

Review of Italo Calvino's *t zero*, translated by William Weaver (New York: Harcourt, Brace and World, 1969). From the *New York Times Book Review* (October 12, 1969).

Introduction to *The Collected Poems of Frank O'Hara*

That *The Collected Poems of Frank O'Hara* should turn out to be a volume of the present dimensions will surprise those who knew him, and would have surprised Frank even more. Dashing the poems off at odd moments—in his office at the Museum of Modern Art, in the street at lunchtime or even in a room full of people—he would then put them away in drawers and cartons and half forget them. Once when a publisher asked him for a collection he spent weeks and months combing the apartment, enthusiastic and bored at the same time, trying to assemble the poems. Finally he let the project drop, not because he didn't wish his work to appear, but because his thoughts were elsewhere, in the urban world of fantasy where the poems came from. Donald Allen's task in tracking them down has not been easy. Sometimes poems Frank's friends remembered having seen had simply disappeared. Some survived only in letters. One of his most beautiful early poems, "Memorial Day 1950," exists only because I once copied it out in a letter to Kenneth Koch and Kenneth kept the letter. But, given the instantaneous quality of the poems, their problematical life seems only natural: poetry was what finally mattered to Frank, and even the poems themselves, like the experiences and personal relationships that went into them, were important but somehow secondary. His career stands as an unrevised work-in-progress; the fact that parts of it are now missing or unfinished is unimportant, except as an indicator of the temporal, fluctuating quality that runs through his work and is one of its major innovations.

For his poetry is anything but literary. It is part of a modern tradition which is anti-literary and anti-artistic, and which goes back to Apollinaire and the Dadaists, to the collages of Picasso and Braque with their perishable newspaper clippings, to Satie's *musique d'ameublement* which was not meant to be listened to. At Harvard he majored in music and did some composing, and although he wrote poetry too, he was more influenced by contemporary music and art than by what had been going on in American poetry. The poetry that meant the most to him when he began writing was either French—Rimbaud, Mallarmé, the Surrealists: poets who speak the language of every day into the reader's dream—or Russian—Pasternak and especially Mayakovsky, from whom he picked up what James Schuyler has called the "intimate yell." So it was not surprising that his work should have initially proved so puzzling to readers—it ignored the rules for modern American poetry that had been gradually drawn up from Pound and Eliot down to the academic establishment of the 1940s. To ignore the rules is always a provocation, and since the poetry itself was crammed with provocative sentiments, it was met with the friendly silence reserved for the thoroughly unacceptable guest.

It is true that much of Frank's early work was not only provocative but provoking. One frequently feels that the poet is trying on various pairs of brass knuckles until he finds the one which fits comfortably. It is not just that it is often aggressive in tone—it simply doesn't care. A poet who in the academic atmosphere of the late 1940s could begin a poem

> At night Chinamen jump
> On Asia with a thump

was amusing himself, another highly suspect activity. But these poems, so "French" in the pejorative sense the word so often had in America, were essential in the early, muscle-flexing period of his work. Just as he was constantly interested in a variety of people, in several branches of the arts at once and in an assortment of writers of whom one had never heard (Beckett, Firbank, Jean Rhys and Flann O'Brien were among the then almost unknown writers he was reading when I first met him in 1949), so he was constantly experimenting in his poetry in different ways without particularly caring whether the result looked like a finished poem.

The first four or five years of Frank O'Hara's writing—from about 1947 to 1952—were a period of testing, of trying to put together a tradition to build on where none had existed. Except for some rather pale Surrealist poetry written in England

and America during the 1930s, and an occasional maverick poet like John Wheelwright or Laura Riding; except for Hart Crane in his vatic moments and the more abandoned side of Dylan Thomas and the early Auden, there was nothing like a basis for the kind of freedom of expression that Frank instinctively needed. One had to look to France, and even there the freedom was more often an encouraging sentiment expressed in poetry ("Il faut être absolument moderne"* or "Plonger au fond du gouffre"†) than a program actually carried out in search of new poetic forms. Even French Surrealist poetry can be cold and classical, and Breton's call for "liberté totale" stopped short of manipulating the grammar and syntax of the sacrosanct French language.

So it was natural for Frank to turn to other branches of the arts, closer to home, where a profounder kind of experimentation was taking place. One of these was American painting, which was just then in what is now called the "heroic period" of Abstract Expressionism. This art absorbed Frank to such a degree, both as a critic for *ARTnews* and a curator at the Museum of Modern Art, and as a friend of the protagonists, that it could be said to have taken over his life. In return it gave him a conception of art as process which, if not exactly new (it was close to Gertrude Stein's definition of creative thinking, which applied both to her own work and to Picasso's: "Real thinking is conceptions aiming again and again always getting fuller, that is the difference between creative thinking and theorizing"‡), still had never before been applied in America with such dramatic results. Frank O'Hara's concept of the poem as the chronicle of the creative act that produces it was strengthened by his intimate experience of Pollock's, Kline's and de Kooning's great paintings of the late forties and early fifties, and of

---

*Arthur Rimbaud, from "Adieu," in *Une saison en enfer.*

†Charles Baudelaire, from "Le voyage," in *Les fleurs du mal.*

‡Quoted by Leon Katz in his text for the catalogue of the show of the Stein collections, *Four Americans in Paris* (New York: Museum of Modern Art, 1970).

the imaginative realism of painters like Jane Freilicher and Larry Rivers.*

Frank also listened constantly to music, not only to composers of the recent past as diverse as Rachmaninoff and Schönberg (his elegies to both of them are in this volume) but to contemporary avant-garde composers such as Cage and Feldman. We were both tremendously impressed by David Tudor's performance at a concert on New Year's Day 1952 of John Cage's "Music of Changes," a piano work lasting an hour and consisting, as I recall, entirely of isolated, autonomous tone-clusters struck seemingly at random all over the keyboard. It was aleatory music, written by throwing coins in a method adapted from the *I Ching*. The actual mechanics of the method escaped me then as it does now, what mattered was that chance elements could combine to produce so beautiful and cogent a work. It was a further, perhaps for us ultimate proof not so much of "Anything goes" but "Anything can come out."

This climate—Picasso and French poetry, de Kooning and Guston, Cage and Feldman, Rachmaninoff, Schubert, Sibelius and Krenek—just about any music, in fact—encouraged Frank's poetry and provided him with a sort of reservoir of inspiration: words and colors that could be borrowed freely from everywhere to build up big, airy structures unlike anything previous in American poetry and indeed unlike poetry, more like the inspired ramblings of a mind open to the point of distraction. The result has been a truly viable freedom of poetic expression which, together with other attempts at technical (Charles Olson) and psychological (Allen Ginsberg) liberation, has opened up poetry for today's generation of young poets. In fact

---

*James Schuyler takes issue with my estimate of the role of painting in Frank's work. He says in a letter to me, "I think you are hampered by a feeling of disapproval, or irritation (also felt by others—Schuyler, Koch . . .) for Frank's exaltation of the New York painters as the climax of human creativity, as something more important than his own work and talent. Perhaps the kindest (and it may even be true) way of seeing it would be along the lines of what Pasternak says about life creating incidents to divert our attention from it so that it can get on with the work it can only accomplish unobserved."

without the contribution of poets like these, and O'Hara in particular, there probably wouldn't be a young generation of poets committed to poetry as something living rather than an academic parlor game.

It is not surprising that there should be experiments which didn't work out among these early poems, considering they were part of an attempt to plot a not-yet-existent tradition with reference to what it was and what it wasn't. The posturing that mars "Oranges" and the obfuscation that makes reading "Second Avenue" such a difficult pleasure were useful because they eventually turned out to be unsatisfactory; it would not be necessary to try them again. That it was nevertheless worthwhile to do so once is proved in poems like "Easter"—an example of what I think of as Frank's "French Zen" period, where the same faults don't impair but rather make the poem—whose form is that of a bag into which anything is dumped and ends up belonging there.

What was needed was a vernacular corresponding to the creatively messy New York environment to ventilate the concentrated surrealist imagery of poems like "Hatred," "Easter" and "Second Avenue." Though a conversational tone had existed in his poetry from the beginning, it had often seemed a borrowed one—sometimes with overtones of home-grown surrealism, as in "Poem" ("The eager note on my door"); sometimes veering into Parisian artiness ("Oh! kangaroos, sequins, chocolate sodas! / You really are beautiful!"). It was not yet a force that could penetrate the monolithic slipperiness of the long poems, breaking up their surreal imagery and partially plowing it under to form in the process a new style incorporating the suggestions and temptations of every day as well as the dreams of the Surrealists. In the poems he was to write during the remainder of his life—from about 1954 to 1966, the year of his death—this vernacular took over, shaping his already considerable gifts toward a remarkable new poetry—both modest and monumental, with something basically usable about it—not only for poets in search of a voice of their own but for the reader who turns to poetry as a last resort in trying to juggle the contradictory components of modern life into something like a livable space.

The space, in Frank O'Hara's case, was not only the space of

New York School painting but of New York itself, that kaleido-scopic lumber-room where laws of time and space are altered—where one can live a few yards away from a friend whom one never sees and whom one would travel miles to visit in the country. The nightmares, delights and paradoxes of life in this city went into Frank's style, as did the many passionate friendships he kept going simultaneously (to the point where it was almost impossible for anyone to see him alone—there were so many people whose love demanded attention, and there was so little time and so many other things to do, like work and, when there was a free moment, poetry). The term "New York School" ap-plied to poetry isn't helpful, in characterizing a number of widely dissimilar poets whose work moreover has little to do with New York, which is, or used to be, merely a convenient place to live and meet people, rather than a specific place whose local color influences the literature produced there. But O'Hara is certainly a New York poet. The life of the city and of the millions of relationships that go to make it up hums through his poetry; a scent of garbage, patchouli and carbon monoxide drifts across it, making it the lovely, corrupt, wholesome place New York is.

Another way in which his work differs from that of other New York poets is that it is almost exclusively autobiographical. Even at its most abstract, or even when it seems to be telling someone else's story (see Donald Allen's footnote to the poem "Louise," whose title was suggested to Frank by a louse he says he "found on my own immaculate person"), it is emerging out of his life. Yet there is little that is confessional about it—he does not linger over aspects of himself hoping that his self-absorption will make them seem exemplary. Rather he talks about himself be-cause it is he who happens to be writing the poem, and in the end it is the poem that materializes as a sort of monumental backdrop against the random ruminations of a poet seemingly caught up in the business of a New York working day or another love affair. This is the tone in great poems like "In Memory of My Feelings," "For the Chinese New Year and for Bill Berkson"; this is the tone of the Odes, Lunch Poems and Love Poems (love is as important as lunch). Half on contemptuously famil-iar terms with poetry, half embarrassed or withdrawn before its strangeness, the work seems entirely natural and available to the multitude of big and little phenomena which combine to make that almost unknowable substance that is our experience. This openness is the essence of Frank O'Hara's poetry, and it is why he is read by increasing numbers of those who, in Kenneth Koch's phrase, are "dying for the truth."

From *The Collected Poems of Frank O'Hara*, edited by Donald Allen (New York: Knopf, 1971).

North Light: Louisa Matthiasdottir

Louisa Matthiasdottir is one of a number of highly gifted, independent artists who flourish unmolested if unencouraged on the fringes of the fashion-conscious New York art world, and who will be remembered long after the big names of this season or next season are as forgotten as those of the *pompiers* of yesteryear. Not that this artist herself seems in the least occupied with questions of art-world politics or her own reputation. Unlike her husband, the painter Leland Bell (see my article in *ARTnews*, February 1970), who is an ardent polemicist, she is seldom inclined to argue aesthetic questions. In fact she is an extremely reticent woman who seems to possess an inner peace, born perhaps out of a deep preoccupation with her work.

Louisa, or Ulla as her husband calls her, was born in Reykjavik in 1917. In the 1930s she studied art in Copenhagen and later in Paris with Gromaire, returning to Iceland when the war broke out. (Recently she and her husband unearthed some copies of a Danish Sunday supplement published in the thirties, with reproductions on the cover of landscapes of Iceland done by Louisa during her student days in Copenhagen. Their bold, reductive monochrome fields, a little suggestive of Milton Avery, were perhaps done with the printing requirement of the newspaper in mind, but they are also prophetic of the work she is doing today.) In 1942, since further study in Europe was impossible, she left Iceland for America. Although she doesn't mention it, her decision to travel across the Atlantic at the height of the U-boat war must be indicative of a powerful will to develop her art.

Once in New York she enrolled at the Hans Hofmann school, where she met her husband in 1943—he himself was not a Hofmann student but had heard reports about a beautiful Scandinavian girl studying there and had to check them out. Today they live with their daughter Temma, also a painter, in a pleasant, unpretentious brick house on one of the blocks in New York's Chelsea district that have their ups and downs, from townhouses to tenements. All three of the Bells have studios in it. Comfortably but simply furnished, with no touches of luxury except for the art they have collected (Derain, Giacometti, Hélion, Léger), it has a northern thriftiness and cleanliness. Homes in Iceland must be like this.

Much of the imagery in Louisa Matthiasdottir's paintings is derived from her childhood in Iceland, a past remembered with accuracy, rather than nostalgia, for its painterly potential. Her pictures sometimes seem to be taken from old snapshots (two men holding up a catch of fish, a girl standing with her bicycle on a country road, a picnic, a father helping his two little daughters across a brook). In fact some are, and others are done from memory, both kinds usually beginning as sketches which are worked up into larger studies which sometimes become large paintings. They have no connection with the campy blowups of family album photos which one sometimes sees in New York galleries. She is not dwelling on the past or exploiting its picturesqueness, but rather using it because it is, as evocative potentialities. An example is *Reykjavik Bus Stop*. The two figures in the foreground, posed by Louisa's mother and Temma, cast an enigmatically long shadow; the street is surreally empty (perhaps streets often are in Reykjavik); the houses behind suggest the ones in Munch's *Girls on the Bridge*, but perhaps only because Scandinavian houses tend to look alike. Everything prepares one for an epiphany such as the Munch painting seems to convey, but on further examination it turns out that the subject is only two ladies waiting for a bus; in fact it is hardly even that but is closer to pure painting—one has a strong sense of the joy of covering a canvas with long sweeps of paint and simultaneously capturing the vagaries of particular light and space with generalized accuracy.

Similarly, *Reykjavik Stroll,* posed by the same models, has the "mystery and melancholy of a street" of a de Chirico, which may again be but a realistic assessment of local color. There is almost a moment of high drama in the gestures of the two figures (whose features, as frequently, are left undelineated): the older lady's white-gloved hands clasped emphatically before her; the young one's left raised in an airy gesture, as though she were explaining a point. (A similar gesture, of an almost Poussinesque poignancy, occurs in the marvelous painting of the girls and their father crossing a brook; the younger one—Louisa herself—raises her hand in a moment of excitement which the camera caught long ago and which is now transmitted into the more permanent and universal medium of paint.) Yet the drama is not in the gestures but in the precise if low-profile fidelity with which they have been recorded.

The views of the Icelandic countryside oscillate between being mere pretexts for lush, cold sheets of not too worked-up pigment: green, blue, indigo (if a kodachrome postcard on the Bells' mantelpiece can be believed, the mountains in Iceland really are that shade of indigo), capturing as if incidentally the freshness of the air that sweeps directly down from the Arctic; and landscapes whose *genii loci* and spatial mysteries are close to the preoccupations of a Caspar David Friedrich. *Man in a Landscape* is an example. The pasture is not really a pasture but connected planes of green with no attempt made to suggest grass; perspective is indicated by the most summary means: the large animal (a horse?) in the foreground, the smaller one behind, with the tiny shapes of buildings further back, and the whole traversed and brought together by the figure of the man, whose feet touch earth in the foreground and whose hat grazes the distant mountains. It could be a Wordsworthian celebration of nature, a volumetric proto-abstraction or an exercise in painterly improvisation. In fact, it is all three, each element curbing the others so that the final result has a richness stemming from a basic, functional ambiguity.

It is this ambiguity, projected not for its own sake but as a means of getting more content into the picture, that is one of the major rewards of Louisa Matthiasdottir's painting. At a time when artists tend increasingly to consider single aspects to the detriment of wholeness, she reminds us that it is not only possible to be and to do many things while being oneself and doing one thing, it is also impossible not to.

In the American Grain:
A. R. Ammons and
John Wheelwright

The pure products of America don't always go crazy. Dr. Williams himself is a demonstration of this. But the effort of remaining both pure and American can make them seem odd and harassed—a lopsided look characteristic of much major American poetry, whose fructifying mainstream seems at times to be peopled mostly by cranks (Emerson, Whitman, Pound, Stevens), while certified major poets (Frost, Eliot) somehow end up on the sidelines. This is suggested again by the unexpected appearance of two voluminous *Collected Poems* by two poets who now seem destined to pass abruptly from the status of minor to major cranks.

Both John Wheelwright and A. R. Ammons are full of tics and quirks; both frequently write as though poetry could not be a vehicle of major utterance, as though it were itself a refutation of any such mythic nonsense; with both, the poem is not so much a chronicle of its own making as of its unmaking. Often, as in Ammons's "Working Still" or Wheelwright's "North Atlantic Passage," the final product looks like a mess of disjointed notes for a poem. Yet each poet finishes by stretching our recognition of what a poem can be and in so doing carries the notion of poetry a little higher and further. Each seems destined to end up, albeit kicking and struggling, as classic American.

Unexpected is perhaps not the right word for the publication of Wheelwright's *Collected Poems;* it was first announced on the jacket of a small pamphlet of his *Selected Poems* published by New Directions in 1941, a few months after Wheelwright was killed by a drunken driver in Boston at the age of forty-three. Why the present volume has been in the works for so long is not explained, and is all the more inexplicable in view of Wheelwright's close ties with so many well-known writers of his time, to whom many of the poems are dedicated: Robert Fitzgerald, Malcolm Cowley, Matthew Josephson, James Agee, Archibald MacLeish, Allen Tate, Howard Nemerov, Horace Gregory, and Wheelwright's brother-in-law (and literary executor) S. Foster Damon, to name a few. If at least some of them were his close friends it seems strange that no one, including James Laughlin (another dedicatee), has managed until now to rescue this brilliant poet's work from obscurity.

Perhaps there was some kind of opposition from the family, and one suspects also that many of the writers with whom "Jack" was on close terms appreciated his engaging personality and odd political views (Boston Brahmin–Anglo-Catholic-Trotskyite) but drew the line at his "recalcitrant" (the apt word is that of his editor, Alvin Rosenfeld) verse. Three volumes—*Rock and Shell, Mirrors of Venus, Political Self-Portrait*—were published in his lifetime by the Boston publisher Bruce Humphries in tiny editions and have long been unobtainable, as has the New Directions pamphlet. A fourth collection, *Dusk to Dusk,* which was ready for publication at the time of Wheelwright's death, now appears for the first time in the *Collected Poems,* along with some hitherto uncollected poems.*

Besides the mystery of the book's long-delayed arrival, Mr. Rosenfeld's thoughtful preface leaves several other questions

---

*Alas, a marvelously funny poem that satirizes the cultural pretensions of Beacon Hill, "There Is No Opera like 'Lohengrin,'" is not included, though it appears in *The New Yorker Book of Poems* (New York: Viking, 1969). The poem was first published in *The New Yorker* (May 6, 1939).

unanswered. Where are the original texts of the previously unpublished poems, and how were the present readings established? The fact that a poem published in the 1941 *Selected Poems* as "Staircase Thoughts" appears here in somewhat different form as "*Esprit d'Escalier*," while another now called "In the Bathtub, to Mnemosyne" was printed in the earlier volume as "Bathtub Thoughts" with a final stanza which has here been omitted, suggests that significantly different versions of other poems might well exist.

One wonders too about the sketches for a long poem on St. Thomas (the skeptic-believer, Wheelwright's favorite saint) which Mr. Rosenfeld says were "deemed too fragmentary for publication," and whether there are other such fragments. What happened to the book on American architecture which Wheelwright, whose father was for a time city architect of Boston and built among other things the Stadium Bridge in Cambridge and the troubadour-style Lampoon Building, was working on at the end of his life? These are, of course, secondary questions which will have to await a later stage of Wheelwright scholarship; meanwhile one hopes that the present volume will initiate that stage.

Wheelwright is a difficult poet, not merely for the erudition he presupposes, though this in itself is intimidating. His own footnotes usually compound the difficulties. One poem, he says, "is a literal contradiction to Oliver Wendell Holmes's *The Voiceless*"; another "quotes the Hymnal, the Psalter, the Bhagavad Gita, Oliver Wendell Holmes, Stonewall Jackson, and an anonymous ejaculation made at the Jamestown [*sic*] Flood." Elsewhere it is a question of Baring-Gould's *Lost and Hostile Gospels,* "Walker's translation of a Nestorian novel on the Acts of Thomas," "Maurice Samuel's translation of Edmond Flegg's *Jewish Anthology*," Boehme, Engels, Dietzgen, "the *Journal* of Pastor Higgenson," and even more to the point, episodes from the poet's private life: "'Lobster Cove,' an essay in pastoral, represents what occupied the end of a day at the Madame Goss House in Annisquam, on Cape Ann, while the Author was brushing up some chores for the Damons." (The reader will look in vain for a poem with this title in the *Collected Poems;* it was one of the titles, here omitted, of the nine groups of poems that comprise *Political Self-Portrait*.)

I say even more to the point because Wheelwright's literary

references, if they could be tracked down, would finally be of as little help in explicating the poetry as are the unstated facts of his biography, which are given the same telescoped, allusive treatment. This is not to say that the references don't matter; they, or their abstruseness, matter crucially in the long theological epics, where there are stretches unrelieved by the chiaroscuro glitter of the equally obdurate but less programmatic lyrics. But the difficulty proceeds less from arcane allusions than from Wheelwright's peculiarly elliptical turn of mind which convolutes and compresses clarities to the point of opacity. There is no more point in doing one's homework first than there is with the *Cantos:* one has to wade in, grasping at what is graspable and letting the extraordinarily charmed lyrical climate accustom one little by little to the at first blinding brightness or darkness.

Ellipsis is not a principle of construction, as with Pound, nor is there a willful, romantic obscuring impulse like Crane's. Wheelwright demands that we follow a logic perceptible to him but only intermittently so to us, and that we be prepared to abandon it without warning for another kind of poetic logic. If Crane's poetry presents a baroque façade, Wheelwright's is the architectural underpinnings and calculations that would support such a façade, which we glimpse only rarely in his calmer, lyrical moments. Meanwhile the feats of engineering that we can take in are almost enough in themselves.

It is best perhaps to start with the shorter, seemingly easier poems, not because they are actually much easier but because they contain some of his most radically original poetry unburdened by a narrative or dialectical function. This one, "Familiar," is from *Dusk to Dusk:*

> O, gilded Boston State House; O, gleaming Irish hair!
> I saw Lady Bountiful taking a walk in clean sunlight.
> A goodlooking girl, if only she hadn't lips for eyelids.
> I thought I saw two persons, and I got all mixed up.
> You see, it was this way . . . Lady Bountiful was modestly,
>   even stylishly
> dressed in two dimensions. But Lady Bountiful's shadow
> had three dimensions, and crept behind like
> pickpocket stenches of belches of Welch wenches.

Even while beginning to wonder what this is all about, one notes its crotchety sense of conviction. I think it succeeds, just as I think the very next one, "Stranger," doesn't:

> (While Boston blossoms into one brown rose)
> how is it, Girlie, on your way
> from Saroyan's whimsy play
> *Over the Hills and Far Away*
> to suffocate black incubator babies
> that you carry a tall walking stick
> embossed with the many-breasted Artemis;
> but rubbed on its prepuce nether tip?
> Did you lift it from my steady's mother?

In both cases I am unsure of what is being said, but also fairly sure that it doesn't matter, that we are in the presence of something as dumbfounding as Cubism must have seemed to its first spectators and as valid as it now looks in retrospect.

Even at his most direct Wheelwright is up to something other than what appears, as in "Dinner Call," a poem about a posthumous visit from Amy Lowell. The setting owes something to the Eliot of "Aunt Helen" and "The *Boston Evening Transcript*." The specter of the poetess arrives "while my Aunt and I were sitting round the house / waiting for the time to come for us to be sitting / and waiting for the time to drink our tea, / what brought her to Nantucket seven months after decent burial? / Digging up color for *Scrimshaw and Jade Fish*?" Miss Lowell gossips about her recent post-mortem activities as this seemingly prosaic but incredible domestic scene unfolds:

> When Anna carried in the urn, the lamp, slop-bowl, the pot,
>   *et cetera* for tea, the Sacrament of tact, Aunt Dolly lit the
>   alcohol
> Whereat, from that oracular orifice and steaming snout of
>   repartee, the kettle's grape tendril of vapor gushed:
> "Amy's got next the tripod of cookies,—great girl; she helps
>   herself while helping others . . . (It's hot spit shut my eye.)
> Let's let her let us help ourselves,—look how she takes up the
>   entire settle . . ." (The lamp went out.)

She departs and the narrator accompanies her for a while until their paths separate:

> But I turned for "Good-bye" to Amy Lowell, Biggest Traveling
>   One-Man Show since Buffalo Bill caught the Midnight
>   Flyer to contact Mark Twain:
> "One would be inclined, at moments, to doubt the entire
>   death!" I shouted.
> Grinning from ear to ear, she shouted back: "Mr. Brooks, you
>   are perfectly right;—one would be."

We know, because Matthew Josephson mentions it in a recent memoir of Wheelwright in *Southern Review,* that Wheelwright met Amy Lowell at the home of one of his aunts; that he once nettled her at a lecture she gave at Harvard by asking, "Miss Lowell, how do you write when you have nothing to say?" and that he later explained he had merely meant, "How does one write when one has nothing to say?" Yet the poem, which Josephson calls "a rather jocular elegy for Miss Lowell," seems to work on a number of levels: first as anecdote, though even here much remains to be explained. Why is the ghost returning? Why the sarcastic parting at the end? Wheelwright alludes to their exchange at Harvard, but a reader unfamiliar with the incident might well take it as another fictive bauble and miss the point.

Obviously the poem is satirical, but who or what is being satirized? If it is Miss Lowell, we are not told why. Wheelwright's attitude toward her and her poetry is tongue-in-cheek but uncommitted. And what is the function of the ghastly evocation of her corpse, straight out of the film *El Topo:* "As the lime rose, her neck turned grey, like stale ashes of cigars; but gushes of dead blood mounted her neck. / They flowed through her head; the cheeks turned red; the lips glowed like scars. But her eyes? Her eyes were frightened." Yet finally these questions scarcely matter. What matters is that the poem is alive and crackling with satire loosened from its object; it stands free of its narrative armature, though it could scarcely have come into being without it.

This is true of much of the poetry, including the long poems, and it points to a central problem: that lacking the precise reference, which is often not literary but autobiographical, we are forced back on the tributary beauties of the language, which are however frequently substantial enough to carry the poem alone. In this Wheelwright resembles another rediscovered Yankee crackpot genius, Charles Ives, whose gifts didn't rule out occasional lapses into tedium which cannot and should not be isolated from the rest, because they too stem from an ambitious plan which was completely apparent only to its author but whose energy enlivens even the barren passages. Nevertheless there will have to be a study of Wheelwright's sources before major poems such as the arcane closet drama "Morning," published here for the first time, can be appraised for more than their coldly felicitous Landor-like purple passages.

Still, almost any random page from Wheelwright makes one want to persevere. A suggestion of the difficulties and delights ahead can be found in the remarkable *ars poetica* (of a sort) called "Verse + Radio = Poetry," published by Rosenfeld and S. Foster Damon in *Southern Review* (Spring 1972):

> The music of poetry is more than sound—its music consists in the presentations of ideas as themes repeated, contradicted, and developed like musical ideas . . . Ideological music is closely related to disassociation of associated ideas and the association of the disassociated. This philosophical process must constantly go on, in answer to constantly changing society, for ages and generations and for individuals from childhood to old age and from mood to mood. This makes spirits athletic, not only to guard against the change but to welcome change. The poetry keeps you awake. If it makes you dream, it warns you that you are half asleep.

I can't leave Wheelwright without quoting in full one of his most beautiful poems, "Why Must You Know?" from *Rock and Shell*, to which one can return again and again, savoring it without penetrating its secret:

> —"What was that sound we heard
> fall on the snow?"
> —"It was a frozen bird,
> Why must you know?
> All the dull earth knows the good

that the air, with claws and wings
tears to the scattered questionings
which burn in fires of our blood."
— "Let the air's beak and claws
    carry my deeds
far, where no springtime thaws
    the frost for their seeds."
—"One could fathom every sound
that the circling blood can tell,
who heard the diurnal syllable,
while lying close against the ground."
—"My flesh, bone and sinew
    now would discern
hidden waters in you
    Earth, waters that burn."
—"One who turns to earth again
finds solace in its weight; and deep
hears the blood forever keep
the silence between drops of rain."

The clear mystery, the cold passion, and the warm intelligence
are there in equal proportion.

A. R. Ammons's *Collected Poems* comes almost as unheralded as
Wheelwright's sudden belated materialization. Ammons's first
book, *Ommateum,* published in 1955, seems not to have attracted much attention; his second appeared nine years later.
Recently he has been more prolific, and critics, particularly
Harold Bloom and Richard Howard, have considered his work
seriously and at length, but few had probably anticipated a *Collected Poems* of such dimensions (almost four hundred pages, to
which must be added the recent Norton reissue in a separate
volume of his two-hundred-page poem *Tape for the Turn of the
Year*). If his importance was suspected before, it is now, as so
often happens, confirmed merely by the joining of several volumes in one—not only because the solidity and brilliance are at
last fully apparent but because, as also often happens, the occasionally weaker early poems somehow illuminate and give access
to the big, difficult later ones.
    Without wishing to fall into the trap of comparing Wheel-

wright and Ammons merely because of the hazards of publication, one cannot help being struck by certain resemblances. Both are American originals (in the French sense of *un original* as someone who is also quite eccentric), and they are products as much of the American landscape as of its poetic tradition, via devious ways. Wheelwright's aesthetic relation to New England is as tenuous but as real as Ives's cacophonous "The Housatonic at Stockbridge" is to the bucolic scene which prompted it. The relation lies deeper than resemblance. Ammons's landscape is American sidereal; a descendant of Emerson, as Bloom has pointed out, he is always on the brink of being "whirled / Beyond the circuit of the shuddering Bear" from the safe confines of backyard or living room. But the fascination of his poetry is not the transcendental but his struggle with it, which tends to turn each poem into a battleground strewn with scattered testimony to the history of its making in the teeth of its creator's reluctance and distrust of "all this fiddle."

Reading the poems in sequence one soon absorbs this rhythm of making-unmaking, of speech facing up to the improbability of speech, so that ultimately Ammons's landscape— yard, riverbed, ocean, mountain, desert, and soon "the unseasonal undifferentiated empty stark"—releases the reader to the clash of word against word, to what Harold Bloom calls his "oddly negative exuberance." The movement is the same, from the visible if only half-real flotsam of daily living to the uncertainties beyond, but one forgets this from one poem to the next; each is as different as a wave is from the one that follows and obliterates it. One is left, like the author at the end of his best-known poem, "Corsons Inlet," "enjoying the freedom that / Scope eludes my grasp, that there is no finality of vision, / that I have perceived nothing completely, / that tomorrow a new walk is a new walk."

The poet's work is like that of Penelope ripping up her web into a varicolored heap that tells the story more accurately than the picture did. And meanwhile the "regional" has become universal, at an enormous but unavoidable cost; the destructiveness of the creative act in Ammons ("what / destruction am I / blessed by?") permits him to escape, each time, the temptations of the *paysage moralisé*. Much has been written about the relation of the so-called New York School of Poets to the painting of men like Pollock, but in a curious way Ammons's poetry seems a much closer and more successful approximation of "Action Painting" or art as process ("The problem is / how to keep shape and flow").

Marianne Moore pointed out that "inns are not residences," and a similar basic corrective impulse runs throughout Ammons, giving rise to a vocabulary of pivotal words. "Saliences" (the title of one of his best poems), "suasion," "loft," "scary," "motion," and "extreme" are a few which assume their new meaning only after a number of encounters, a meaning whose sharpness corrects a previous one whose vagueness was more dangerous than we knew. A "loft" (also frequently used as a verb) is not a summit, but a way station and possibly the last one; saliences are pertinent and outstanding but not necessarily to be confused with meanings; suasion is neither persuasion nor dissuasion. The corrective impulse proceeds as much from prudence as from modesty; in any case it can coexist with occasional outbursts of pure egotism: "I want a squirrel-foil for my martin pole / I want to perturb some laws of balance / I want to create unnatural conditions" (but the poem of which this is the beginning is entitled "The Imagined Land"), just as Ammons's frugality and his relentless understatement are countered by the swarming profusion of the poems.

This austerity could lose its point in the course of such a long volume: the restricted palette; the limited cast of characters (bluejays, squirrels, and other backyard denizens figure prominently, along with the poet's wife, child, and car, not to forget the wind with whom he has dialogues frequently in a continuing love-hate relationship); the sparse iconography of plant, pebble, sand, leaf, twig, bone, ends by turning the reader back from the creature comforts he might have expected from "nature" poetry to the dazzlingly self-sufficient logic which illuminates Ammons's poetry and in turn restores these samples from nature to something of their Wordsworthian splendor—but Wordsworth recollected in the tranquillity of mid-century mindless America, and after the ironic refractions of Emerson, Stevens, and Williams. For despite Ammons's misgivings, his permanent awareness of "a void that is all being, a being that is void," his "negative exuberance" is of a kind that could exist only after the trials of so much negation.

> I can't think of a thing to uphold:
> the carborundum plant snows
> sift-scum on the slick, outgoing river
> and along the avenues car wheels
>
> float in a small powder: my made-up
> mind idles like a pyramid . . .
>> —from "Working Still"

But if he is unable to find a saving word for the polluted (in so many ways) American scene, his speech elevates it even as it refuses to transform it. "No American poet," writes Harold Bloom in an essay on Ammons, "When You Consider the Radiance," in his book *The Ringers in the Tower*, "not Whitman or Stevens, shows us so fully something otherwise unknown in the structures of the national consciousness as Ammons does." And for Americans who feel that America is the last truly foreign country, this something comes startlingly alive in poem after poem, as in the magnificent "One: Many":

> . . . and on and on through the villages,
> along dirt roads, ditchbanks, by gravel pits and on to the
>   homes, to the citizens and their histories,
> inventions, longings:
> I think how enriching, though unassimilable as a whole
> into art, are the differences. the small-business
> man in
>   Kansas City declares an extra dividend
> and his daughter
>   who teaches school in Duquesne
> buys a Volkswagen, a second car for the family:
> out of many, one:
> from variety an over-riding unity, the expression of
> variety:

How perfect and how funny in its Whitmanesque nod to the automotive industry is that "buys a Volkswagen, a second car for the family": it seems as much by its music as by its sense to sum up everything that is beautiful and wrong in our vast, monotonous, but very much alive landscape. And Ammons knows this well; he ends the poem with an unemotional summation that, in its reluctant acceptance of the "opaque" world that is still "world enough to take my time, stretch my reason, hinder / and free me," can also stand for the work:

> no book of laws, short of unattainable reality itself,
> can anticipate every event,
> control every event: only the book
> of laws founded against itself,
> founded on freedom of each event to occur as itself,
> lasts into the inevitable balances events will take.

Review of *Collected Poems of John Wheelwright* (New York: New Directions, 1972); and A. R. Ammons's *Collected Poems 1951–1971* (New York: Norton, 1972) and *Tape for the Turn of the Year* (New York: Norton, 1972). From the *New York Review of Books* 20, no. 2 (February 22, 1973). Excerpts reprinted in *A. R. Ammons,* Modern Critical Views: Contemporary American, edited by Harold Bloom (New York: Chelsea House, 1986). "Familiar," "Stranger," and "Why Must You Know" by John Wheelwright, copyright © 1971 by Louise Wheelwright Damon. Reprinted by permission of New Directions Publishing Corp.

Jacques Rivette:
Rivette Masterpiece(s?)

> But I was thinking of a plan
>   To dye one's whiskers green,
> And always use so large a fan
>   That they could not be seen.
> So, having no reply to give
>   To what the old man said
> I cried, "Come, tell me how you live!"
>   And thumped him on the head.
> —Lewis Carroll

Jacques Rivette's *Out One / Spectre,* together with his very different *Céline and Julie Go Boating,* is not only a magnificent film, a film totally unlike anything one has ever seen, but also one that seems to mark a turning point in the evolution of the art of the film. How could it have been shown in New York without word leaking out that something extraordinary was happening? Of course, the guardians of orthodoxy at the *Times* have unusually sensitive nostrils for anything truly original and therefore subversive. Their policy of containment (to put the kindest construction on it) was to be expected, but I know of no enthusiasm for the film in any other publication, including this one, which is apparently going to publish an unfavorable review of it. So maybe *I'm* crazy. Still I would like to present my reasons for considering *Out One* a masterpiece.

Since it has been called formless and isn't, I'll begin by giving some account of its shape. A young deaf-mute named Colin (Jean-Pierre Leaud), who makes a living by peddling "the message of destiny" to café patrons, begins receiving some peculiar messages himself—typewritten pages which speak incoherently of Balzac's *Histoire des treize* and Carroll's *Hunting of the Snark*, when they speak of anything at all. He tries to decipher the messages.

One of his first discoveries is a coded address, "2 Place Sainte-Opportune," which turns out to be the address of a hippy boutique called L'Angle du Hasard run by a beautiful, affectless blonde (Bulle Ogier), whose name is sometimes Pauline and sometimes Emilie. The shop is seemingly a front for a revolutionary underground newspaper, which is in turn, we soon realize, a front for something far more obscure and dangerous.

Meanwhile we have been meeting a raft of other characters, some louche, some respectable: a Balzac scholar (Eric Rohmer); Lucie, a lawyer (Françoise Fabian); Frédérique, a part-time pickpocket (Juliet Berto); Thomas, an avant-garde theater director who is staging a Grotowskian version of *Prometheus* (Michel Lonsdale); Lili, an actress who has left Thomas's troupe to put on her own Living Theatre version of *Seven against Thebes* (Michèle Moretti); Sarah, a novelist with writer's block (Bernadette Lafont); and an assortment of businessmen, actors, loafers, professors and revolutionaries, some of whom appear to know one another.

Quite soon we begin to feel that the deaf-mute (who to no one's surprise turns out to be in possession of all his faculties) isn't so mad after all. The situation is that of a James novel such as *The Sacred Fount,* where everything hinges on whether or not the narrator is imagining the whole thing: by the time we realize that he isn't we are somehow more deeply involved than he in a distressing situation.

Gradually we learn that there is indeed a secret society of thirteen members, as Colin suspects. But we never learn much about their activities, or what their ultimate aim is. (The only clue is offered by Frédérique, not a member of the group, when she speculates that they "want to blow up the whole world.") Only two incidents suggest that the group has a potential for violence: once when Pauline blackjacks (and perhaps kills) an unwelcome visitor to the shop; again when Frédérique, who has been tepidly trying to blackmail one of the thirteen, gets beaten up by a thug in black leather—though there is actually no reason to link this event to the group.

When things get tense Pauline and Lili split to a seaside villa called L'Aubade, where nothing "really" happens either, though there is talk of a ghost and a recurring dream of being strangled. We begin to suspect that the members of the group whom we have seen are of secondary importance in its structure. Much seems to depend on the doings of a certain Pierre and Igor, who never appear. At the end, Pauline/Emilie, who may be Igor's wife, talks to him on the telephone and rushes off to meet him, though one doubts that the meeting will take place. Meanwhile it turns out that it is the unseen Pierre who has been sending Colin those messages, as a sort of Byzantine way of communicating with the rest of the gang.

That's where we are left at the end, after four and a half hours. A great many things have been said; a few have actually happened; but the thing, the explanation for all this, hasn't made its appearance, as it seldom does in life. Colin, clever but never clever enough (like the detectives in Feuillade's serials, to which Rivette is certainly indebted), sinks deeper into justified delusions, wandering the streets of Paris muttering, "Treize pour chasser le SNARK!"

Apparently the Snark was once again a Boojum (is there any other kind?), and Colin's fate is "to softly and suddenly vanish away." But he seems not unhappy. Toward the end he tells a politely skeptical member of the thirteen that the thirteen has to exist, otherwise the magic and terrible universe through which he is advancing would evaporate, "and that would be *intolerable.*"

One feels meanwhile that the group is on the wane: the members lose touch with one another and tend to forget why they teamed up in the first place. Igor's ominous absence and Pierre's suspicious one aren't reassuring. Pierre seems to be the strong man, but since he has nothing better to do than torment Colin with cryptograms (at least, we never see any other evidence of his activity), we must conclude that the days of the group's importance as a vital (or lethal) force are numbered. Only Colin, at the end, has improved his lot through the felicity of being duped; the luck of his opponents has eroded (though this is never clearly stated). What is suggested (but only sketchily) is that the fate of victims (Colin and Frédérique) is pleasanter than that of their oppressors. (I forgot to mention that Frédérique manages to pick her assailant's pocket in the middle of getting beaten up, in a café under the eyes of two indifferent barmen, and this success seems to reward her amply for the pain and humiliation.)

That is the story of *Out One / Spectre* (the title, according to festival director Richard Roud, refers to the film term "outtake" and the fact that this four-and-a-half-hour version of the film is only a specter of the original thirteen-hour one which Rivette made hoping—incredibly enough—to interest a television network in it as a series). It probably sounds no better and perhaps even worse than the "concepts"of many ambitious movies.

What makes the film a great one (in my opinion) is not the story but the telling. Rivette has a genius for rendering a viewer hypersensitive to details: the pattern of a woman's blouse, furniture, cars, flowers, the gait of a passerby. Since 95 percent of the film is details, and since we unexpectedly find ourselves in the position of reacting violently to them, it becomes quite an experience.

The conversation flows endlessly *à la* Rohmer; the typical French *bavardage* about politics, the theater, the relative merits of rhubarb jam and rhubarb pie, is superbly improvised by a cast who had apparently been provided only with the general outline of each scene. What they say is sometimes boring, sometimes funny, but always slightly out of focus, off balance. The reaction and the reply are never quite what one would expect, nor are they so far-fetched that one quite dismisses them. "It's strange, the trees have blossomed twice this year," says Hélène, an actress in Lili's troupe, to Lili as they are sitting together at a sidewalk café. But then she adds something like: "How silly I am, mixing up memories of last spring with this one," fudging the surrealist tone of her first sentence but still leaving us wondering what has been said and where we are.

As the festival blurb said, *Out One* "shows us a world which looks like the real world but isn't," which is also the striking feature of Feuillade's silent serials. (Rivette apparently dislikes being compared to Feuillade, which could be just another example of what Harold Bloom calls "the anxiety of influence.") In Feuillade's films, especially his final masterpiece *Barabbas,* which also deals with a secret society of criminals who move freely through a world of elegant Paris salons, the contrast is probably even more unnerving in retrospect since the "real" world is an old-fashioned, bourgeois, cozy-looking one—an unlikely setting for the endless beautiful atrocities. (I remember a scene in *Ti Minh* where a frock-coated, bearded gentleman is seen sauntering along the Promenade des Anglais at Nice. Suddenly an airplane materializes; a rope-ladder is let down and a man descends it, grabs the bearded gent and lugs him back up into the airplane before the horrified gaze of a crowd of fashionable onlookers. The scene was shot on location and nothing was faked.)

In Rivette's two new films the background is contemporary but an equally improbable decor for nightmare. The glittering cafés, the Sonia Rykiel fashions, the elegant Vuillard-like apartments, the powder-blue sky of a sea resort in spring allude to a reality we know exists from having read about it in *Travel and Leisure* and the Sunday *Times;* the next moment everything is in doubt, the rules of life have changed, only to shatter and reform further on. Rivette's superb orchestration of minutiae has made one so aware of the passage of time that a trivial piece of action can have the force of a pistol shot, an important one the force of an explosion.

Rivette seems to have reached a plateau where he can do anything and have it come out right. His last long film, *L'amour fou,* was ambitious but flawed: madness was viewed from a case-history viewpoint rather than as a condition of the world. Now that it has triumphed it can afford to be less visible, and Rivette is able to juggle a whole Larousse of fructifying influences, from such masters of the enigmatic as Carroll, Gaston Leroux and Raymond Roussel (the animated corpses programmed to re-enact the same skit forever in *Locus Solus* are the ancestors of the strange inhabitants of the villa at 7 *bis,* rue du Nadir aux Pommes in *Céline and Julie*) to Cocteau to the Godard of *Alphaville* to Robert Wilson to Hollywood (am I wrong in seeing shreds of that chestnut *Home before Dark* in *Céline and Julie,* where the repeated line "Vous êtes le meilleur parti de la Nouvelle Angleterre!"—"You're the best catch in New England!"—takes on a *certain* significance?).

Unlike Buñuel, whose new film, *Le fantôme de la liberté* (1974), simply reverses the expected order of things, so that once the black humor pattern is established one can only sit back and chuckle occasionally while admiring the craftsmanship of his film rather than its non-existent substance, Rivette never completely turns the tables and so keeps his spectator enthralled, wedding-guest-like. Just when it all starts to get too incongruous he deftly tacks back into the "real" world for a moment before his next, more outrageous sortie. One advances along an ever-narrowing ledge between disbelief and acceptance until the two merge.

Review of Jacques Rivette's *Out One / Spectre* and *Céline and Julie Go Boating.* From the *SoHo Weekly News* 2, no. 3 (October 24, 1974).

Introduction to E. V. Lucas and George Morrow's *What a Life!*

In a volume of literary reminiscences called *Reading, Writing and Remembering,* published in 1932, Edward Verrall Lucas gives the following account of the composition of *What a Life!:*

> In 1911 George Morrow and I hit upon the device of forcing the blocks in a store's catalogue to illustrate a biography, and produced *What a Life!* . . . We applied first to Harrod's for

permission and, being refused, went to Whiteley's and were made welcome. The next thing was to get scissors and paste and let ourselves go; and the process of bending the material to our will was, I can assure you, very exhilarating.

The book had very little popularity, but it won a few very faithful friends, and I know one house where a copy of it is chained to the side of the mantelpiece like a Bible in church.

A year or so ago it formed the basis of a lantern lecture at the Grafton Theatre, the arranged fee for which has not yet been paid.

It would be amusing to give the joke a second chance, but the illustrated shilling book is dead, killed by the rise in the prices of production which set in during the War; and to ask more than a shilling would be foolish.

Here one may take issue with Mr. Lucas, who is not the first man of letters to underestimate his lighter productions. The illustrated shilling book is gone, but *What a Life!* is very much alive. The object of a small but enthusiastic cult, it has become a collector's item and certainly deserves to be reprinted at the present going rate. In fact this tiny classic of proto-Dada seems likely to outlive all of Lucas's other books (more than sixty altogether, with titles like *A Wanderer in Paris* and *Roving East and Roving West*), if indeed anybody still reads them.

What a Life! is a very funny book and deserves a niche in the pantheon of British nonsense. It also has a certain place in the history of modern art, predating by almost a decade the collages of Max Ernst, who also drew inspiration (but for very different ends) from the engravings in illustrated catalogues. The fact has been noted by Herta Wescher in her monumental history of the medium entitled *Collage*. And Raymond Queneau, the French novelist and former member of the Surrealist group, has a brief essay on *What a Life!* in his book *Bâtons, chiffres et lettres,* citing its publication date (August 17, 1911) as the moment of the first conjunction of scissors and glue-pot "with disinterested ends in view." The book's importance as an object of fantastic art was consecrated in the 1936 Museum of Modern Art exhibition "Fantastic Art, Dada and Surrealism," where two of its illustrations were included at the suggestion of the writer Jay Leyda, who was at that time on the museum's staff and had discovered *What a Life!* in a London bookshop a few years before.

Although there is no evidence that Max Ernst knew Lucas and Morrow's little book, the resemblances between it and such a work as Ernst's collage novel *Une semaine de bonté* are striking. Of course the raw material—those old steel engravings—was already charged with disturbing suggestions, waiting to be incorporated into fantasy. Queneau mentions the "memory of the precise uneasiness" produced by the catalogues his mother received from the Grande Maison de Blanc. And Marcel Jean in his *History of Surrealist Painting* has noted that at the time when Ernst first began cutting up steel-engraved illustrations, this method of reproduction was already old-fashioned and evocative of childhood memories for the people of his generation: "possessing a picturesque quality that is both derisive and very engaging, and which becomes enhanced, revivified by the very humor of the collage." Yet there is terror in Ernst's collages, for example in the "Cour du dragon" sequence of *Une semaine de bonté*, where an already turbulent *drame bourgeois* is complicated by the bat's wings and reptilian members that its elegant characters keep sprouting. The terror is heightened by the fact that these figures who once stood as symbols of taste and correctness have changed character and are now rampaging in a world of nightmare.

There is no terror in *What a Life!*, but there are veiled suggestions of the *trouble* mentioned by Queneau, and it is present not only in such gothic touches as the "headless apparition" of Sir Easton West's Tudor manor and the bloody hand-print that figured in the stolen diamonds case at Closure Castle. It can be felt throughout in the dislocations, sometimes farcically broad but sometimes very slight, that separate the pictures from the text.

Marcel Jean says of Ernst's collages that "his point of departure is literally a cliché."* Lucas and Morrow's work is even more deeply rooted in the cliché: in addition to the cliché reproductions of visual stereotypes from Whiteley's catalogue, the story itself is a continuous literary cliché, deftly sabotaged on every

---

*"Cliché" in French also means a photographic reproduction.

page by the authors' finely honed scissors and pen. Here as usual the satirist's attitude toward his material is ambivalent—a "love-hate relationship." Lucas was precisely a writer "entrapped by teatime fame and by commuters' comforts," in Marianne Moore's phrase. He wrote compulsively and continually, using the proceeds to live well in the manner suggested by the frock-coated gentlemen and aigretted ladies who stare from the pages of the catalogue, surrounded by those solemn and superfluous luxury goods which sometimes seem so essential to life. Yet he is constantly ridiculing the upper classes or rather the ambition to belong to them which the catalogue meant to insinuate into its readers.

The visual satire is effected through various techniques. One is the collaged juxtaposition of incongruously unrelated objects (in the manner of Lautréamont's famous "fortuitous encounter of an umbrella and a sewing machine on a dissecting table"). There are relatively few examples of this kind of pre-Surrealist collage in *What a Life!* One of them depicts the unfortunate Lady Goosepelt, a chronic invalid who lived at Bournemouth "in a charming villegiatura." But the illustration shows a horse-drawn trash can from which emerges, as in Beckett's *Endgame,* the head of a lady of quality wearing an ostrich-trimmed hat. Another example is the picture of Lord Crewett, "who was never out of riding breeches," and whose breeches are in fact a pair of inverted cruets. But the authors' usual method is to present a single image from the catalogue, diverted from its original context by the accompanying caption. Sometimes the text ridicules the very crudeness of the reproduction, as in the illustration of Lady Goosepelt's eccentric husband Sir William, a figure standing under a shower from which heavy lines of water issue, with the legend: "Among his other odd ways he often indulged in the luxury of a treacle bath." Throughout, it is the proliferation of consumer goods deemed indispensable to the well-stocked Edwardian household that is under attack. An elaborate jellied prawn salad turned out of a mold from Whiteley's becomes a new hat sent down from London for the narrator's bride; on the same page a hideous scrollwork *bonheur-du-jour* laden with gewgaws is billed as his "unique collection of Sèvres." The occasional moments of a slightly darker humor such as the headless apparition (actually a dress on a hanger emerging from a steamer trunk) and the Paticaka railway disaster are strikingly premonitory of Ernst's *La femme 100 têtes* (a pun on "La femme sans tête"). Yet, in the absence of any known link one must assume that Lucas and Ernst were simply in touch with the same zeitgeist and received emanations of the same absurdity through the medium of a popular imagery, although what in Lucas's work are only polite suggestions of anarchy have become destructive paroxysms in Ernst's.

This bit of "shilling nonsense" as Lucas called it was but one of a number of collaborations between him and George Morrow. The latter, born in Belfast in 1869, was a popular illustrator and a regular contributor to *Punch* from 1906 almost to his death in 1955. Morrow's style is neat, fluent and idiomatic without any obvious tics; it is somewhat reminiscent of the French caricaturist Caran d'Ache whose work was popular in France at the time Morrow was a student there. It seems likely that the crisp *mise en page* of *What a Life!* was more Morrow's creation than Lucas's, though both probably collaborated on the "plot" and the jokes; like Lucas, Morrow had a reputation as a wit.

Lucas's daughter Audrey left a memoir of her father which tells us very little about him (though considerably more than Lucas's own volumes of "reminiscences"). We learn from her that he was rather irritable, hated draughts and believed in the importance of masticating bread with one's meals. Somehow he himself sounds a likely tenant of Frisby Towers, the cardboard castle where the narrator of *What a Life!* finally settles with his bride ("We were idyllically happy at Frisby Towers, in spite of its outward air of gloom"). An anecdote Audrey Lucas tells of Lucas's later years (he died in 1938 at the age of seventy), after he had left his family for an undisclosed reason and set up housekeeping on his own, suggests that he may finally have ended up living out the fantasies he had pilloried so wittily years before.

He did, I suppose, go in for a good many of the frills of life; but at these he was quite able to laugh, almost to sneer even. Part of his house in the country had been converted from a cottage, occupied many years before by a shepherd; and E.V.,

157

telling me one day that his dining-room, which had in it a great open fireplace, and had been in the shepherd's time the kitchen, went on to say, "Sometimes when I'm having dinner here, I imagine the shepherd's ghost coming back to have a look round. I suppose if he peeped in and saw me sitting here alone, in a dinner jacket, drinking champagne and being waited on by Watkins, he would think it a disgusting spectacle." He paused for a split second, before adding, "As indeed it is."

Indeed it may have been, but the story pinpoints the drama behind the surface of *What a Life!*: the conflict between our fascination with the appurtenances of physical comfort, that always seem to hold out the promise of a better life, and our knowledge that neither they nor anything else is going to alter the facts of our existence on earth. One of this century's greatest poets, Osip Mandelstam, wrote in a letter from Switzerland in 1906: "I have strange taste: I love the patches of reflected light on Lake Leman, respectful lackeys, the silent flight of the elevator, the marble vestibule of the hotel and the Englishwomen who play Mozart with two or three official listeners in the half-darkened salon. I love bourgeois, European comfort and am devoted to it not only physically but emotionally." Yet his "devotion" never allowed him to abandon the poetry which eventually led him to death in a Siberian prison camp after years of hardship. This tragic ambivalence—the contradictory allegiances to physical and spiritual well-being—exists in all of us and is the core of the situation which Lucas and Morrow elaborated within the confines of their exiguous comic masterpiece. What a life, indeed.

From E. V. Lucas and George Morrow's *What a Life!* (New York: Dover, 1975), an autobiography of an imaginary Edwardian with pictures from Whiteley's catalogue, first published by Methuen and Co. (London, 1911). An adapted version of the introduction was published in *Horizon* 17, no. 1 (Winter 1975).

The Figure in the Carport:
Kenward Elmslie

Kenward Elmslie's *Tropicalism* is the finest collection so far from this wonderful and singularly under-appreciated poet, and in my opinion it is one of the most important books of poetry in recent years. It also has a shapeliness lacking in his earlier collections, partly no doubt because of the hazards of small press publishing: *Album,* as its title implies, was a grab bag of brilliant fragments, drawn from many different sources including Elmslie's librettos for operas and the musical *The Grass Harp. Motor Disturbance,* published in 1971 in the Columbia University Press Frank O'Hara Award series, included poems from as far back as Elmslie's 1961 pamphlet *Pavilions,* making at times for disconcerting clashes in style. Not that a collection of poems need have anything resembling a plan or a structure, but the one uniting the separate poems of *Tropicalism* is so beautiful that one is apt to feel its lack in the next book of poems one chances to open.

This structure, which may or may not be there, is a kind of long conjugation, a ringing of changes on "tropicalism," a term Elmslie uses in the spirit of Frank O'Hara's "personism," and which is associated with Caetano Veloso's and Gilberto Gil's Brazilian cultural movement from the late sixties. The voice of the poet in *Tropicalism* (and in much of Elmslie's work, including his prose masterpiece *The Orchid Stories*) is, precisely, that of some freaked-out Lévi-Strauss, a mad scientist who has swallowed the wrong potion in his lab and is desperately trying to get his calculations on paper before everything closes in: in other words, the voice of today's *homme moyen sensuel.* Man has construed nature with the help of a set of complex devices and diagrams; nature of course has other ideas and a set of quite different and more formidable devices and diagrams. Elmslie lives on a geological fault which forms the common frontier of these two contending systems. Sometimes he falls in and disappears briefly, but mostly he displays an extraordinary sense of brinkmanship forced on him by the circumstances.

Elmslie's tropiques are far from *tristes;* too much is happening, for one thing. The poems are the result of extreme attentiveness and require extreme attentiveness from the reader: they aren't difficult but they are dense, and attentiveness leaves no room for *tristesse*. Also, though I imagine Burroughs has been an influence (along with the more obvious, and long ago assimilated, influences of Koch, O'Hara, and perhaps too the vivid present tenses of Ginsberg), Elmslie's tone is very different. It is as though Burroughs's permanent apocalypse were being observed by someone else: not a closet Savonarola but someone motivated by the humor, sensuality, and *joie de vivre* of an O'Hara, for instance. The world may be an industrial swamp, but Elmslie's dazzling one-step-ahead induction of it is a cause for rejoicing and even joy:

> Chaos has one bonus,
> somehow prevents total decay.
> Frills that loomed major
> are reduced to a single focus:
> flashbulbs popping around
> an ill-conceived plant-torture episode.
> We have something on everyone,
> something that will sound better,
> like all fairy stories,
> after it stands the test of time.
> Subliminal fear goes unnoticed:
> rocket into sun.
> —"Middle Class Fantasies"

The attentiveness comes with the reading; it is a skill that develops itself. The poem comes out like an electrocardiogram of the universe, puzzling to the untrained eye until one discovers one is reading it with the trained eye of the poet himself. Necessarily puzzling too because everything inessential has been left out; we are not seeing a landscape, for instance, but hearing about the only things in it that need concern us—he knows which they are. But very soon this fragmentary scene comes to seem natural since one has nothing arbitrary or optional to consider, or rather the arbitrary has now been brought into focus. I keep speaking of his poetry in visual terms, which is somewhat misleading, for although he is indeed a master of the memorable *aperçu* ("The figure in the carport"; "Bumblebees crawling around the empty Bumblebee Tuna Can"), the images are always closely meshed with revelations of the new laws of thermodynamics:

> The gigantic ghost scissors clacked away at the Olympic Team on the glacier, youngsters engrossed in their summer beverage. Screened by sandy lashes, their eyes vanished under their upper lids, up, up, slick but not *quite* right—maimed buck look. But that's what comes of years of flopping down anywhere, California-style, new professions zinging past, combinations and possible combinations that make you drool (gasp), aghast. Dumb come-on, none-the-less, to bank on the built-in climax that comes from realizing the death seizure is just a simulated orgasm moue.
>
> —"Visual Radios"

The scenery and the principle ordering it or deranging it are the same: this is visionary poetry which proceeds not by describing but by calling into being. The rapid syncopated rhythms of the passage just quoted are typical of Elmslie's style: his guided tour of chaos is conducted via roller-coaster—no question of going back or stopping to examine more closely some particularly enchanting specimen of lunar asparagus. You commit yourself to the poems at the very beginning; it is a one-way street and there is no waste space, nothing left over. At the end you have experienced what the poet wanted you to experience and, no matter how distasteful this may have been (and it often is), you feel distinctly refreshed.

I said before that this seems to me Elmslie's most satisfying book and that I felt it had a thematic unity. The unity may be nothing more than a feeling of a tone of voice building in intensity as it moves through ever more complex situations and civilizations, with the primitive past and the sci-fi future wedged inextricably together:

7.

The authorities here are highly susp—SHUSH! OK TAKE THIS DOWN. Che is going into market research, more relevant than doctoring the poor. OK TAKE THIS DOWN, THEY DON'T GIVE A

FLYING FUCK. Every life saved broadens the base of the population pyramid that much more, until its sub-strata . . . slimy and fetid but with more energy than the "thin-out" line near top . . . OK TAKE THIS DOWN FRIEND, OK? Roaches, tarantulas, roaches, tarantulas: in convoys of ten each they hurry along the traffic lane marked with day-glo dots, and down the starveling's throat. The Big Divvy according to the (TRANS-MISSION PROBLEMAS, AMIGO, BEAR WITH ME)—in the fields at low enough level to circumvent the inevitability of mechanization taking command (SORRY, PAL, DIFFERENT FEEDER CHANNEL FOR NONCE—ERRATUM: NUNS) in which case the population pyramid (BYE, FOLKS, TIME TO GO UNDERGROUND AGAIN) will be restructured into an obelisk, squeezing the hierarchy into a more nakedly vertical pattern that makes it impossible for them to reproduce themselves in sufficient numbers—less intermingling, less sloppy pecking-order infighting, more intra-bureau phoning, more non-destruct memos, more solitude at one's booth to which one is assigned early in life, but the obelisk isn't practical yet (HI BACK AGAIN IT'S ME)—pyramid has years to go as long as its base keeps widening (say) five percent per annum—then its weight is sufficiently defused to reduce the rate of sinkage to (say) ten percent per annum, which gives us (say) oh, 2050 may be a bit much and the pyramid may have to be converted into a rectangle: sarcophagus, with the lid hooked from the inside to cut down on hanky-panky (NO NEED TAKE REST DOWN: MESSAGE OVER, BYEBYE)—golf pro has yen for daughter, not her flabby henna mama—only daughter and school chum—gov't censor demands X number pesetas leave in snatches throbbing, with one girl tracing on other girl's boob: CHE—invisible finger-writing. Audience assumes its AMOR—except for politics buffs.

8.

Regular paintings in front of the arch with the discreet black curtain. Most interesting, such a hard glare beating down on the lilies (Utrillo), with the ballerina electric mixer (Duchamp) floating over the Tudor bed and its inviting sateen spread, reflected in the mirror, and the pretty couple in the background, their bodies lightly touching, staring at the dawn

from the balcony, pronunciation, and the subjective tenses
coming up so fast—

—"Tropicalism"

It may be the arrangement of the book, wherein one moves from short, lighter poems through long, major ones ("Winter Life," "Tropicalism," "Topiary Trek"), always aware of a deepening, an increasing tension which also becomes progressively lighter and funnier. There is also a new seamlessness to his language. I have liked his poems from the beginning, but having read the new ones, I now feel in some of the very early ones a somewhat high-pitched resonance, a not always justifiable vehemence, a skittishness which I might never have noticed had not the effortless mastery of the recent poems underscored them. Here absolutely everything works, and although Elmslie's vision of the world as a grotesque, picturesque, and very busy junkyard has changed little from the early "Shirley Temple Surrounded by Lions" and "The Dustbowl" ("The Harvey Girls invaded Kansas that spring of the famine / nudged by sweet memories of cornfields in the snow"), his elaboration of it has become progressively surer, stronger, more involving; sometimes (as in "Winter Life") almost austere, but classically cool in contrast to the "hot" materials he is working with, which is one reason why this poetry is so profoundly arresting. *Tropicalism* is on the same high level as *The Orchid Stories*. Both are evocations of a rococo world of banality and nightmare which, thanks to the almost loving understanding which the poet has brought to focus on it, always anticipating its next spasm or cataclysm correctly, comes in the end to seem like paradise enow.

Review of Kenward Elmslie's *Tropicalism* (Calais, VT: Z Press, 1975). From *Parnassus: Poetry in Review* 5, no. 1 (Fall–Winter 1977).

163

Second Presentation of
Elizabeth Bishop

To call Elizabeth Bishop a writer's writer is to pay her an ambiguous compliment. We all know about writer's writers, though we are perhaps incapable of really defining that term. But we perhaps do feel, even as we say it admiringly, that it somehow diminishes the writer. Should he be placed so far above the mass of readers, not to mention the mass of writers? Mightn't such exaltation be harmful to him, even taking into account the fact that he himself hasn't asked for it and may not know precisely what to do with it?

To call Elizabeth Bishop a writer's writer's writer is perhaps to compound the audacity of the compliment, to imply that her writing has sophistication—that somehow unfortunate state of felicity in whose toils most of us wallow from time to time even as we struggle to cast them off. Yet this is the first thing that strikes me about Miss Bishop's unique position among American poets, one might even say among American writers. That is, the extraordinarily intense loyalty her work inspires in writers of every sort—from poets like myself, sometimes considered a harebrained, homegrown surrealist whose poetry defies even the rules and logic of Surrealism, and from a whole generation of young experimental poets to experimenters of a different sort and perhaps of a steadier eye, such as Robert Duncan and James Tate, and to poet-critics of undeniable authority like Marianne Moore, Randall Jarrell, Richard Wilbur and Robert Lowell. It shouldn't be a criticism leveled at Miss Bishop that her mind is capable of inspiring and delighting minds of so many different formations. We must see it as her strength, a strength whose singularity almost prevents us from seeing it.

I first read Elizabeth Bishop's book *North and South* when it was published in 1946, and I had the experience in the very first poem, "The Map," of being drawn into a world that seemed as inevitable as "the" world and as charged with the possibilities of pleasure as the contiguous, overlapping world of poetry. Here, as in so many of her poems, the very materials—ink and paper—

seemed to enlarge the horizons of the poem as they simultaneously called it back to the constricting dimensions of the page,
much as a collage by Schwitters or Robert Motherwell triumphs
over its prosaic substance by cultivating its ordinariness and the
responses it can strike in our minds, where in a sense everything
is ordinary, everything happens in a perpetual present which is
a collage of objects and our impressions of them.

> Land lies in water; it is shadowed green.
> Shadows, or are they shallows, at its edges
> showing the line of long sea-weeded ledges
> where weeds hang to the simple blue from green.
> Or does the land lean down to lift the sea from under,
> drawing it unperturbed around itself?
> Along the fine tan sandy shelf
> is the land tugging at the sea from under?

> The shadow of Newfoundland lies flat and still.
> Labrador's yellow, where the moony Eskimo
> has oiled it. We can stroke these lovely bays,
> under a glass as if they were expected to blossom,
> or as if to provide a clean cage for invisible fish.
> The names of seashore towns run out to sea,
> the names of cities cross the neighboring mountains
> —the printer here experiencing the same excitement
> as when emotion too far exceeds its cause.
> These peninsulas take the water between thumb and finger
> like women feeling for the smoothness of yard-goods.

> Mapped waters are more quiet than the land is,
> lending the land their waves' own conformation:
> and Norway's hare runs south in agitation,
> profiles investigate the sea, where land is.
> Are they assigned, or can the countries pick their colors?
> —what suits the character or the native waters best.
> Topography displays no favorites; North's as near as West.
> More delicate than the historians' are the map-makers' colors.

In the last line of this first poem in her first collection Elizabeth
Bishop has, I think, given us the nucleus from which the dazzling
variety of her poetry will evolve. Like the highest kind of poetic
idea, it presents itself in the form of a paradox. How could the

map-makers' colors be more delicate than the historians'? How could the infinity of nuances and tones which is finally transformed into history, a living mosaic of whatever has happened and is happening now, prove less delicate—and not in the sense of softness or suavity but in the sense of a rigorously conceived mathematical instrument—than the commercial colors of maps in an atlas, which are the product, after all, of the expediencies and limitations of a mechanical process? Precisely because they are what is given to us to see, on a given day in a given book taken down from the bookshelf from some practical motive.

As the critic David Kalstone has said, Bishop's poems "both describe and set themselves at the limits of description . . . Details are also boundaries for Miss Bishop . . . Whatever radiant glimpses they afford, they are also set at the vibrant limits of our descriptive powers. [The poems] show us what generates that precarious state, and what surrounds us. 'From this the poem springs,' Wallace Stevens remarks, 'that we live in a place that is not our own and, much more, not ourselves, and hard it is in spite of blazoned days.' Miss Bishop writes under that star, aware of the smallness and dignity of human observation and contrivance. She sees with such a rooted, piercing vision, so realistically because she has never taken our presence in the world as totally real."

It is this continually renewed sense of discovering the strangeness, the unreality of our reality at the very moment of becoming conscious of it as reality, that is the great subject for Elizabeth Bishop. The silhouette of Norway unexpectedly becomes the fleeing hare it resembles; the names of cities conquer mountains; Labrador is yellow on the map not by chance but because the Eskimo has oiled it so as to make it into a window for an igloo; the universe is constantly expanding into vast generalizations that seem on the point of taking fire with meaning and contracting into tiny particulars whose enormous specific gravity bombards us with meaning from another unexpected angle.

> But surely it would have been a pity
> not to have seen the trees along this road,
> really exaggerated in their beauty,
> not to have seen them gesturing

like noble pantomimists, robed in pink.
—Not to have had to stop for gas and heard
the sad, two-noted, wooden tune
on disparate wooden clogs
carelessly clacking over
a grease-stained filling-station floor.
(In another country the clogs would all be tested.
Each pair there would have identical pitch.)
—A pity not to have heard
the other, less primitive music of the fat brown bird
who sings above the broken gasoline pump
in a bamboo church of Jesuit baroque:
three towers, five silver crosses.
—Yes, a pity not to have pondered,
blurr'dly and inconclusively,
on what connection can exist for centuries
between the crudest wooden footwear
and, careful and finicky,
the whittled fantasies of wooden cages.
—Never to have studied history in
the weak calligraphy of songbirds' cages.
                         —from "Questions of Travel"

In a group of memorable poems about Brazil, Miss Bishop, like Darwin, whom she admires, has sought not so much to come to grips with the frightening, teeming discipline of nature as it can be experienced raw in the South American landscape as to let herself be permeated and perhaps ultimately ordered by the lesson of that swarming order. Speaking of what the act of writing might be, she has said: "Dreams, works of art, (some) glimpses of the always-more-successful surrealism of everyday life, unexpected moments of empathy (is it?), catch a peripheral vision of whatever it is one can never really see full-face but that seems enormously important. I can't believe we are wholly irrational—and I do admire Darwin—but reading Darwin one admires the beautiful solid case being built up out of his endless, heroic observations, almost unconscious or automatic—and then comes a sudden relaxation, a forgetful phrase, and one feels that strangeness of his undertaking, sees the lonely young man, his eye fixed on facts and minute details, sinking or sliding giddily off into the unknown. What one seems to want in art, in experiencing it, is the same that is necessary for its creation, a self-forgetful, perfectly useless concentration"—a formulation not unlike Gauguin's "placing oneself in front of nature and dreaming." Only out of such "perfectly useless concentration" can emerge the one thing that is useful for us: our coming to know ourselves as the necessarily inaccurate transcribers of the life that is always on the point of coming into being.

In many of her poems Bishop installs herself as an open-minded, keen-eyed, even somewhat caustic observer of the life that is about to happen, speaking in a pleasant, chatty vernacular tone which seeks in no way to diminish the enormity of it, but rather to focus on it calmly and unpoetically. In the three short prose poems spoken from the point of view of three creatures much lower on the scale of human consciousness—"Giant Toad," "Strayed Crab," "Giant Snail"—she gives us the mystification of an elemental eye that is being steeped in it to the point of bemused utterance. The Giant Snail gives this account of its limited but basic perception:

The rain has stopped. The waterfall will roar like that all night. I have come out to take a walk and feed. My body— foot, that is—is wet and cold and covered with sharp gravel. It is white, the size of a dinner plate. I have set myself a goal, a certain rock, but it may well be dawn before I get there. Although I move ghostlike and my floating edges barely graze the ground, I am heavy, heavy, heavy. My white muscles are already tired. I give the impression of a mysterious ease, but it is only with the greatest effort of my will that I can rise above the smallest stones and sticks. And I must not let myself be distracted by those rough spears of grass. Don't touch them. Draw back. Withdrawal is always best.

The rain has stopped. The waterfall makes such a noise! (And what if I fall over it?) The mountains of black rock give off such clouds of steam! Shiny streamers are hanging down their sides. When this occurs, we have a saying that the Snail Gods have come down in haste. I could never descend such steep escarpments, much less dream of climbing them.

That toad was too big, too, like me. His eyes beseeched my love. Our proportions horrify our neighbors.

Rest a minute; relax. Flattened to the ground, my body is like a pallid, decomposing leaf. What's that tapping on my shell? Nothing. Let's go on.

My sides move in rhythmic waves, just off the ground, from front to back, the wake of a ship, wax-white water, or a slowly melting floe. I am cold, cold, cold as ice. My blind, white bull's head was a Cretan scare-head; degenerate, my four horns that can't attack. The sides of my mouth are now my hands. They press the earth and suck it hard. Ah, but I know my shell is beautiful, and high, and glazed, and shining. I know it well, although I have not seen it. Its curled white lip is of the finest enamel. Inside, it is as smooth as silk, and I, I fill it to perfection.

My wide wake shines, now it is growing dark. I leave a lovely opalescent ribbon: I know this.

But O! I am too big. I feel it. Pity me.

If and when I reach the rock, I shall go into a certain crack there for the night. The waterfall below will vibrate through my shell and body all night long. In that steady pulsing I can rest. All night I shall be like a sleeping ear.

A sleeping ear—that is as good a metaphor as any for the delicate but imperfect instrument the poet has to use in order to construe the bewilderingly proliferating data of the universe that is continually surging up around him, threatening to submerge him at the moment he in turn threatens to pierce it through with a ray of interpretation. The ear hears but sleeps and cannot know that it hears; yet it hears nevertheless. Not until the senses have all but eroded themselves to nothing in the process of doing the work assigned to them can anything approaching a moment of understanding take place—as meaningless perhaps as the glimpse of the girl at the window which is the ultimate vision of the condemned hero in Kafka's *Trial*, but as crucial because it is what is finally there.

In another poem where, as in "The Map," Miss Bishop shows a series of pictures which are sometimes illustrations in an old gazetteer (the poem is entitled "Over 2,000 Illustrations and a Complete Concordance") and sometimes real scenes remembered from an actual voyage—memories and illustrations overlap inextricably here—she elaborates the dilemma of perception versus understanding in a sustained, almost painfully acute argument that is one of the summits of her poetry. "Thus should have been our travels: / serious, engravable," she begins. But "The Seven Wonders of the World are tired / and a touch familiar, but the other scenes, / innumerable, though equally sad and still, / are foreign." Throughout the poem, which dips freely back and forth from a steel-etched "Holy Land" to the coast of Nova Scotia to Rome to Mexico to Marrakesh, we are never sure that the landscape we are in is the real world or the "engravable" one. Finally travel, the movement on which so much of her poetry hinges, dissolves into a bewildering swarm of particulars.

> Everything only connected by "and" and "and."
> Open the book. (The gilt rubs off the edges
> of the pages and pollinates the fingertips.)
> Open the heavy book. Why couldn't we have seen
> this old Nativity while we were at it?
> —the dark ajar, the rocks breaking with light,
> an undisturbed, unbreathing flame,
> colorless, sparkless, freely fed on straw,
> and, lulled within, a family with pets,
> —and looked and looked our infant sight away.

The last line still seems to me to somehow contain the clue to Elizabeth Bishop's poetry. Just as the crumbling gilt of the books seems, disturbingly, to pollinate our fingers, endow them fleetingly with life, so is flame—freely fed on straw (in the illustration)—colorless, sparkless, unbreathing and undisturbed. It would have been nice, at this point, to have *seen* the nativity, and not only to have seen it but to have participated in it to the point of self-effacement—to have looked our infant sight away.

David Kalstone has glossed the line thoughtfully and pointed out the similarity to a line in another key poem in Bishop's oeuvre, "The Imaginary Iceberg," where she describes the monstrous perfection of the iceberg as "a scene a sailor'd give his eyes for," mentioning that both lines convey a mysterious yearning to stop observing, which they also guard against. "What will it mean," he asks, "to look and look our infant sight away?" Where or when is *away*? Is it a measureless absorption in the scene? Or on the contrary, a loss of powers, as in "to waste away"? Or a welcome relinquishment, a return to "infant" sight, keeping its Latin root of "speechless"?

It is no doubt all these things, and a perfect summation of the poet's act—the looking so intense that it becomes something like death or ecstasy, both at once perhaps. Behind the multiple disguises, sometimes funny, sometimes terrifyingly unlike anything human, that the world assumes in Elizabeth Bishop's poetry, this moment of almost-transfiguration is always being tracked to its lair, giving the work a disturbing reality unlike anything else in contemporary poetry.

From *World Literature Today* 51, no. 1 (Winter 1977). Written for the special issue in honor of the 1976 Neustadt Prize Laureate at the University of Oklahoma in Norman. "Giant Snail,""The Map," and excerpt from "Questions of Travel" from *The Complete Poems 1927–1979* by Elizabeth Bishop. Copyright © 1979, 1983 by Alice Helen Methfessel. Reprinted by permission of Farrar, Straus and Giroux, LLC.

A Reminiscence: Frank O'Hara

I first met Frank at a cocktail party at the Mandrake Book Shop in Cambridge in the spring of 1949. I believe the occasion for the party was an exhibition of watercolors by Edward Gorey, who at that time was Frank's roommate. I had known who Frank was for some time—he had submitted poems and stories to the *Advocate,* of which I was an editor, and we had published some. I had thought several times of introducing myself when we passed each other on the street, but each time I held back. Frank's normal expression—the one into which his face settled when he was thinking about something—was a tough, aggressive one which I later found out did not necessarily reflect his mood (though it certainly *could* on occasion!). So it was rather a surprise when I overheard a ridiculous remark such as I liked to make uttered in a ridiculous nasal voice that sounded to me like my own, and to realize that the speaker was Frank. He said:

"Let's face it, *Les Sécheresses* is greater than *Tristan.*" I knew that *Les Sécheresses* was a vocal work by Poulenc which had been performed recently at Harvard; I also knew, back in those dull days, that nobody at Harvard took Poulenc or any other modern composer (except Hindemith, Piston, and Stravinsky) seriously, and that this assertion was in the way of a pleasant provocation. Also, I felt somehow, it summed up a kind of aesthetic attitude which was very close to my own. I knew instinctively that Frank didn't really believe that *Les Sécheresses* was greater than *Tristan,* and that he wanted people to understand this, but at the same time he felt it important to make that statement, possibly because he felt that art is already serious enough; there is no point in making it seem even more serious by taking it too seriously.

But I was struck, as I said, not only by his remark but also by the voice in which it was uttered. Though we grew up in widely distant regions of the Northeast, he in Massachusetts and I in western New York state, we both inherited the same twang, a hick accent so out of keeping with the roles we were trying to play that it seems to me we probably exaggerated it, later on, in hopes of making it seem intentional. I don't know what the significance of this was, but it fascinated us and was doubtless one reason why we became friends so quickly after our first meeting. On the telephone, I was told, we were all but indistinguishable. Once when I was at Frank's apartment in New York I picked up the phone and impersonated Frank to Joe LeSueur, one of Frank's closest friends, pretending to pick a quarrel with him for several minutes during which he was entirely taken in. Another time when Frank came to visit my parents' farm in upstate New York he walked into the kitchen one evening when my mother was washing dishes and asked if he could help; without turning around from the sink my mother said, "No, John, go back in and talk with your friends."

Having determined that Frank's somewhat intimidating punk-angel look was an anomaly, partly the result of a broken nose which gave him the look of a scrappy boxer, I decided to try to spend as much time as possible in his company during the few weeks that remained before my graduation from Harvard.

(Frank, whose college days had been interrupted by a two-year stint in the Navy toward the end of the war, stayed on another year after I left.) Not since I had met Kenneth Koch a couple of years before had I encountered anyone so stimulating, with such a powerfully personal way of looking at art and poetry and at the world. He was an insatiable reader with a knack for discovering unknown writers who, later on, came into their own. Shortly after we first met I ran into him in Widener Library carrying a stack of books by various writers I had never heard of, including Samuel Beckett, Jean Rhys and Flann O'Brien, who were in fact all but unknown in 1949. He also introduced me to the work of Ronald Firbank, whom I had avoided reading up until then because people said he was frivolous and silly. Frank corrected this misconception and somehow allowed me to see what a major writer Firbank was. I was interested in modern music but hadn't really heard very much; recordings of it in that early LP era were relatively few. Frank played the piano quite well, albeit somewhat percussively as was the fashion then, and we used sometimes to go to a music room in Eliot House, where he lived, and I got to hear for the first time works by Satie, Krenek, Sessions, Schönberg, and others, as well as some of Frank's own compositions (including a "sonatina that lasts about three seconds"), which have apparently disappeared. I think he was rather careless with his work; he had a tremendous energy and zest for it while he was working on it, and then seemed to rather lose interest once it was done. One work that seems to have been lost was a play called "Dig My Grave with a Golden Spoon," of which I remember only that the action was to take place behind a fishnet curtain, and that one character said to another, "I don't think we're ever going to get out of here," to which the latter replied, "Why not? I don't see any 'No Exit' signs anywhere." So much for Sartre.

We were serious but we were also a little unintentionally funny in our aesthetes' pose, and a little pathetic. Nobody but ourselves and a handful of adepts knew or cared about our poetry, or seemed likely to in the future. Though Cambridge teemed with poets who would later become celebrated (Bly, Creeley, Donald Hall, Adrienne Rich, Richard Wilbur) we did not know them well, if at all, except for Koch who had already graduated the year before, and V. R. Lang whose close friendship with Frank had only just begun. And despite their presence, Cambridge seemed to me then a place where anything adventurous in poetry or the arts was subtly discouraged: I mentioned in my preface to Frank's *Collected Poems* how some friends of his in the music department had made fun of him for attending the premiere of a work by Schönberg. Later on, in the more encouraging climate of New York, we could begin to be ourselves, but much of the poetry we both wrote as undergraduates now seems marred by a certain nervous preciosity, in part a reaction to the cultivated blandness around us which also impelled us to callow aesthetic pronouncements.

Nevertheless I look back on that remote period as an almost idyllic one for a number of reasons. One was that I had discovered a wonderful new friend and we gave each other attention and encouragement. Another was that we didn't know so many people and could often be alone together—later on, when Frank moved to New York, it was difficult to see him alone. New York discovered him and his radiant magnetism almost as soon as he moved there. Everybody wanted to be with him, so that it was difficult to get a private audience. If one made a date for dinner with him there would usually be six or seven other close friends along, all secretly resentful of each other's presence. And after a few years I left for France on a Fulbright and ended up staying there for ten years, during which I saw him only on the rare occasions when I came home or he went to Europe. By the time I moved back to New York, he had only a few months left to live. And during those months, alas, we seldom had or took the opportunity to see each other. Frank's job at the museum had become more time-consuming; he was busy with the Nakian retrospective which opened just a few weeks before his death; his circle of business and personal acquaintances seemed to be constantly expanding at a geometrical rate. I was having problems of my own readjusting to New York and my new job at *ARTnews* after a decade abroad, finding and furnishing an apartment, picking up the threads of interrupted friendships, re-learning the New York *patois*. Our moments together were few and far between. One that sticks with me was a bleak Sunday afternoon in the spring of 1966; Frank had just returned from a business trip to Holland with a mysterious ailment. He was lying in bed surrounded by the unread Sunday *Times*. I had never seen him so "down," or at any rate, never for reasons of his own health: more often his moments of depression grew out of empathy with other people's misfortunes. I tried, not too successfully, to cheer him up, and left after an hour or so. Probably his mood was short-lived; Frank was too curious about what was going on around him to remember his depressions or anxieties for very long. I have often envied this quality of his.

Unfortunately, this rather sad occasion is one of the last memories I have of him, except for the gala opening of the Nakian show shortly afterward, where I kept catching sight of him (in black tie) at a distance, moving from group to group with the purposeful but effortless grace of a Balanchine dancer. The last time we spoke was, I believe, the Friday he left for the fatal weekend at Fire Island. He suggested that we have lunch at Larré's as we often did. I was trying to clear up my desk before going to Maine for a few days and suggested another day the week after the following one. Shortly afterward, eternity intersected time. How could I have known it was our last chance to gossip in the bar of that hectic but pleasant restaurant (the setting of so many "lunch poems"), where the French waiters didn't mind replying in French to one's French, where the paté (as Jimmy Schuyler once wrote in a poem) was really meat loaf and where Frank usually had a Ricard and the *oeuf à la russe*? I can never go there now without imagining him across the dinky table for two, responding to some gambit of mine with a favorite rejoinder like "Oh, so *that's* the way it is, is it?" At which we both burst into laughter, not because anything funny was said, but from the special happiness that comes with being with an old friend in a familiar place and making the same remarks that have warmed and mildly amused us so many times before—the *olim meminisse juvabit* syndrome. How cruel and unjust it seems that we cannot do it again.

From *Homàge to Frank O'Hara,* edited by Bill Berkson and Joe LeSueur (Bolinas, CA: Big Sky, 1978).

Schubert's Unfinished:
David Schubert

I first encountered David Schubert's work in the early 1940s, when I was in high school and trying to find out as much as I could about contemporary poetry. This included reading the annual Oscar Williams anthologies and as many little magazines as I could lay my hands on in rural upstate New York. Schubert was one of the poets who impressed me the most then, though I continue to believe that there was a lot of very exciting poetry being written in the thirties and forties by poets who, like Schubert, have been forgotten since.

At some point in the sixties I picked up a paperback copy of *Initial A*—marked down to 75 cents from its original price of $1.50—and discovered Schubert anew. Since being asked to contribute to the present volume, a year or so ago, I have discovered him a third time and now carry *Initial A* with me on travels. For me it's one of those books that poets keep for themselves, to remind them of what poetry can be when the writing isn't going well and one feels out of touch with the possibilities of poetry. To sit down for a little while and reread some of Schubert's rare and poignant verse is like opening a window in a room that had become stuffy without one's realizing it.

Schubert presents a specifically American experience that reminds one of certain contemporaries—poets such as Delmore Schwartz and Hart Crane (though there is a ponderous side to Schwartz that Schubert doesn't have; nor are there echoes in Schubert of the portentousness that for me mars Crane's poetry), but also artists like Walker Evans, Arthur Dove, Hopper and Reginald Marsh and composers like Ruth Crawford Seeger. That is to say that it's recognizably of the same climate and period. In reality, Schubert's poetry, both wildly disjunct and secretly cohesive, is like no one else's art. Who else could have written these lines, and what is happening in them?

And over tight breath, tighter eyes,
The mirror ebbs, it ebbs and flows.
And the intern, the driver, speed
To gangrene! But—who knows—suppose
He was beside her! Please, star-bright,
First I see, while in the night
A soft-voiced, like a tear, guitar—
It calls a palm coast from afar.

His poetry is made up of moments like these, that are like a complex, dissonant, astringent musical chord. Analyze it and it falls apart, or at any rate the analysis does. The parts have to be kept together, their possibilities allowed to remain open-ended, for the full range of the chord's savor—bitter to acidulous to perilously sweet—to register.

I don't think it's demeaning to call Schubert a "poet's poet"—a poet whom poets in particular treasure for the knowledge of the craft of poetry he can give to a practitioner of it, but also one whose work is open and available to everybody. He is always kindly and tactfully ushering us back to square one, reminding us that we have to start all over again at the beginning when we approach the writing or reading of poetry.

"What in the world are you trying to do
In the small room, shivering so.—But
It won't hurt it really won't, tell me!—
I'll touch you with my thought and we—
We'll walk out on the sea as one
Crosses the street, and on the sun
In amber day, before!—but run!—
The road can catch and catches us—
But the black buoys! And before
Those buildings lean down grabbing us—
Run! It won't hurt. Learning's like
Learning to walk after a long
Sickness, singing, happy as
Happy children all day long."

From *Works and Days,* edited by Ted Weiss and Renée Karol Weiss, *Quarterly Review of Literature,* fortieth anniversary issue (1983). Written March 8, 1983.

On the Poetry of F. T. Prince

That a great poet could write and publish three collections of poetry over a period of twenty-five years and still remain undiscovered is an idea we find hard to accept today when we imagine ourselves to have reached the level of maximum receptiveness, when poetry has finally "caught on" after all these centuries and when even *poètes maudits* have a hard time remaining so for very long. And yet it can happen. In our country, one of our finest poets, Robert Fitzgerald, remains unknown or at least unread, which is almost the same thing. In England, where at the moment "the languid strings do scarcely move," F. T. Prince suffers the even worse fate of being somewhat known and a little read, if only so that he may be all the more quickly dismissed without the slightest twinge of conscience. The fault of both poets is that they cannot be attached to any group; therefore, their excellence confuses people. Fitzgerald's voice is lost in America where the loyalty-oath mentality has infiltrated even poetry, where you cannot see the poet for the disciples. And Prince is simply alone in England.

Although he has occasionally contributed to *Poetry,* Prince's only book published in the U.S. as of 1983 (except for a scholarly work on Milton's Italian influences distributed by Oxford) was for a long time a pamphlet published in 1941 in New Directions' Poet of the Month series. With one exception, a beautiful early poem called "The Babiaantje," these poems are taken from his first volume, *Poems,* published in 1938 by Faber. A second British collection, *Soldiers Bathing,* published in 1954, included only eleven new poems, three earlier ones and three extraordinary translations from St. John of the Cross. His *Collected Poems* of 1979 (Sheep Meadow Press) is again short on new poems—only thirteen, alas—but it includes "all he wishes to preserve" from the previous books and will thus be convenient except for readers like me who believe that everything he writes is worth preserving.

There is rarely anything obscure in his poems, but their final effect remains mysterious. Looking back over poems by Prince, we can discern the path we have taken, the general architecture, but an individual poem will seem to hover in a cloud of gold motes. The essence of Prince is already in the three "early poems": "The Babiaantje," "The Moonflower," and "Cefalù." The first is an extremely simple lyric in three eight-line stanzas. It was probably written in the early thirties, but nothing in its language suggests either Auden or the Georgians: its cool elegiac smoothness is closer to Arnold or Landor. The narrator has returned to a wood he knew as a boy to hunt for the babiaantje, "a pale blue / Wild hyacinth that between narrow gray leaves / On the ground grew." Here is the final stanza:

> The flower will be breathing there now, should I wish
> To comb the grass beneath those trees,
> And having found it, should go down
> To snuff it, on my knees
> But now, although the crested hoopoe
> Calls like a bell, how barren these
> Rough paths and dusty woodlands look to one
> Who has lost youth's peace.

(This is the version printed in the New Directions pamphlet: the later one substitutes "search" for "comb," "ways" for "paths," and adds an exclamation point at the end, which gives a clue to the phenomenal sensitivity of Prince's ear and also shows how he likes to pair off concrete and abstract words.) There is nothing in either version to startle any but the most finicky reader, but the latter will note a delicate but consistent disparity between the sense of the words and the *sprachgitter*, or feeling of the language, as in the rather crude word "snuff," whose reverberations come to be dominant. Once alerted by the language, we begin to probe the meaning. Is it so very clear? Will the flower be there even if he decides not to look for it? Would the woods look even more barren without the call of the hoopoe? And is peace a characteristic of youth? Perhaps the answer is yes in all three cases, but at any rate the poet has stirred our curiosity. We begin to suspect that his poem is far less classic than it seems to be. Its conventional surface is striated with uncertainties, mined by shifting, opposing forces, as in the music of Busoni, the one composer to meaningfully fuse classicism and atonality, and who is thus a spiritual forerunner of Prince.

The question of forerunners could—and should—be the subject of a separate essay. Once examined, it would help to explain why Prince's poetry seems so subtly different from that of his English contemporaries. First of all is the fact that he is, or was, not English but South African, meaning that he grew up amid the endless spaces of that country, in his case in an ambience of privilege and isolation, which allowed him to pursue the literature that attracted him. Some of it was French—notably Rimbaud and Valéry—and Italian—Ariosto and Tasso, whose influence culminated in his study of Milton and in the poem "Strambotti." And of course, the English, from Donne (the love poems in *Soldiers Bathing*) to the Victorians to Eliot. One major inspiration seems to have been that strange and neglected hybrid masterpiece, Eliot's translation of St.-John Perse's *Anabase*. It would be interesting to trace the repercussions on the thirties generation of this collaboration between the most French of twentieth-century English poets and the most English of French ones. At any rate we can feel it in Prince's landscapes of migration and the history outside of recorded history, of the engulfing and engulfed past that is lost to us. It sighs in monologues like "Chaka" and in the anonymous but precise wilderness settings of shorter poems like "For the Deserted" and "For Fugitives."

It would be easy to invent a title for F. T. Prince like "best poet working in England today"—but is this necessary? Let's leave it at this: Prince is one of the best twentieth-century poets. Like Landor, he stands somewhat apart from mainstream modern poetry; like him, he is a poet to whom poets turn when they cannot write, that is, he is a source of poetry. He is an artist.*

---

*Frank Templeton Prince, 1912–2003.

From *PN Review* (Fall 2002). Based on an introduction to a reading Prince gave of his poems at the Church of the Transfiguration in New York City (1983).

Introduction to Fairfield Porter's *The Collected Poems with Selected Drawings*

Read and enjoy these poems. Fairfield Porter was a great painter. He was also a fine poet. His poetry didn't always equal his painting, but it is something special. It is uneven, but its very unevenness is preferable to the dull uniformity that afflicts so much poetry today. In that, Porter resembles Emily Dickinson, whose best work has been compared to a period of fine weather—wonderful, and subject to change. Perhaps this is to be expected—after all, shifts of weather are a force in the paintings.

The unevenness can occur in the course of a single poem, such as the first of two poems to the painter Leon Hartl, which begins awkwardly: "The son of an alien baker valued for his skill," and ends in a heart-catching burst of song:

> Only by watching a flower fade can you know it and
>   understand it,
> Its perfume changes:
> Dry touches of crispness in an airy sky.

The last line reminds us of his painting, of course, which is one reason why it is so good to have these poems in a book. But this is not always the case with his best lyric passages: they are often quite unlike the paintings and unlike anyone else's poetry, like the marvelous sonnet that begins:

> The train rolls jouncily towards the city
> With a slight tilt against the landscape seen on both sides.

I am envious of those lines and those that follow, and especially of the word "jouncily"—so perfect, so unexpected. Is it possible that anyone ever used it before?

To the best of my recollection, Porter's poetry mattered a lot to him, while remaining a *violon d'Ingres*. In one poem, "I Wonder What They Think of My Verses," he indeed wonders what various friends think of his verses, but doesn't seem too worried about it. He is more interested in characterizing each friend with a couple of deft, light strokes; in saying their names for the pleasure of saying a friend's name. (I am the John in the poem, described as "lazy" and "quick.") In the first of the "Letters to Kenneth Koch," one of his many sestinas, he begins by saying: "Because I am not so vers / atile as Kenneth, at least in verse, I prefer to stick compulsive / ly to the same unvarying sestina form"; and he ends the poem, "As for painting, well, that is something else."

Well, it is. But both paintings and poems are animated by the same quiet urgency, regulated by "the losing clock of the tide," as he so memorably puts it in "Great Spruce Head Island," by "the compass / following a way that it knows without knowing" ("To the Mainland"), by "the darkness advancing between the lamps like adventure"("In the Suburbs"). Much of life is loosely bundled in these poems, but Porter, as was his way, gives us vibrant samples, not an inventory:

> the smell of bushes
> A barking dog, footsteps, the slam of car doors
> A latching door, newspapers and boxes
> The color of food on the colored tablecloth
> And music, and musical voices.
>
> —"At Night"

Like his pictures, Fairfield Porter's poetry invites us "to contemplate this color both rare and familiar" ("A Few Leaves Fall"). We shall not be disappointed if we accept the invitation.

From Fairfield Porter's *The Collected Poems with Selected Drawings,* edited by John Yau with David Kermani (New York: Tibor de Nagy Editions— The Promise of Learnings, Inc., 1985).

Introduction to Marcel Allain and Pierre Souvestre's *Fantômas*

Stretching his immense shadow
Across the world and across Paris
What is this gray-eyed specter
Rising out of the silence?
Fantômas might it be you
Lurking on the rooftops?
　　—Robert Desnos,
　　　"Complaint of Fantômas"

From the moment it was published in February 1911, *Fantômas* (and the thirty-one sequels which immediately followed it) was a phenomenon: a work of fiction whose popularity cut across all social and cultural strata. Countesses and concierges; poets and proletarians; Cubists, nascent Dadaists, soon-to-be Surrealists: everyone who could read, and even those who could not, shivered at posters of a masked man in impeccable evening clothes, dagger in hand, looming over Paris like a somber Gulliver, contemplating hideous misdeeds from which no citizen was safe. Plastered on billboards, on kiosks and *colonnes Morris,* on walls of corridors in the Métro, his image multiplied throughout the city. In short order five Fantômas films directed by the incomparable Louis Feuillade further celebrated the exploits of the "king of the night," his mistress Lady Beltham, his mysterious daughter Hélène, and his implacable foes, Inspector Juve and the daredevil young reporter Jérôme Fandor (soon to become romantically involved with Hélène). There have been endless reprints of the novels, frequent remakes of the films until as recently as the mid-sixties (though none bears comparison with Feuillade's), not to mention theatrical adaptations, photo-novels, and translations into umpteen foreign languages, including Czech, Greek, and Serbian. (The present translation is a modernized version of one published in 1915 by both Stanley Paul in London and Brentano's in New York.) In France, the Fantômas phenomenon is a live issue even today: co-author Marcel Allain was an honored guest at a conference of intellectuals at Cerisy in 1967, two years before his death, and at least two serious literary reviews have published special Fantômas issues (*La tour de feu* in December 1965 and *Europe* in 1978). I am particularly indebted to the latter for information given here; in addition, a 1951 book entitled *Les terribles* by Antoinette Peské and Pierre Marty has valuable material on Fantômas and on kindred spirits like Maurice Leblanc's Arsène Lupin and Gaston Leroux's Chéri-Bibi. It would seem that the *empereur du crime*, whose fate was naturally left in doubt at the end of each novel, is still alive and well and living in Paris.

Fantômas was the chance creation of two inspired hacks, both of whom had studied law before turning to the French equivalent of Grub Street. Pierre Souvestre was born to a well-to-do family at the manor of Keraval in Brittany in 1874; after being admitted to the bar he apparently grew bored with that profession and entered the new field of automotive journalism, first at a magazine called *L'auto* and then with another called *Poids lourds* (Heavy Trucks), while also serving as drama critic for the newspaper *Le soleil*. In search of a secretary, he happened on Marcel Allain, a clever young man almost ten years his junior who amazed him by producing a seventeen-page article on a new truck (the "Darracq-Serpolet"), about which he knew nothing, in the space of two hours. So their collaboration began, and soon Allain was made managing editor of *Poids lourds* as well as ghostwriter of a column by Souvestre in *L'auto;* shortly both joined the editorial staff of the newly created theatrical review *Comoedia*. The withdrawal of an advertiser from *L'auto* left the magazine with a number of blank pages which the resourceful authors rapidly filled with a "Hindu" serial called *Le rour.* This proved so successful that they supplied a pseudonymous parody of it for yet another vehicular journal, *Le vélo* (The Bike). That sequel, entitled *Le four* ("The Oven," or, in popular parlance, "The Flop"), brought them to the attention of the publisher Arthème Fayard, who commissioned them to write a series of five fantastic novels having a common theme. The day after meeting with Fayard they put their heads together and came up with a lot of ideas but no title; later, in the Métro, Allain seized on the name *Fantômus*. Souvestre wrote it down in a notebook and subsequently showed it to Fayard, who misread it *Fantômas*—doubtless a lucky accident, for *Fantômus* doesn't seem quite to make it, while *Fantômas* is somehow pregnant with mystery.

Thanks to a blockbusting publicity campaign, the first novel was an instant success and the sequels, frequently dictated by the authors to save time and sometimes produced in the span of a couple of days, were awaited with an impatience rivaling that with which upper-class Frenchmen of the time of Louis XV awaited the arrival of the first green peas in spring. Feuillade's films of 1913–14 fanned the craze; then Souvestre died suddenly of Spanish influenza in 1914, the war arrived a few months later, and Allain was off to the trenches. He survived to produce eleven more Fantômas novels on his own as well as an immense amount of ephemeral fiction on other themes (some six hundred novels as well as innumerable stories and articles), eventually marrying Souvestre's widow. He died in 1969 three weeks short of his eighty-fourth birthday, apparently still an amused and adventurous spirit, content with his singular career and active almost to the end of his life as a pulp writer and compulsive driver of the cars he collected.

What is most surprising about the Fantômas tales is the gap between their crude narratives, appropriately garbed in hackneyed prose, and the deep impression they left on the work of poets and painters. As early as 1912 Apollinaire founded the Société de Amis de Fantômas (SAF); in 1914 he wrote in the august *Mercure de France* of "that extraordinary novel, full of life and imagination, lamely written but extremely vivid . . . From the imaginative standpoint *Fantômas* is one of the richest works that exist." And Cocteau later wrote of "the absurd and magnificent lyricism of *Fantômas*." It is true that Apollinaire and Cocteau were, in the words of one critic, "always afraid of missing the boat." But what of more reserved spirits such as Max Jacob, an active member of the SAF who wrote poems about Fantômas; of Blaise Cendrars, who called the Fantômas series "the modern *Aeneid*"; of Desnos, whose "Complaint of Fantômas," quoted above, was set to music by Kurt Weill? (What, one wonders, has happened to the score? Was it a Gallic version of Weill's "Ballad of Mackie Messer"?) To say nothing of Aragon, Colette, Raymond Queneau and Pablo Neruda, all of whom are reported to have been fans of the beastly hero, as were the painters Picasso, Juan Gris, and Magritte.

It is all somewhat puzzling, since a case can easily be made against the "absurd and magnificent lyricism" of the novels. Fantômas was a late-blooming *fleur du mal* on a vine whose roots extended back to the mid–nineteenth century and beyond, if we want to include the Gothic period and such ancestors as Melmoth and Manfred. But Fantômas isn't just a personage, superhuman or not, but a place, an atmosphere, a state of mind: this tradition too goes back to Eugène Sue's *Mystères de Paris* (1842–43) and to Ponson du Terrail (1829–71), whose hero Rocambole gave the French language the adjective *rocambolesque,* still used to describe anything farfetched. In Hugo's *Les misérables* we have the reverse prototypes of Fantômas and Juve in Jean Valjean, the long-suffering convict-hero, and the evil Inspector Javert; while Maldoror in Lautréamont's *Les chants de Maldoror,* a proto-Surrealist *chanson de geste,* has often been seen as a forerunner of Fantômas, though it is unlikely that Allain and Souvestre had ever heard of him. As the century drew to a close the genre of the novel of terror, often with Paris as the important backdrop, reached new heights with such writers as Maurice Leblanc (Arsène Lupin), Gaston Leroux (Chéri-Bibi), and the amazing, recently discovered, and aptly named Gustave Le-Rouge, author of such gory treats as *The Mysterious Dr. Cornelius* and *The War of the Vampires.* (LeRouge, who wove a strain of science fiction into his incredible and interminable novels, seems to have had a love-hate affair with America, which he never visited but often used for his settings; his energetic young American villains are the exact antitheses of America's Nick Carter, also immensely popular in France at the time, and perhaps prefigure one of Fantômas's alter egos, the American detective Tom Bob in *Le policier apache*—"The Hoodlum Policeman," but published in England as *Slippery as Sin.*)

It is safe to say that any of the above writers were superior to Messrs. Allain and Souvestre, even as purveyors of popular entertainment. For all their crimes, Arsène Lupin (who, one critic has said, used the same tailor as Fantômas) and Chéri-Bibi had their sympathetic, Robin Hood side; even Leroux's Phantom of the Opera is a not-inhuman monster. LeRouge's villains are certainly beyond redemption, but the dreamlike atmosphere of his narratives lightens the terror. But with Fantômas, terror almost becomes monotonous. He really has no redeeming traits;

greed and vengeance are his chief motivations, despite a knee-jerk paternal attachment to the ambiguous and ultimately unconvincing Hélène. His sadism seems especially directed toward women, and it doesn't matter whether they are young or old, virtuous or wicked, marchionesses or streetwalkers. But of course men aren't spared either. In *The Daughter of Fantômas,* the eighth novel in the series, Fantômas is off to South Africa with Juve in hot pursuit; once there he does away with his daughter's elderly female guardian and almost simultaneously provokes the lynching of Jupiter, a black "noble savage," having meanwhile infected the luxurious ocean liner *British Queen* by injecting rats with plague germs and watching its five hundred passengers die ghastly deaths.

In an article titled "The Morality of Fantômas" in the review *Europe,* Louis Chavance summarizes the case against the antihero. The enduring popularity of the novels for literati and just plain folks is justified "neither by the clarity nor the vigor of their style, which, in its density, resembles a layer of volcanic ash into which one sinks to the ankles; nor by their imagination nor their extremely simple construction, wherein a single 'climax' per volume (the phantom hansom cab; the singing fountains of the Place de la Concorde) constitutes the central point around which the other events turn; nor by the extremely conventional and simplistic characters, including that of Fantômas himself . . . which is ultimately reduced to his penchant for atrocities and his morality: that of a *petit bourgeois* who prefers crime to bowling."

Chavance explains that our fascination with Fantômas is due to the Surrealists' having welcomed him into their cénacle, though given his low opinion of the series, he offers no very good explanation for their having done so. He also attributes the success of the stories in part to the exploits of the *bande à Bonnot,* a gang of anarchist criminals whose crimes horrified and fascinated the French, and in whom he sees the germ of the Fantômas series—but eleven of the novels had already appeared by the time the Bonnot gang burst on the scene in December 1911. Still, Chavance alone among the contributors to *Europe's* Fantômas symposium raises an interesting issue: given their shortcomings, what is the secret of the fascination these books have had for so many of the great creators of our time? Why not, indeed, the far more promising LeRouge, who seems to have been ignored by the intelligentsia, except for Cendrars, who managed to strike up a friendship with the self-effacing author?

Well, LeRouge was too much on the way to being a *surréaliste sans le savoir* to have satisfied the populist longings of that group: we must remember how Breton carried *encanaillement* to the point of eulogizing (in *Nadja*) a forgotten Hollywood serial about a giant octopus, starring Ben Wilson and Neva Gerber. The prose, the plots, the personages of what has come to be known as the *geste de Fantômas* were constructed of the requisite industrial-strength fustian. And besides, Fantômas was more than the sum of the thirty-two novels of the original series. He was, first of all, an image: the unforgettable one of the masked man with a dagger brooding over Paris, inspired perhaps by Félicien Rops's famous engraving, *Satan Sowing Tares.* The artist, an Italian named Gino Starace, continued to provide lurid cover illustrations for each sequel, and no doubt contributed in large part to their success. (Some notable examples were his covers for *The Marriage of Fantômas*—a group of gendarmes laying hands on a woman in a white bridal gown and a black mask; *The Gold Stealer*—two men stripping gold from the dome of the Hôtel des Invalides; and *The Severed Hand*—a bloody hand clutching the roulette wheel of a casino.) The films of Feuillade extended the repertory of images, and are if anything more like the novels than the novels themselves. Indeed, Feuillade's later serials based on different sources (*Judex, Les vampires, Barabbas*) are not only superior to his Fantômas films, which were made at a time when he was still learning the tricks of his trade, but develop their atmosphere, so that in watching them one keeps expecting the characters from Fantômas to appear. Actually Feuillade was but one of a number of filmmakers working this vein. Stills from Monca's *The Prey* and Gance's *The Madness of Dr. Tube* partake of a similar ambience of exotic terror at odds with the reassuring naturalism of the settings: humble estaminets, the concierge's loge, the writing rooms of grand hotels, vast Parisian department stores such as the Galerie de Paris where Fantômas substitutes sulfuric acid in the atomizers of the perfume counter, trains, ocean liners, industrial suburbs, or elegant faubourgs.

The authors' uncanny sense of *genius loci* is one of the principal ingredients of the novels' potent charm. If the five principal characters—Fantômas, Juve, Fandor, Lady Beltham, and Hélène—remain hieratically frozen in their relation to one another, like figures in a romanesque frieze, they are nonetheless constantly on the move, traversing the landscapes of the world by every available means of locomotion. The effect is not unlike that of a passacaglia, whose fixed underlying motive allows for ornamentation above that can all but obscure it. In Fantômas what we savor most are the details and decor including subordinate characters and subplots, while the basic situation remains the same. The atmospheres and landscapes, particularly those of Paris, are brushed with remarkable sensitivity, and these extensions of the personage of Fantômas and of his friends and foes are the real characters in the epic. The facility with which Fantômas can become an object was noted by Max Jacob in one of two Fantômas prose poems in his collection *The Dice Cup:* "On the burnished silver knocker of the door, darkened by time, by the dust of time, was a kind of chiseled Buddha with a too-high forehead, with pendulous ears, with the look of a sailor or a gorilla: it was Fantômas." And this physicality was transmitted into film by Feuillade so flawlessly that what one critic has written about the Fantômas films could apply equally to the novels themselves. Feuillade, in the words of Francis Lacassin, "had discovered before Antonioni the secret of grisaille. He had understood that nothing is more beautiful than a certain suburban poetry that emanates from disjointed paving stones, from working-class districts, from a dismal suburb, silent and deserted, from vacant lots beyond which, at a distance, the blurred profiles of buildings under construction are silhouetted against the sky."

It is possible that French place-names are more suggestive than those of other countries; at any rate the names of Paris streets have a life of their own in fiction and in real life. Crimes are named after them: thus the first of the Bonnot gang's bloody exploits has gone down in history as "l'attendat de la rue Ordener," conferring a kind of immortality on an otherwise undistinguished thoroughfare. French newspapers keep their readers abreast of late-breaking developments in "le drame de la rue Raynouard" or "l'affaire du boulevard Saint-Jacques" until it seems that the places themselves are actually actors in the events described. No doubt the earliest readers of Fantômas shuddered delightedly at the thought that dire acts were being committed in the next street or one they walked along to work every day, its sober façades a seeming denial of fantastic goings-on behind them. Frequently it is enough for the authors to name a place, in Paris or elsewhere in France, or even in London (though not in locations with which they were obviously unfamiliar, such as Durban), for the magic to start. Space that extends and amplifies the human figure, meanwhile mingling it with printed words and mundane objects, was an invention of the Cubists, the exact contemporaries of Fantômas, and it is not at all surprising that Juan Gris should have painted a *Fantômas Still-Life*.

But one shouldn't analyze too closely the charms of this superb charade, as flimsy as they are durable. Lacassin is surely close enough when, speaking again on the films, he observes that their dreamlike quality almost makes us forget their extraordinary realism. "Perhaps the most beautiful scene in *Fantômas*," he writes, "isn't the struggle with the boa constrictor and the latter's death pangs, nor the gunfight among the wine-barrels nor the masked criminal slipping into a cistern, but simply that in which a policeman is expertly unscrewing the grill of a ventilating duct, holding on to the fastened side of the plaque and testing from time to time the resistance of the screws, then carefully placing them beside the piece of metal once it has finally been removed. In this marvelous poetic anthology, each of us has at our disposal beforehand an image that is destined to thrill us. And for each of us it will never be the same one."

BIBLIOGRAPHY

Cocteau, Jean. *Opium*. 1930. Translated by Margaret Crosland and Sinclair Road. New York: Grove Press, 1958.
Europe 590–91 (June–July 1978).
Fauchereau, Serge. *La révolution cubiste*. Paris: Denoël, 1982.
Jacob, Max. *Le cornet à dés*. Paris: Gallimard, 1945.
Lacassin, Francis. *Louis Feuillade*. Cinéma d'aujourd'hui, no. 22. Paris: Seghers, 1964.

Marty, Pierre, and Antoinette Peské. *Les terribles.* Paris: Chambriand, 1951. *Tour de Feu* 87–88 (December 1965).

From Marcel Allain and Pierre Souvestre's *Fantômas* (New York: William Morrow and Co., 1986; Bantam Books, 1987).

Featured Poet: Nicholas Moore

Nicholas Moore was born in Cambridge, England, in 1918. His father was the philosopher G. E. Moore and his uncle the poet T. Sturge Moore. While still a student at Cambridge, he became internationally known as a poet (1939–41) and he edited the magazine *Seven*. By 1942 he had produced three books of poetry and two pamphlets and was the editorial assistant to Tambimuttu of *Poetry London*. He published frequently in American periodicals, including *Poetry* (Chicago) which awarded him its Harriet Monroe Prize in 1947. He also wrote a pamphlet on Henry Miller (1943) and edited the *PL Book of Modern American Short Stories* (1945). Due to personal circumstances, Moore wrote little in the 1950s and fell out of fashion. He contracted diabetes which crippled him and restricted his movements. He began to write poetry again in the mid-1960s, but very little of the later work is published. There are nine unpublished books of poems prepared by Moore, three of them dating from the 1940s and one of them lost. Work is in progress on a *Collected Poems* edited by Peter Riley (to whom I am indebted for this biographical information), but there are no plans as yet for publication. Moore was also a horticulturalist and a world expert on irises and sempervivums; his book *The Tall Bearded Iris* was published in 1956. Two of his other enthusiasms are cricket and jazz, and he has written on both. He was married twice; his second wife died several years ago.

Moore's poetry has its roots in the brilliant and jarring British poetry of the 1930s, particularly that of Auden. (One is reminded also of the lyrical passages from Auden's and Isherwood's plays *The Dog Beneath the Skin* and *The Ascent of F6*.) Eliot, Yeats and Durrell are also influences, but Moore is perhaps unique among English poets of the forties in his awareness of contemporary American poetry, especially Wallace Stevens, with whom he corresponded and to whom he dedicated at least two poems. He also said that he owed a great deal to southern poets such as Robert Penn Warren and John Peale Bishop. Other American poets who were important to him are Weldon Kees, Howard Nemerov and Dunstan Thompson. There are even trace elements of American pop culture in his writings, such as the titles of songs of the forties ("I Get Along Without You Very Well"; "I Heard You Cried Last Night"). Moore is, I think, a tremendously exciting and unaccountably overlooked poet. At his best, he transmutes the malaise of the thirties (Auden's "low dishonest decade") and the agony of the subsequent war years into mercurial poetry: feverishly bright, pulsating with jazz rhythms and sometimes laced with vitriol. Of his many pamphlets and collections of poetry, the principal ones are no doubt *The Island and the Cattle* (Fortune Press, 1941), *The Glass Tower* (Editions Poetry London, 1944) and *Recollections of the Gala* (Editions Poetry London, 1950).*

Song

A little onion lay by the fireplace,
It had a burning mansion painted on one side,
On the other it had a rat and a pair of whiskers.
I said, My love, this reminds me of you,
But she put out the candle and said, Go to bed.
I cannot remember, said the madman.

The mouse on the floor and the bat on the ceiling
Batten on my memory, O make my bed soon,
Before I see her again, or before the doctor shoots me,
Or the white nurse straps me to my bed like mother.
The midnight lady has lost her echo.
I only remember the onion, the egg, and the boy.
O that was me, said the madman.

---

*Nicholas Moore died in London on January 26, 1986, while *Poetry Pilot* was going to press. Two of Moore's books of poems, edited by Peter Riley, are in print: *Lacrimae Rerum* (Cambridge, England: Poetical Histories and Open Township, 1986), last poems; and *Longings of the Acrobats* (Manchester, England: Carcanet Press, 1990), selected poems. A third collection, edited by Anthony Rudolph, is available as a PDF file online at www.ubu.com/ubu/moore_spleen.html: *Spleen* (London: Menard Press, 2nd ed. 1990; Ubu Editions, rev. 2nd ed., 2004), thirty-one versions of a Baudelairian sonnet.

Pastoral

Watch how in the lazy air, the mist-filled air
The birds waver their autumn wings. Rooks,
Who are cold in the ice-laden air,
Sparrows and robins who spring and chirp;

And how the spiky chestnuts hang on trees,
Or fall for the small boys to find,
Red, burnished shapes, and marked like jewels!
And how the horses swish their tails!

And then remember the sly mind
Of Autumn, the last singing in the air
Of summer joys, of flowery hats and silk
Dresses, and how the Autumn holds them all

To its will, with the last whistle of birds,
The long spikes of the goldenrod,
And the lashes of rain. How they fall!
And in the last hazy and wish-filled air

Men totter home to tea and warmth and buns,
After an afternoon at the end
Of summer, while in the mist revolve pale suns,
Lemon-yellow, and the fireside is a friend.

Interlude with a Pu-pu Bird

There are moments when we can truly say
"This is an interlude between dreams."
Then the trees stand elegant in gardens,
And the young girls forget their names

Or the names of their lovers. Then the absurd
Becomes the general. The young men speak
Elegantly and in elegant attitudes
The young women stand and are weak.

What is the truth we seek? Exact
Chronology is the historian's habit.
For us who write in elegant poetry
Such strictness would, I fear, inhibit

That which so clearly we want to say.
Is it a day of emerald skies, of yellow

Asters, geraniums pink in pots, or is it
Merely that our hearts are honest and hollow?

However it is, however it may be, there are times
When the real world indeed seems far away.
The young girls seem to stand like trees in gardens,
And we—the birds in them—what can we say?

Song

The disease is too acute for you, my dear.
Everywhere behind you, standing near
  Is the shadow, the shadow.

It is no good saying it's spring.
Spring's lovely, but it won't change a thing,
  Nor the crocuses' yellow.

Not the tulips tall as slender ladies,
Not the lilies with their cool bodies
  Can make you less bitter;

Not the new dress or the new lover;
The past is there, though everything's over:
  The future isn't any better.

No, it's no use pretending you're detached:
You can lock the door, but the window isn't latched,
  And the shadow's so clever.

You may take delight in Graham Greene
Or the deceptions of Ellery Queen,
  But there's still the murder.

You may hate them, and let them hate you,
But it's no good, whatever you do.
  As the shadow grows longer:

You become less yourself every day.
You'll be going the same old way.
  No. You weren't any stronger.

The shadow is dogging you, too.
And there isn't a thing that you can do
  To draw the curtain.

O, my dear, you are lovely as wine,
And, wherever you dance or you dine,
          There's just one thing that's certain:

You will never evade the shadow
In any dark room or bright-eyed meadow.
          You'll never be careless again.

The disease will begin to ride like a fever,
Unless you remain yourself. O, the clever
          Only bring pain.

It's no use, it's no use, it's no use forever.
You can't be good, if you're going to be clever.
          The shadow alone will remain.

I Get Along without You Very Well

Of all old men, of all ancestors
We speak the word, and it is done.
Laughing, eager, the young girls reach the stars,
And everywhere begin to dream

Of strange beasts, animals
Without tails, tortoises and manx
Cats: they say "This is the style of evening,
When the heart is already nude."

And you will be deluded
Into thinking them wonderful, their hair
Will be black, will be yellow.
You will not be an old man.

Yet everywhere will be dreams of old men,
And the ancestral willows will weep
By the deep house and the clematis
Climb efflorescent upon

The tiled roofs. It will be
In anger that you stand and sharply say:
"You are too nude in your dreams, yet
Not nude enough in the real." And they will cry,

The long tears like spears edging against
Your heart. "It is the evening. It is blue
With an odour of rains. It is not us
But the evening that fails you." And they

Stand about like marbles, infinitely pure.
Their hands caress the sides of air.
They are carved in a terrible deception
Of all old men, of all ancestors.

Paul Bannows Thinks of His Honeymoon

Lying together in the heather,
Drinking together in the night,
Coffee together in the morning.
Every whisper spells "delight."

Records together on the grama-
-phone, "My heart beats like a hammer,"
The familiar yammer
Of gossip, and the great Bean's tone;

The morning on the hillside alone.

Thanks for the memory; thanks
For the cool, soft drinks,
For all the buns and dreams of salmon,
For each wry stammer.

Now I recline here like a swimmer
On the Far Eastern bank.
Gold in the morning, red sunsets,
The small rain, and the moon's white wink

Remind me, remind me of you,
Of purity, coffee and beaches,
Of the hillside, the winds, and the reaches
Of thought, and they leave me quite speechless

Now in this shadowy blue.

Lying together in the sighing
Grasses, the kisses, the crying:
What is there left but denial
Now in the bed's blank smile?

What is there left to do?

From *Poetry Pilot* (February 1986), the newsletter of The Academy of American Poets. "Song" ("A little onion lay by the fireplace . . .") from *The Island and the Cattle* by Nicholas Moore, copyright © 1941 by The

An Unpublished Note: Raymond Roussel

Tuesday

Dear Sir

Agreed for tomorrow Wednesday at seven.

Thank you for your astounding sonnet. So many rhymes for "Roussel"! It is a tour de force and "lis braire"[1] is terrific. It reminds me of this couplet of twelve-syllable lines:

> Dans ces meubles laqués, rideaux et dais moroses
> Dans, aime, bleu laquais, rit d'oser des mots roses.[2]

> fondly,
> Raymond Roussel

NOTES

1. "Read to bray," a pun on *libraire,* "bookseller."
2. "Amid this lacquered furniture, these gloomy curtains and canopies / Dance, make love, blue lackey, laugh to venture blushing words."

The two lines are almost identical phonetically. By an odd coincidence, Breton, who couldn't possibly have known of this letter, quotes this same couplet in his preface to Jean Ferry's *Essay on Raymond Roussel,* attributing it to Charles Cros and citing it as a precedent for Roussel's linguistic experiments. Breton however gives *ris,* the familiar imperative of the verb *rire,* "to laugh," rather than Roussel's *rit,* the third-person singular, which here makes no sense grammatically. The lines were published in an article by Charles Cros in his *Revue du monde nouveau* (April 2, 1874), but according to the editors of the Pléiade edition of his works, are "undoubtedly not by him." They formed the first and fourth lines of a quatrain; the two inner lines are similarly constructed "totally rhyming" verses. The article satirizes the formal strictures of the Parnassian poets.

From *Atlas Anthology* 4 (1987). The letter was probably written by Roussel to Pierre Frondaie. Translated and annotated by John Ashbery.

A Note on "Variation on a Noel"

Variation on a Noel

"when the snow lay round about,
deep and crisp and even . . ."

A year away from the pigpen, and look at him.
A thirsty unit by an upending stream,
Man doctors, God supplies the necessary medication
If elixir were to be found in the world's dolor, where is
  none.

A thirsty unit by an unending stream,
Ashamed of the moon, of everything that hides too little of
  her nakedness—
If elixir were to be found in the world's dolor, where is
  none,
Our emancipation should be great and steady.

Ashamed of the moon, of everything that hides too little of
  her nakedness,
The twilight prayers begin to emerge on a country
  crossroads.
Our emancipation should be great and steady
As crossword puzzles done in this room, this after-effect.

The twilight prayers begin to emerge on a country
  crossroads
Where no sea contends with the interest of the cherry trees.

As crossword puzzles done in this room, this after-effect,
I see the whole thing written down.

Where no sea contends with the interest of the cherry trees
Everything but love was abolished. It stayed on, a stepchild.
I see the whole thing written down
Business, a lack of drama. Whatever the partygoing public
    needs.

Everything but love was abolished. It stayed on, a stepchild.
The bent towers of the playroom advanced to something
    like openness,
Business, a lack of drama. Whatever the partygoing public
    needs
To be kind, and to forget, passing through the next doors.

The bent towers of the playroom advanced to something
    like openness.
But if you heard it, and if you didn't want it
To be kind, and to forget, passing through the next doors
(For we believe him not exiled from the skies) . . . ?

But if you heard it, and if you didn't want it,
Why do I call to you after all this time?
For we believe him not exiled from the skies.
Because I wish to give only what the specialist can give,

Why do I call to you after all this time?
Your own friends, running for mayor, behaving outlandishly
Because I wish to give only what the specialist can give,
Spend what they care to.

Your own friends, running for mayor, behaving outlandishly,
(And I have known him cheaply)
Spend what they care to,
A form of ignorance, you might say. Let's leave that though.

And I have known him cheaply.
Agree to remove all that concern, another exodus—
A form of ignorance, you might say. Let's leave that though.
The mere whiteness was a blessing, taking us far.

Agree to remove all that concern, another exodus.
A year away from the pigpen, and look at him.
The mere whiteness was a blessing, taking us far.
Man doctors, God supplies the necessary medication.

I first came across the word "pantoum" as the title of one of the movements of Ravel's "Trio," and then found the term in a manual of prosody. I wrote a poem called "Pantoum" in the early fifties; it is in my book *Some Trees.* "Variation on a Noel" is the only other time I have ever used the form.* The poem was written in December of 1979. I was attracted to the form in both cases because of its stricture, even greater than in other hobbling forms such as the sestina or canzone. These restraints seem to have a paradoxically liberating effect, for me at least. The form has the additional advantage of providing you with twice as much poem for your effort, since every line has to be repeated.

*Other pantoums followed: see, for example, "Hotel Lautréamont."

From *Ecstatic Occasions, Expedient Forms,* edited by David Lehman (New York: Macmillan, 1987). "Variation on a Noel" is from *A Wave,* by John Ashbery (New York: Viking Penguin, 1984). Copyright © 1984 by John Ashbery.

Foreword to *The Third Rose: Gertrude Stein and Her World*

Few writers' lives have been so frequently and, it would seem, so thoroughly documented as that of Gertrude Stein. She has been the subject not only of innumerable biographical and critical studies, but also of plays, a recent film, and even a comic strip. Rosalyn Drexler, reviewing the film in the *Nation,* claimed to have contacted Alice Toklas via ouija board and been told: "Au revoir, Mme. Drexler, and please do what you can to stop this unholy use of our lives by those who want to ride to fame and fortune on our skirt-hems."

A result of this situation is that persons having barely a nodding acquaintance with twentieth-century literature are likely to imagine that they have actually visited the formidable *doyenne* of 27 rue de Fleurus in her art-cluttered atelier, and sat through her monologues and the subtler probings of the equally formidable Miss Toklas. We feel we have picked up just about all there is to know about her by osmosis. We are almost tempted to reproach her for being so little mysterious.

And yet a mystery, or at least a paradox, subsists. Gertrude Stein is famous and unread. She is one of those writers one prefers to read about rather than to read, and one suspects that very few of the consumers of Stein studies have ever ventured into the work itself much beyond such relatively undemanding classics as *Three Lives* and *The Autobiography of Alice B. Toklas*. Nor are they necessarily to be faulted for their neglect: Miss Stein—a further paradox—is both arduous and exciting. That is to say, some of her work is arduous, some of it exciting, and much of it a stubbornly entangled mixture of both. Yet even at her most perverse and inaccessible, she cannot be ignored. To open a book like *Tender Buttons* or *How to Write*, read a few pages, and then smartly snap the book shut (I am convinced that this is not just my own method) is to experience a wry, faintly distressing, but altogether singular pleasure that can be found nowhere else.

John Malcolm Brinnin's book is about Gertrude rather than Miss Stein. It isn't the densest or most detailed account of either her life or her work, nor does it make any claim to be, but it is the most enjoyable one I have encountered. As Mr. Brinnin explains in an afterword, it is the result of happenstance. A passionate fan of Gertrude from his teens, he happened one day in 1946 on a first edition of *Geography and Plays* in a small bookstore in upstate New York. After spending a happy afternoon with the book, he learned from a radio broadcast that Gertrude Stein had died that day. Stirred by the coincidence, he eventually began to write *The Third Rose*, a task for which he must have been long prepared without realizing it. The result is a marvelously fluid and engaging study by an admirer who, though he never met her, was obviously on such familiar terms with her that he felt no compunction about pointing out the flaws as well as the merits of her writing and her character, confident no doubt that the evident love from which he wrote would rectify any imbalance.

As indeed it does. Mr. Brinnin can be a charmed listener, but he can just as easily slap Gertrude on the wrist when she begins to natter. He is severe in dealing with the failure of works like the best-selling *Wars I Have Seen.* Judgments such as this one of *Mrs. Reynolds*—"The style of the novel is clear, but its interminable small talk is apt to give most readers the feeling that they are listening for days and weeks on end to one side of a telephone conversation"—would be almost too sharply accurate were it not for the spontaneous generosity that buoys his assessment of the whole writer. One encounters it throughout his book, as in this beautiful evaluation of another late work, *The Mother of Us All:* "Gertrude Stein has come out of the depths of the nineteenth century and her last and most eloquent utterance glowed with her pleasure, and even love, for all that she had spent a lifetime escaping."

This generosity, indeed, seems to be the most striking quality that the two writers share. Mr. Brinnin's poetry, such as his limpid "Little Elegy for Gertrude Stein," published in the afterword, inhabits a world of order and neoclassical sweetness many light-years removed from Gertrude's. They would seem at first glance a very odd couple. Yet the enduring warmth, laughter, and spunk that he identifies in her resonates in his own writing as well. He breathes her work as if it were air. That is no doubt why he has been so successful at inundating with light and air a body of work that for too long has been fenced round with a redoubtable palisade of mingled ignorance and scholarship. For this, all those wishing to explore one of the most exciting and elusive adventures of our century must be in his debt.

From John Malcolm Brinnin's *The Third Rose: Gertrude Stein and Her World* (Reading, MA: Merloyd Lawrence–Addison Wesley, 1987).

Introduction to *The Best American Poetry*

One of the minor disadvantages of being a poet (as opposed to the major ones, which everybody—every poet at least—already knows about) is being continually asked who reads one's poetry. Or who reads poetry. This is annoying not so much because the question cannot be answered, but because the interrogator invariably assumes that the poet *must* know, with the implied assumption that if he doesn't there must be something wrong with him. Closely related to this question is another unanswered and unanswerable one: for whom do you write? Again the implication is that the writer of course knows, that any writer who doesn't ought to get out of the business of writing. There is a special anguish here for the poet: who wouldn't like to know for whom one is writing? If that were possible we could try to please them, tailor our writing not perhaps to their individual tastes but at any rate to a general profile of our actual and potential readers. Then they might like what we wrote; even critics might, and there would be an end to literary misunderstanding.

It never seems to occur to anyone that each reader is different, and that even those who might be said to resemble each other will each bring an individual set of experiences and references to their reading, and interpret and misinterpret it according to these. Alas, even to suggest that such a state of affairs exists is to invite further misunderstanding. It's no use trying, as I have done, to answer the question "for whom do you write?" with Gertrude Stein's brilliant, ask-a-simple-question-and-you-get-a-simple-answer formulation: "for myself and strangers." Like Cordelia's truthful answers, this one can infuriate the questioner, leading to charges of elitism, arrogance, and sedition.

Still another question that poets must be prepared for is some variation of: Is something happening in poetry today? Is poetry coming out of the closet, or the trunk? Why does it seem that people are suddenly bothering about poetry? Why am I asking you this question? Would you please account for the fact that your work interests me, perhaps only a very little but enough to make me curious about it? In the late 1950s my friend Frank O'Hara was invited for an after-work drink by a reporter from *Time* who cross-examined him in this fashion; O'Hara replied: "Sure there's something going on in poetry. Otherwise you wouldn't be buying me this drink." As far as I know, *Time* didn't print that.

After more than forty years of observation, I have come to the conclusion that there is always something happening in poetry, but it always seems as though it had just begun to happen. The main difference between then and now is quantity or volume: there are more places for poets to publish, hence more poets and poems—or does it work the other way round? And poets are certainly more visible now. In the forties there were few poetry readings, with only a handful of elder statesmen of poetry ever called upon to read in public. Probably the Beat generation changed all that: poets, a few of them at least, performed in public and became celebrities, and then others, not necessarily media material, joined their ranks, and suddenly in the larger cities there were readings in bookstores and churches and cafés almost every night. This happened when I was out of the country; returning to New York from France in 1963 for a visit after an absence of five years I was startled when asked to give a reading, and more surprised to discover how commonplace such events had become. And the poetry-reading industry continues to thrive. Poets are no longer faceless; many have become public figures, of a sort, and they are expected to perform. After every reading members of the audience come forward with copies of the poets' books for them to autograph. It's not even always a book—sometimes it's a photocopy of a poem from a magazine or even a paper napkin. On one occasion a man asked me to autograph a book which, it turned out, I had already autographed for him at a previous reading. When I pointed this out, he asked me to sign it with a fresh autograph. And recently in Washington, D.C., I was approached after a reading by a young man who said he was on a limited income and had already bought a book last week when another poet had been there, and would I please autograph it? It turned out to be Allen Ginsberg's *White Shroud*. When I balked at autographing someone else's book, he became so insistent that I finally did sign my name on the back endpaper, leaving the flyleaf for Allen to sign should he pass through Washington again.

Even taking the ordinary zaniness of American life into account, such occurrences can stir up suspicions about the so-called poetry revival: Once again, *is* something happening in poetry? Or is it only one more fad in a series of so many in our history? Are these fans merely the avatars of those who mobbed Jenny Lind and Oscar Wilde when they toured the country, and promptly forgot about them the next day? Poetry publications abound, stacks of books are sold after readings, but does anyone read them? Or are they meant never to be opened, like the limp-leather volumes of Emerson's essays and *Lalla Rookh* that adorned "library tables" in thousands of American homes at the turn of the century?

More to the point, do even poets read poetry? Having taught writing classes for quite a few years, I have my doubts. The reading lists I give out seldom get examined very closely. Frequently when I tell a student that, on the basis of his work, he must have been reading William Carlos Williams recently (or Pound or Moore or Bishop or Auden), I am met with a blank stare: the student has not read the poet he seems influenced by, has perhaps not even heard of him, but like an unwitting version of Borges's Pierre Ménard, has produced his own *Don Quixote* while remaining uncorrupted by knowledge of the original.

But I don't wish to belittle students: how many "mature" poets read each other's work? I have to confess to some laziness in this regard, and therefore can't really condemn the writing student who wants to be heard without listening to others. I hasten to add that I am perhaps an extreme case: I know scholar-poets who manage to "keep up" with the bewildering proliferation of contemporary poetry; people like John Hollander or Richard Howard or the late Robert Duncan, whose knowledge of poetry is encyclopedic, who live and breathe poetry every day and in whom poetry begets poetry. But what of the others? Many, perhaps the majority, respond to other stimuli which also result in poetry: poets who mostly listen to music or look at movies or pore over newspapers or travel literature or scientific journals (as Marianne Moore did), or who perhaps do not do much of anything but write poetry. Is their poetry any better or worse because of this? Certainly one wouldn't have wished Miss Moore to have proceeded otherwise, given the results, nor wished Dr. Williams away from his patients or Wallace Stevens from the offices of the Hartford Insurance Company. Who knows, perhaps they would have been better if circumstances had allowed them to keep their noses permanently "stuck in a book," but in the absence of proof to the contrary let's settle for them as they are.

Yet it can do no harm for us poets to come to know each

other's work. Reading through the poetry of 1987 I was struck, perhaps for the first time, by the exciting diversity of American poetry *right now*, and by the validity of this diversity, the tremendous power it could have for enriching our lives—I hesitated before using this hoary phrase but am going to let it stand. And what a pity that so few of us avail ourselves of it. For I think that even the most literate of readers of American poetry tend to confine themselves to a narrow segment of it. In traveling around the country I have noticed that the landscape of American poetry is strangely fragmented and gerrymandered, its partisans frequently blinkered. It is odd that in the age of the global village, a quaint regionalism stubbornly prevails. In New York, audiences like to listen to poetry of the New York School; the spirits of Frost and Lowell are alive and well in New England; in Tennessee, poetry other than that of Tate and Warren is viewed with suspicion; in the Pacific Northwest it is felt that poetry should be modeled after that of Roethke and William Stafford—two poets who, except for that accident of geography, would not seem to have much in common. Further down the coast one can almost hear the assertive voices of Duncan and Rexroth speaking out of the San Francisco fog. And of course Olson, who turns up elsewhere as well, as do the relatively recent Language Poets (no one seems to be able to define this term, so I won't try), many of them based in southern California, though they have chapters in Michigan, New England, and New York. Otherwise the reasonable voices of the writers associated with the Iowa Writers Workshop have the Midwest pretty much to themselves—except for a Chicago-style funk which turns up both in poetry and the visual arts.

Instead of congratulating ourselves on so much diversity we tend, as so often in America, to choose sides and ignore anyone not on our team, much as "single-issue" voters choose their political candidates. At the risk of producing cacophony, I have tried to bring together a number of poets of different persuasions in this anthology. I like things that seem to me good of their kind, and don't especially care what the kind is. I have enjoyed juxtaposing poets as unlike each other as Richard Wilbur and Kenward Elmslie, Joseph Brodsky and Kenneth Koch; young, unknown poets (at least they were to me) like Joe Ross and Lydia Tomkiw with established ones like Donald Hall and Donald Justice. I have some prejudices: there is not much "political" poetry that I like, for the reason that the political sentiments reiterated in it are usually the exact ones I already harbor, and I would rather learn something new. Still, there are exceptions to this rule as to every other, and politics in the poems by Alan Williamson, Wanda Coleman, and Philip Levine reprinted here sounds fresh and newly minted to me.

I like the light these poets involuntarily shed on each other. I think we read them differently in such mixed company, where they are inflected by the tuning-forked vibrations of their neighbors. Leafing through this anthology one can be reminded that red looks very different when placed next to green; that a d-sharp and an e-flat sound different in different contexts. One doesn't approach an anthology in the same way one approaches a collection of poems by a single poet: in the former case a "rubbing off" happens that can be disorienting but—I hope—also stimulating, and of course we can always return to our favorite poets for more concentrated scrutiny on some other occasion.

In discussing the supposed gulf between abstract and representational art, the late French painter Jean Hélion wrote in his journal: "I wonder . . . whether all the valid painting being done today doesn't bear certain resemblances which escape us at the present time." One could wonder the same thing about poetry, but in the meantime, while we await that uniform utopia, the dissimilarities—the splintering, the impurity—could be those of life itself. Life is what present American poetry gets to seem more like, and the more angles we choose to view it from, the more its amazing accidental abundance imposes itself.

From *The Best American Poetry,* edited by David Lehman, guest editor John Ashbery (New York: Charles Scribner's Sons, 1988).

Introduction to a Reading by James Schuyler

I knew someone in college who refused to listen to any chamber music because he wanted to save up at least one major aesthetic experience for late in life. Tonight I think many of us are in for a treat not unlike that of experiencing one's first chamber music at a ripe age. James Schuyler doesn't ordinarily give poetry readings; as far as I know this is the first public one he has ever given. Until now, at least, he has resisted the urge to public utterance that has turned the heads of so many poets ever since poetry readings became popular in the late fifties, and which has resulted in a kind of performance-art of poetry parallel to the private consumption of poetry that one had known previously.

This is not the place to debate whether poetry readings are good or bad, and indeed I'm sure that everyone here tonight is very glad to at last be able to see and hear Mr. Schuyler read his poems. I will only say that I think that the fad for seeing and hearing real live poets give utterance to their works is good insofar as it has drawn attention to poetry and resulted in a wider audience for it in the past few decades, and bad insofar as it can tempt the poet to undertake the kind of poetry he or she might not have attempted without the lure of the limelight that even modest tours on the remoter poetry circuits can provide. In any case, Schuyler has avoided these pitfalls, not out of principle, probably, but simply because they interfere with the business of living daily life as he means to lead it. And though I am myself ambivalent about the value of poetry readings, I can't help regretting that his decision has possibly slowed the growth of Mr. Schuyler's audience in a time when performance and personalities tend to upstage the written word. Perhaps that situation is already changing as of tonight, however.

I have known Mr. Schuyler so long that it is difficult to remember a time when I was writing and wasn't his friend. We collaborated over a period of many years on a novel called *A Nest of Ninnies,* and today there are many lines in it that we can't be sure which of us wrote. That's rather fun in a way, and it's nice to have a writer to whom one feels so close both personally and aesthetically that asking advice from him is only a step removed from consulting oneself. At the same time, I feel he is very different from me, and I'm jealous. Because he's somehow managed to draw on the whole arsenal of modernism, from the minimalism of Dr. Williams to the gorgeous aberrations of Wallace Stevens and the French Surrealists, and still write in what Marianne Moore calls "plain American which cats and dogs can read." He makes sense, dammit, and he manages to do so without falsifying or simplifying the daunting complexity of life as we are living it today.

He has been called a nature poet, and it's true that nature observed does play a large role in his poetry, but he's about as far from Wordsworth as you can get. He's closer to Elizabeth Bishop, with whom he has sometimes been compared: for both these superb poets, nature is merely what is adjacent, what one looks out on all the time, whether it be trees, people, vehicles or odd happenings that one happens to witness. Schuyler is at the antipodes of romanticism because nature is merely the medium he lives in, and nature in that sense is sometimes troublesome and more often boring. Schuyler, however, is on such intimate terms with it that he can easily afford to give it a slap on the wrist when it tends to run on, as it so often does. The two are like a married couple whose occasional spats look disconcerting to outsiders but for themselves are merely another kind of smooth sailing. What else is there to do but go about one's business, observe and reflect and jot down notes that in Schuyler's case are an inspired utterance couched in everyday terms. In one of his poems he asks,

> But
> what if it is all "Maya,
> illusion?" I
> doubt it, though. Men are not
> so inventive. Or
> few are. Not knowing
> a name for something proves nothing. Right
> now it isn't raining, snowing, sleeting, slushing,
> yet it is

doing something. As a matter of fact
it is raining snow.

—from "Empathy and New Year"

I give you a poet who knows the names for things, and whose knowing proves something.

From a reading given at the Dia Art Foundation, New York City (November 15, 1988). First published as "An Infrequent Pleasure," *Poetry Flash* 191 (February 1989). Reprinted in *Denver Quarterly* 24, no. 4 (Spring 1990).

Poetical Space

I have been asked to discuss two topics I know very little about: one is "poetical phenomenology," the other is "Ashbery himself." It is true that I might be expected to know something about them since poetry is a kind of phenomenology ("a branch of science dealing with the descriptions and classification of phenomena," according to Webster's dictionary), and I am probably a poet. In addition to which, I am also "Ashbery myself," if not "himself." But it is also true that I know relatively little about poetry, despite or perhaps because of having been a poet for almost half a century. How can this be? I am not sure. Perhaps somewhere I have a superstitious dread of knowing too much about what it is that I do—a fear that if I can explain it I won't be able to do it. Or perhaps—and I somewhat incline toward this view—being a poet or making poetry somehow precludes the most intimate knowledge of what poetry is, of how it affects people other than the poet. In fact, being a poet seems to disqualify or disequip one for so many of the practical aspects and tasks of life. In my case, it is very difficult for me to answer letters or pay bills or even make plans for the immediate future, not because I am so very busy or even because I am immobilized by continually waiting for a poem to happen, like a fisherman sitting for hours on the bank of a stream. It is simply that poetry, in granting one a kind of power no poet would willingly give up, also disempowers, in ways that are ill understood. The resulting situation for the poet has been brilliantly defined by John Keats as "negative capability."

The painter Barnett Newman, when asked once to characterize his painting, replied in words to the effect that "birds don't make good ornithologists." And though this is more or less my view regarding my own poetry, I recognize that there are occasions—such as this one—when it becomes necessary and even decent to do so if one wants to remain on good terms with one's audience. This is something every poet ought to do, since a poet without an audience, or at least a potential one, is nothing: that is, poetry is not a stationary object but a kinetic act, in which something is transferred from somebody to somebody else. (No doubt this is true of all writing, though I have heard of, but never met, writers who claim to write "for the drawer," i.e., for themselves, and desire no other public.) So I shall try to deal in my fashion with the topic at hand, with the hope of at least ending up slightly wiser myself, if not illuminating you on a subject that remains dark to me.

Dr. Takachi had originally proposed another topic to me, since I have for much of my life earned my living as an art critic (in an attempt to support my "poetry habit"); this was "Poetic Space in Contemporary Painting." And as I thought about this topic, it occurred to me that I am a somewhat unusual case since I originally intended to be a painter, and when I was young thought of myself as a painter—well, as a potential or future painter. I read poetry as a child and as an adolescent, but at that time poetry didn't interest me as it does today; that is, I enjoyed it but felt no desire to make it. When I was eight years old I wrote a rhyming poem about a snowstorm which seemed excellent to me. I felt I had achieved what I set out to do, and the result was so perfect that there would be no point in pursuing this branch of the arts any further. So I returned to my crayons and watercolors and wrote no more poetry until several years later.

As I thought about this it occurred to me that there was something strange in my early imperviousness to poetry, and in my gradual indifference to visual art later on after I had found myself becoming a poet. When I use the terms "indifference" and "imperviousness," I am not referring to my feelings as a creative person, nor to my attitude as a consumer of art and literature, since I have at all times enjoyed both forms of expression, and music as well, perhaps even more so—*as a spectator.* But that particular feeling of close involvement, which makes one want to create something and in doing so chases away other urges or at least demotes them to secondary status, has been different for me at different times. The reason for this may be hidden in the topic that was proposed to me—the poetic space in contemporary painting. Let me see if I can figure out how.

What strikes us all immediately in painting is space, or rather the illusion of space, or rather how the artist has tried to convey that illusion. This has been a primal concern from very early on, and the desire to communicate a sense of space must have been for primitive artists one of those all-consuming but seemingly impossible-to-satisfy urges, like man's attempts to fly. Some of the Roman wall painters were pretty good at it and discovered techniques of perspective and the coloristic rendering of distance that would be perfected by artists of the Renaissance. For several centuries, however, these techniques would be lost, as they are in Byzantine art and so-called Italian Primitive painting. Of course, work of these schools is often deeply moving, sometimes even because of the artist's inability to render the illusion of space. Particularly so are works of Giotto and his contemporaries, which strive to tell the story of a saint's life, for instance, by showing him at different positions in a landscape, which correspond to different stages in his career. Here, the artist appears to confuse the rendering of space with that of time, as the Surrealists would do purposely in our time—Dali's *Persistence of Memory* is an example. Or the incorrectly rendered space would turn out to be something far more enchanting than space in the world could ever be, as in Chinese landscape scrolls, where we are permitted to glimpse vast expanses of mountains and rivers which would scarcely be visible from a single vantage point in the real world.

It is not until fairly recently, however, that artists have sought to alter traditional, received notions of what space actually looks like, first in the interests of a more scientific objectivity, as with the Impressionists, who tried to second-guess the eye's irregular ways of taking in information, but later gradually left these attempts at a "new realism" behind. In Cézanne, for instance, we feel at first that he is grappling with an urge to express space more accurately (both for the eye and the mind) than has ever been done before. But, gradually, it seems as though he is leaving this "objective" goal behind as he embarks on new adventures in which space becomes distorted, not out of an urge for more exact description but in order to express something, a feeling no doubt rather than an idea. Suddenly, tabletops that should be lying down peacefully under their assortment of jugs and apples are rearing up on their hind legs like a horse. The effect now is not one of greater naturalism, but of nature twisted out of shape by the artist in order to make a point, or perhaps just to satisfy an unnamed urge which, strangely, strikes chords within us. We realize that we have always wanted to see things this way without knowing why. It makes us glad. We are free from the slavish description of former times; at the same time, this seeming waywardness also tells us something new about how the visible world feels, if not how it looks.

I am not going to summarize the permutations through which twentieth-century artists have put space, for they are common knowledge—so common, in fact, that we are sometimes in danger of losing sight of their originality. A landscape by Soutine, for instance, in which trees and houses dance upside down and mountains roll over like kittens waiting to have their belly scratched, no longer seems novel; it may even seem perfectly straightforward and prosaically descriptive, so accustomed are we to seeing its like in museums and reproductions. We have indeed grown accustomed to inhabiting bizarre spaces and finding them sane and comfortable. We are "corner dwellers," in Gaston Bachelard's phrase. The paper-thin layers of space in an "analytical" Cubist still life (and let us not forget that such works analyze nothing, despite the scientific sobriquet, but are sheer fantasy) are as comfortable and habitable as an overstuffed easy chair. The seeming distortions please us; if they didn't, we wouldn't have responded to them as legitimate—and supreme—modes of expression, almost as remote from us in time now as nineteenth-century realism, and constantly elaborated on and stretched even further by new kinds of expressiveness breaking over us like the waves of a sea with increasing frequency.

Poetry, however, isn't bound even by the tenuous veins of advanced painterly expression but is even freer than the visual arts to make up its own universe and then make up the laws that govern it. At least, it has been so for the last sixty or seventy years, always following the visual arts a little but then making even greater strides once it had assimilated the changes there. Unlike a picture, a poem can "put a girdle round the earth in forty minutes"—even technology has a hard time keeping pace with that. Yet, at the same time, it needs the tethering influence of comparing itself with the other branches of the arts in order to keep from running amok and losing the patience of audiences, who may tire of following it in all its transformations. That is where the concept of "poetical space" as observed in painting, sculpture, or even music comes to rescue poets when they are in danger of leaping the track. As art grows more fantastic, poetry has to ballast itself using the discoveries the artists have made. One artist who used the two forms of expression to modulate each other is Giorgio de Chirico, a great poet as well as a great painter, though hardly anybody knows his long poem-novel, *Hebdomeros.* It is, however, full of useful observations on the character of space drawn from his experiences at the easel, and as such helps illustrate how the two disciplines can cross-pollinate each other. Here are two examples taken from *Hebdomeros:* "The sea of stars stretched into the distance, as if the sky no longer seemed to be a dome but a ceiling instead," and again: "At noon in those transitional seasons, autumn and spring, the sky was as blue as a piece of taut paper; it was no whiter near the horizon; it was blue all over from top to bottom; a veritable ceiling stretching over the town."

How satisfying to feel that one lives in these flattened spaces, as flat as the café terraces of Analytical Cubism. But why? One would have thought it more inspiring to feel one was living in a dome, where depth would equal freedom, rather than under a claustrophobic ceiling of stars. I can offer no explanation, for painting or for poetry, except that seeing things turn out differently from what we had been expecting is often a liberating experience, even when the resulting situation isn't what we had hoped for. And poetry, following in the wake of painting (if I insist on this point and perhaps distort it just a little to serve my own purposes, it is because in my life poetry followed painting), offers the same unnerving satisfactions. To limit myself to just one example, from Eliot's "The Waste Land":

> The river sweats
> Oil and tar
> The barges drift
> With the turning tide
> Red sails
> Wide
> To leeward, swing on the heavy spar.
> The barges wash
> Drifting logs
> Down Greenwich reach
> Past the Isle of Dogs.

This seems to me an example from among thousands I might have chosen from twentieth-century poetry of the kind of anti-descriptiveness forced to do the work of description that I have pointed out in modern painting. To me, the river scene as Eliot describes it is very hard to see. Lines like "The barges wash / Drifting logs" are strangely out of focus; how indeed does a barge wash a log? Nor do the limp, static rhythms conjure up the movement of a river flowing; we are far from such an onomatopoeic tour de force as Tennyson's "Lady of Shalott" of exactly eighty years previous, whose rippling meters convey the sight and sound of a swiftly flowing stream in a way that seems almost alchemical. Yet Eliot's ungrateful rhythms do convey something, something perhaps more to the point for us today: the blotchy, out of focus scene, the river refusing to roll, the awkwardly laid-on oil, tar, and sweat add up to a picture of crisis that is mental, but just as surely takes in the visual world, transforming it as it does so into a blurred copy that is all the more meaningful for being imprecise and out of focus—accurate in its inaccuracy.

This is perhaps close to the poetical phenomenology that I was asked to address: a process of description and classification that succeeds in its twin tasks precisely by shirking them. The river miraculously caught in the Lady of Shalott's mirror is a wonder, but the semicoherent daubs laid down over Eliot's Thames are of more value to us, for they point a way in which our own inexpert and falsifying accounts of the truth can eventually ring true, describing and classifying all the more searchingly even as they seem to abdicate this task. "You too can be a phenomenologist," he seems to be saying, "if only you'll abandon the task, let it work through you, let the river carry you where it wants to rather than trying to immobilize it." At which point, the truest kind of description has become merely naming, and classifying merely counting. Unpalatable to the savants among us, perhaps, but to the poets the only real way of getting the job done and moving on.

A lecture given at Shirayuri Women's University, Tokyo, Japan (May 19, 1989). The original topic suggested by the hosting moderator, Junichiro Takachi, was "Poetic Phenomenology and Ashbery Himself." First published in *Edge* (Autumn 1989).

Introduction to a Reading by Michael Palmer and James Tate

I feel privileged to have been asked to introduce two of the outstanding poets of our time, Michael Palmer and James Tate. Both are unrepentant modernists, a fact that might have been not worth mentioning twenty years ago when both were at the beginning of their careers, but which bears mentioning today when a new academicism is the fashion in poetry, and a new generation of critics is seeking to turn back the clock beyond Pound, Eliot and Gertrude Stein to Hardy and even Longfellow. Whether this is some distant repercussion of the conservative political climate of the last decade and a half I know not; it is a mistake in any case to equate political and poetical conservatism, since radical politics and traditional prosody often go together. What is certain is that the modernist tradition that Palmer, Tate, and I grew up with and used as a foundation for further experimentation is being treated more and more as though it never existed in the first place. Michael Palmer's last collection, *Sun,* was attacked in the *New York Times Book Review* for its modernist stance, which the reviewer, William Logan, traced back to myself and to Gertrude Stein, observing however that Miss Stein and I had in the fullness of time achieved some kind of acceptance in certain quarters, even though, and I quote, a "delightful whiff of fraudulence" still clings to us both. No such redeeming whiff was allowed Mr. Palmer, perhaps because he is younger and his work therefore seems newer and more fraudulent, his period of benchwarming in the dugout of poetry having not yet expired.

Michael Palmer's recalcitrant brilliance was apparent from the beginning in his collection *Plan of the City of O,* from 1971, and *Blake's Newton* of the following year. Since then his poetry has not so much developed as refined and reduced itself to the elements that were always there. The critic Don Byrd has said of it that "it *cannot* be paraphrased. Its meaning is strictly a function of the complex interrelations of specific linguistic details . . . It is possible to trace local connections, follow this or that line of thought to its frequently absurd conclusion, but there is no closure except with the irreducible stuff of language and the world."

Palmer is one of the most gifted members of the school known as Language Poets, for whom the stuff of language is particularly irreducible, and for whom signifiers and what is signified have tended to go their separate ways, for various reasons and to different ends. This movement is accompanied by formidable critical baggage, another tendency of our time being for the tail of criticism increasingly to wag the dog of poetry. I haven't read much of it, but my reading of the work of the poets involved suggests that Palmer brings a different set of referents and a different agenda to the situation, meaning as it is engaged by language. He owns to many European influences—Heidegger, Hölderlin, Wittgenstein, Bakhtin and Paul Celan are invoked, and Baudelaire and Raymond Roussel, on whose work Palmer wrote a master's thesis. Equally strong in him is the tradition of the American Objectivists—Reznikoff, Oppen, Lorine Niedecker, Carl Rakosi, Zukofsky—yet he approaches their program of "no ideas but in things" with not a little help from Surrealism. This sounds bizarre at first—surely the leanness of Objectivism is at opposite poles from the high-strung and full-blown conceits of the Surrealists—until we remember that Objectivism has its eldritch side—Williams's *Kora in Hell* for one instance—while Surrealism is not just Breton's rodomontades but also Éluard's jagged, lightning-bolt lines as well. The angular quality of Éluard's poetry reminds me very much of Palmer's, but while the dream is still traceable in Éluard, in Palmer one seems to see it reversed, like the "wrong" side of a patterned fabric. We follow the movement of the argument as intently in the latter as in the former, indeed it appears even more urgent to do so, but, as they say, where it stops nobody knows. That "where" is the delightful, dangerous, and ultimately generous place where we end up if we follow Palmer, and I hope we do. He offers us pure excitement.

Like Michael Palmer, James Tate was born in 1943. His first collection, *The Lost Pilot*, whose title alludes to the father he never knew who was shot down in Europe in the Second World War, won the Yale Younger Poets award in 1967. The titles of subsequent collections—*The Oblivion Ha-Ha, Hottentot Ossuary, Viper Jazz*, and *Riven Doggeries*—provide a clue to the directions he's taken since that relatively correct elegiac beginning. His more recent titles—*Constant Defender, Reckoner*, and *Distance from Loved Ones*—suggest a coming full circle, and indeed the work has perhaps done just that, though the palace of wisdom to which the road of excess has led him is studded with some quite surprising-looking gargoyles.

James Tate has said of his work, "I am in the tradition of the Impurists: Whitman, Williams, Neruda . . . I use the image as a kind of drill to penetrate the veils of illusion we complacently call the Real World, the world of shadows through which we move so confidently. I want to split that world and release the energy of a higher reality. There is nothing I won't do because I see a new possibility each day." And in an early poem called "Rescue," he writes: "Danger invites rescue. I call it loving."

I can do nothing but aspire to such a program. Tate is in fact one of the two poets whose work I read when I have trouble writing, the other being Hölderlin. The idea of the poet permanently at risk, splitting a world, seeing a new possibility each day, wading out into the swamp and seeing where it takes him, sounds to me very close to the actual act of writing poetry, which no one ever really comes close to describing. The "doing" is what Tate and his poems are all about. Recently he told me over the phone that he had decided to put a certain important new relationship on hold—it was satisfying, it was more than that, but he needed time to think about it and above all he wanted to write a poem. The simplicity with which he phrased this reminded me of how simple and unnerving it is to write a poem—it is like getting involved with a person in your life who is so close that you seldom think of him or her, and who for that reason engages you more intensely than a romantic stranger ever could, inviting rescue, inviting love. But let's hear the poet tell about it.

From a reading given at the New York Historical Society (April 11, 1991).

Introduction to Raymond Roussel's
Documents to Serve as an Outline

In an essay published in 1962 in the French review *L'Arc*, reprinted in *Atlas Anthology* 4 (1987), I discussed the opening chapter "In Havana" which had been suppressed, at Roussel's request, from the posthumous printed version of *Documents to Serve as an Outline*, and my reasons for overriding Roussel's wishes in this regard. I wrote among other things that "it appears obvious that it was not doubts about the quality of the work that prompted Roussel to write the note quoted above, but a simple desire for symmetry: shorn of their introduction, the six documents form an easily publishable whole."

Today, thirty years later, I am not so sure. It is impossible to know what Roussel would have understood by terms such as "quality" and "symmetry," and I should have realized this. The fact that he considered two early efforts, the poem *L'âme de Victor Hugo* (originally entitled *Mon âme*) and the novel in verse *La doublure*, as the apogee of his work, after which it was all downhill, is proof enough either of his unreliable judgment vis-à-vis his own work or of the impossibility of fathoming what his aesthetic criteria were. Most readers of Roussel would, I think, consider them minor if not downright tedious efforts, especially *L'âme de Victor Hugo*, and agree that his writing career begins immediately afterward, with the long poem *La vue*. Thus any aesthetic judgment of his work ought to come with the warning that it probably contradicts or at least has no bearing on the author's intentions.

Another problem I have in assessing *Documents* is precisely the work's title, which was assigned by Roussel in his note to the printer regarding posthumous publication, and might well have been different of course, if he had lived to complete the book. But why "documents" and why "outline"? "In Havana" apprises us that the documents were to be assembled as evidence by the thirty members of a club whose raison d'être was to prove the superiority of Europe over America (only six of the planned thirty were printed). Yet it is difficult to see in what way they fulfill their purpose, or any purpose. They are merely tales within tales, from which a didactic lesson seems totally absent. There is no mention of North America or Americans (except for the brief appearance of the arctic explorer T . . . in "In Havana," who has nothing to do with the club's stated goal). It is true that most of the tales have a European setting, though some do not. Some take place in imaginary countries ("Eisnark" or "Belotina") while almost all of the fourth document is nominally set in Honduras and is chiefly concerned with narrating the plot of a drama by the great (and fictitious) Honduran poet Angelo Essermos—surely an example of *Central* American superiority, one would have thought; elsewhere a Mexican novel plays an important role. Could this seeming discrepancy between the documents' stated theme and their actual content have been cause for Roussel's decision to excise the first chapter? Doubtless we'll never know (though it will be interesting to see if the recently discovered hoard of Roussel's papers presently being catalogued at the Bibliothèque Nationale includes any which have a bearing on *Documents*).

As for *canevas,* which I have *faute de mieux* translated as "outline," it too seems a misleading if not mystifying appellation. Harrap's dictionary gives other possible translations: "groundwork, sketch, skeleton (of drawing, novel, etc.)." The original meaning is "canvas" in the sense of an embroidery canvas—something to be finished. Harrap's cites the phrase *"broder le canevas,* to embroider the story, to add artistic verisimilitude to a bald and unconvincing narrative." Yet the documents in no way resemble sketches; they are in fact the most drastic examples of Roussel's constant urge to pare his writing down to its barest essentials (brevity being his chief, if not only, aesthetic criterion)—something hardly possible in a first or early draft. In *Roussel l'ingénu* Michel Leiris writes: "As for style, the only qualities Roussel seems to have sought for, beyond the strictest grammatical correctness, are the maximum of exactitude and concision. I remember causing him a lively pleasure by chance, in praising the extraordinary brevity (to the point where, spoken on stage, the text was very difficult to follow) of each of the anecdotes whose linkage constitutes *L'étoile au front:* 'I forced myself to write each story with the fewest possible words' was Roussel's approximate reply."

Perhaps, however, there were other ways in which the documents, despite their radical bouillon-cube condensation (and this is perhaps as good a place as any to apologize for inevitable shortcomings in my translation, which doubtless employs more words than Roussel would have liked in some cases and in others makes his succinctness sound more eccentric than it is in the original) could be read. One possibility is suggested by Leiris in a 1987 addendum to his earlier essay, "Autour des *Nouvelles impressions d'Afrique.*" He speaks of an earlier version of Chant 1 of *Nouvelles impressions d'Afrique* deposited with Leiris's father (Roussel's business manager) on March 6, 1917, which began and ended "exactly like the version printed in the book, but comprising a quite limited number of insertions, so that the reader doesn't find himself entangled in a labyrinth. This text, in flawless alexandrines, presents itself not as a simple first draft but as a considerably shorter though seemingly finished version of the definitive text, making the latter seem the extraordinarily dense result of a kind of phenomenal padding whose aim is above all to demonstrate the power of an imagination." Thus, what appears to us as the stylistic perfection of the documents (from Roussel's point of view, at least) may be misleading: quantity could have been as important as quality, and the relatively brief tales may have been meant to be "padded" to staggering proportions, resulting in a tome of enormous length, since the book if completed on the scale of the documents as they were published would already have been some three hundred pages long. Perhaps that was what was haunting Roussel during what was apparently his last encounter with Leiris, in Mme. Dufrène's apartment at the beginning of 1933, when Leiris found him looking "slumped, and as though speaking from a great distance." On Leiris's asking him whether he was still writing, Roussel replied: "C'est tellement difficile!"

The difficulty may well have been increased for him by the fact that he was intentionally forging a vast cryptogram. In the manuscript of *Documents,* which I examined at the home of some relatives of Roussel, all dates are left blank, and proper names are indicated only by a first initial. This is also the case with the galley proof of "In Havana." In his note concerning the eventual publication of *Documents,* Roussel requests that someone at the publishing firm fill in the dates and proper names; Michel Leiris tells us that he customarily asked this of his publisher, but invariably changed the names himself. A recently discovered manuscript of *Locus Solus,* sold at auction last year, contains many such changes; for instance, the name of the principal character, Martial Canterel, was arrived at only after eight or nine other names (with different initials) had been rejected. These however were normal French names; many of those in the documents are sheer invention. It seems unlikely that an employee at Lemerre would have arrived at names like Ornigec, Tercus de Lal, Bahol de Jic, Dramieuse, Dess and Gléoc. Fanciful names abound in *Impressions d'Afrique;* there, of course, they can be accounted for by the "exotic" locale; moreover, the European characters have conventional names. In the documents, even French characters have outlandish names, suggesting that Roussel himself supplied them, for purposes of his own. Some of the characters however are actual historical figures: Jesus and Mary Magdalene appear twice, and personages from French history such as Barras, Carrier, Desaix and even Napoleon have cameo roles in narratives that are of course dependent to some extent on historical circumstance. (Unfortunately I can't remember whether or not these names were also left blank in the manuscript I saw.)

Thus we are obliged to read these Chinese-box tales with the understanding that we are not being told all; that behind their polished surface an encrypted secret probably exists. I am reminded of the metaphor Henry James used in *The Golden Bowl* for the hidden relationship between the Prince and Charlotte as it appeared to Maggie Verver: that of an elaborate pagoda with no visible entrance. In Roussel's case this persistent feeling of not knowing precisely what he is up to paradoxically adds to the potent spell of the writing. The stories are intriguing in themselves, the strangely crystallized language a joy to savor, and at the same time a kind of "stereo" effect enhances the experience. We are following him on one level and almost but not entirely missing him on another, a place where secrets remain secret—the "republic of dreams" of which Louis Aragon declared him president.

From *Atlas Anthology* 7 (1991), with John Ashbery's translation of Roussel's *Documents pour servir de canevas*. Reprinted in *How I Wrote Certain of My Books and Other Writings by Raymond Roussel,* edited by Trevor Winkfield (Exact Change, 1995).

Introduction to Gerrit Henry's
The Mirrored Clubs of Hell

Gerrit Henry's poems are by turns, sometimes even simultaneously, bitter and very funny, wry and ecstatic, harrowing and soothing. His subjects are pain and alienation; TV and the movies; relationships with friends, lovers, and parents; life in New York City and the price its transitory pleasures exact; cruising in Village bars and celebrating one's birthday in a psychiatric ward;

God and death and AIDS. At times it seems that he is about to tell us more about himself than he should ("I've gotten fat to discourage AIDS"), but he has the knack of stopping just before he does so. (His stops are incredible and heart-wrenching.) But in fact he isn't telling us about himself to make us feel bad, or good, as some confessional poets have done; he's not telling us about himself, not even telling. Witnessing might be a better word, except that it sounds pretentious and constrained. Instead his rhymes and rhythms are those of the ballads of two poets he particularly admires: Cole Porter and Lorenz Hart, yet always slightly off balance. The metrical shoe never falls precisely at the place where we had anticipated it would. This is but one of many strategies toward an openness amounting to suspense, an unresolved chord at the end. And the subjects listed above aren't precisely subjects, but loci that stake out the territory he travels through, a Dante adrift without a Virgil in the mirrored clubs of hell and their surrounding cityscape: a world he never made but has acclimated himself to for the time being. No, the subject of his poetry is poetry itself, in the broadest sense of the word: a voice that moves toward and away from us and finally just stops, leaving us with the feeling that we have just sensed life, though we would be hard put to analyze it—and why not? Life is like that.

Perhaps the quintessential Henry poem is "*The Watchers*," in which the poet is writing the poem and at the same time watching on TV a horror movie so bad that even he considers abandoning it ("I am / Shocked and outraged // By the sheer ugliness / Of it all"). But . . . "Will I turn it / Off? Probably, no. / I am lonely. And, in some // Subtle, subterranean way, / The movie gives me courage, / Just by its viciousness." But he doesn't stop there: at the end he is turning back to the typewriter to "write you, and me, / An alternative, / Write away the horror, / Write away the blood, / The inevitable, quick progression / Of another American night." In talking about writing an "alternative," Henry actually does so. The horror—and humor—of being trapped with a horror movie that can't even manage to be horrifying is quietly subsumed into "another American night" as the voice stops and the film continues to glimmer for a few seconds, like the point of light at the center of a television screen after you turn it off. Celluloid blood and gore, the poet's unrequited love affair with pop culture and his brief apostrophe to an unnamed "you," the traditional trappings of poetry and narrative which Henry is happy to avail himself of when they can further the work—all dissolve in a closure like that of a Brucknerian or Mahlerian adagio, a moment as transparent as a bubble that is about to burst. This is the splendor of his poetry, which is of a kind we haven't seen before.

From Gerrit Henry's *The Mirrored Clubs of Hell* (New York: Arcade—Little, Brown, 1991).

Preface to Mary Butts's
From Altar to Chimney-Piece

I first heard of Mary Butts in the summer of 1949 when, after graduating from Harvard, I had moved to New York and taken a summer job at the Brooklyn Public Library. It was a time when I was looking for contemporary writers, especially fiction writers, who had somehow escaped classification in what is now called "the canon." Only a couple of months earlier my friend Frank O'Hara had introduced me to the then unknown Jean Rhys, Ronald Firbank, Flann O'Brien and Samuel Beckett (this was in pre-*Godot* days), and I had stumbled on Ivy Compton-Burnett, Laura Riding and Henry Green. All of whom began to persuade me that there was a lot more to twentieth-century literature than Harvard was then letting on.

My immediate superior at the Brooklyn Library was a man in his forties named Richard Elliott who, rather unexpectedly, turned out to be an expert guide to the esoterica I was interested in, and was himself a talented author of strange short stories of which only a few, as far as I know, were published, in obscure little magazines. Of the many writers he suggested I look into, two in particular have remained favorites: Jane Bowles and Mary Butts.

Except for Mary Butts, all the writers I've mentioned so far will doubtless be known to most readers of twentieth-century literature; doubtless she will not be. However, that is about to change. As Patricia Beer wrote in the *London Review of Books* recently: "She is one of the current victims of the fashionable drive to exhume 'forgotten women writers.' The category is dreary. Mary Butts is not."

Yet as recently as 1988, Humphrey Carpenter in *Geniuses Together,* his survey of the 1920s expatriate Montparnasse milieu in which Mary Butts moved, referred to her in passing as "a woman named Mary Butts." Still, she was admired and encouraged by Pound and Eliot; Ford Madox Ford published her in his *Transatlantic Review* (she also appeared in the American review *Hound and Horn*); she was a friend of Cocteau (who drew her portrait and illustrations for two of her books, and is the model for the character André in her story "The House-party"); had a close relationship with Virgil Thomson (who reportedly once proposed marriage to her); and seems to have frequented Gertrude Stein's salon. Of course, these credentials wouldn't matter if she were a negligible talent—the pages of 1920s little magazines like *transition* and *The Little Review* are crammed with forgotten names that will doubtless remain so. Butts was an extraordinary original who deserves to be remembered on the strength of her work alone—one of those *femmes maudites* like Jean Rhys or Djuna Barnes, shadowy presences on the fringes of the Lost Generation in Paris. Until recently, despite the efforts of a few stubborn fans (the American poets Robert Duncan, Robert Kelly and Ken Irby among them), none was more spectral than Mary Butts. Then in 1988 her memoir of childhood, *The Crystal Cabinet,* was reprinted in England (Carcanet Press) and America (Beacon Press).

It was not, however, an ideal vehicle to launch a Mary Butts revival, since it will interest mainly those already won over to her fiction. It rambles occasionally when she sets out her ideas on the education of children and Freudian psychology, and tells us almost nothing of her certainly tumultuous adult years in London and Paris. Fortunately, there is now this collection of stories, as well as an omnibus edition of the novels *Armed with Madness* and *Death of Felicity Taverner* with a preface by Paul West (also published by McPherson and Company). The world can now decide whether it wants reprints of her first novel, *Ashe of Rings*—actually quite different from the others, in an "expressionist" style rather like that of the extraordinary novella "In Bayswater," reprinted here—and of her two historical novels, *The Macedonian* and *Scenes from the Life of Cleopatra*, as well as the still unreprinted stories and the uncollected and virtually unknown poems.

A biography of Mary Butts is said to be on the way, but until it materializes, our knowledge of the person behind the fictions will remain tantalizingly slight. The charms of *The Crystal Cabinet* lie mainly in her evocation of memories of early childhood and of the Dorset landscape which recurs constantly as a setting, a character really, in the novels and the stories. Family relationships are not dealt with in depth. Her brother Tony, obviously an important person in her life, barely appears, and though she speaks fondly of him, Virginia Woolf reported he told her that he had always hated Mary. (Tony was the companion of the writer William Plomer, and committed suicide in 1941.) Hence, it's difficult to know whether to look for traces of Tony in Felix, the heroine's sympathetic gay brother in the *Taverner* novels—he sounds more like Felicity's cruel and capricious brother Adrian in the latter one, just as Adrian's mother and several scheming dowagers in the stories resemble, given certain of her traits set down in *The Crystal Cabinet*, Mary's mother.

Mary Butts was born December 13, 1890, at Salterns, the family estate near the Dorset coast. The pleasantly eccentric house was notable chiefly for its collection of William Blake paintings (the phrase, "the crystal cabinet," is taken from Blake). They were acquired by her great-grandfather Thomas Butts, Blake's enthusiastic patron. She was educated at St. Andrews school in Scotland, went to live in London before the First World War, and married the poet and translator John Rodker, by whom she had her only child, Camilla, in 1920. She seems to have lived mostly in Paris in the 1920s, with occasional revivifying visits to Dorset. Divorced from Rodker, she married the painter Gabriel Aitken (who designed the jacket of her book *Several Occasions*); they too were later divorced. She spent the last years of her life in Sennen, Cornwall, where she died in 1937, aged forty-six.

Paul West mentions her disjointed, dislocated style, and

indeed she can be a difficult writer to "follow." Her fondness for double or even triple negatives ("Nothing upstairs makes me believe anything but that you are all mad, but she is too young to tell nothing but lies"; "It is getting more and more inopportune to suppose women have no secrets unconnected with sex"); her occasional carelessness in indicating who is saying what, to the point where we don't always know who is still in the room; a lapidary terseness that verges on mannerism and is sometimes merely mannered: these traits abound in her stories which nevertheless succeed oftener than the novels. Perhaps she was aware of this, since in *Death of Felicity Taverner* she tries harder than elsewhere to construct a plot (in this case one rather like that of a detective novel), but it sags under the weight of too many stylistic *trouvailles,* often beautiful in themselves.

I seem to be building a case against her; that is by no means my intention, but since I've begun I should perhaps point to her other flaws before going on to her virtues. It will be noticed that the same character-types appear throughout her fiction, sometimes with the same names: the gay brother (her brother Tony?); the taciturn painter-husband (Aitken?); the selfish, dominating mother; the Russian gigolo-in-Paris, Boris, who is sometimes *méchant* (to lapse into French, *à la* Butts), sometimes (as in *Felicity Taverner*) a perverse savior; and the central female character, sometimes called Scylla, who must confront Charybdises of her own, through whose eyes we see everything and who is Butts herself. The supporting cast includes a number of sharply etched expatriate Americans, sometimes heroic and almost as smart as the Europeans (like Carston, another savior, in *Armed with Madness*); sometimes victims of European corruptors (Paul in "The House-party"); sometimes victim-tormentors (Cherry in "From Altar to Chimney-piece"). Indeed, her take on Americans is fresh and unconventional, though it is hard to believe that the Stein-Toklas salon was a coven of satanist bolsheviks, as she seems to be suggesting in "From Altar to Chimney-piece."

The problem is that it isn't always possible to sympathize with these decadent darlings, so determined to put up a brave front in their reduced though hardly indigent circumstances, who have secret access to the earth's magic, who "know," as this passage from *Felicity Taverner* puts it rather too bluntly:

The Taverners were the kind of people who, if they have to choose, choose a boat and a library rather than a car or club; cherry blossom before orchids, apples before tinned peaches, wine to whiskey, one dress from Chanel to six "from a shop" . . . They knew what in relation to Chardin has been called "all the splendor and glory of matter." Like him, they were in love.

This is atypical of the author. Usually she brings on her characters without explaining them, especially in the stories, where there is little room to do so. In the amazing one called "Brightness Falls," a character named Max tells the male narrator: "I ask you not to repeat it, because you won't be able to." This is in fact true of "Brightness Falls" and of her stories in general. They start just about anywhere. "This happened in the kind of house people live in who used not to live in that kind of house, who were taught to have very distinct opinions about the kind of people who lived in them" is the first line of "The Warning." They unfold, rather than unroll, with lacunae and bits of seemingly irrelevant information interrupting the flow, and then, having brought us somewhere, they leave us. Thus, at the end of "Brightness Falls," Max has just finished describing his wife's and her girlfriend's hilarity after all three had passed through an episode that seems tinged with witchcraft:

"Anyhow, they got livelier and livelier; out of their clothes and into them again, telephones, taxis, dancing somewhere; more mischief—"
"Did you go out with them?"
"No, I would not do that."

End of story. But meanwhile we have been to some extraordinary places without leaving London: the enchantment scene takes place in Lincoln's Inn, where

The air was wild and mist-softened, moisture everywhere, but without shine. Like a picture that might easily become another picture, and has to be very good to stay put at all. It was all so dull, a London pool, and not deep enough.

Before that, when Parmys, Max's wife, is starting to explain the mystery, he says:

> "I didn't want to listen, but I found myself attending to noises. In November the third week was still, you remember. A few leaves left to fall, and each one I thought was like a little word that you just couldn't catch. Light and brown and so few of them—whispers in the air. I used to stand at the window and watch, until I thought of coral and pearl and how red and white they are."

Where are we? Where have we come from? But the narrator has already warned us in the story's opening sentences: "There is no head or tail to this story, except that it happened. On the other hand, how does one know that anything happened? How does one know?"

Paul West likens Mary Butts to a hummingbird, and he is right: we admire hummingbirds because we can't quite see them; their erratic motion prevents that and is what we like about them. After reading Butts one is left with an impression of dazzle, of magic, but what made it is hard to pin down. Rereading after forty years her marvelous story "Friendship's Garland" (all the stories set in London as well as the London parts of *Ashe of Rings* have a haze of madness in them, the author being indeed "armed with madness"—a phrase, incidentally, that I would dearly love to trace), I found that the only thing I remembered from my first reading was a single metaphor. We are in rather sinister company at a café called the Craven.

> Through the noise and the iron streets, even through the racing wind the sun poured, roaring its heat through the wind at the huge buildings and the crowd. Those are the hours when the city pays for being a city, and is delivered over to the wind and the sun and their jackal the dust. All the earth pays, but principally the city. On the other hand, inside the Craven there is no nature at all. These things are not natural, marble like cheese, red velvet, and plaster gilt.

"Marble like cheese" was all I had retained, except for a sense of the whole story as something evil, glittering, funny and, at the end, surreally beautiful, as the narrator sees her face in a mirror looking "half old, like a child's recovering from a sickness," and later "like a child that has been dipped in dew." To remember the stories, even just after finishing them, necessitates rereading them; there is no other way to hang onto their breathless skittering as it evolves before us.

Though Mary Butts was not exactly unknown during her lifetime, she became so almost immediately afterward. Only now, after more than half a century, is the public discovering her. The very features of her writing that taxed earlier readers—her startling ellipses, especially in conversations; her drastic cutting in the cinematic sense; her technique of collaging bits of poetry and popular song lyrics ("Lady Be Good" and "What'll I Do") into the narratives—make her seem our contemporary. So do the freewheeling and disordered lives of her characters, who can be "wired" in a very 1990s way—the homosexual ones, for instance, whom she treats with a sympathy and openness astonishing for the England of her time. One keeps getting the feeling that these stories were written yesterday.

"The old man belonged to the majority who do not approve—say of cats or earrings or 'bus tickets,'" she writes in "In Bayswater." Today that majority is bigger than ever, but so is the minority that opposes it—the minority who approves. We need Mary Butts now, to guide us, "armed with madness," through mazes and forests to the pure sources of storytelling.

From Mary Butts's *From Altar to Chimney-Piece* (New York: McPherson and Co., 1992).

Review of Mark Ford's *Landlocked*

Mark Ford's *Landlocked* is one of the most refreshing books of poetry I have seen in years. When was the last time you actually felt refreshed? *Landlocked* will do it for you. Waves and waves of refreshment coming at you, like those "curiously strong" mints they have (or used to have) in England. We know about "strong" poets; attention must now be paid to the "curiously strong" like James Tate and Charles Simic in America, and England's Anthony Howell and Peter Robinson (like Ford currently residing in Kyoto), especially in his recent collection *Leaf Viewing*.

Before continuing I ought to mention that I've met Ford several times, twice in England and twice in America where his parents have been living for the past decade. More to the point, he has written a dissertation on my poetry at Oxford, a copy of which he sent me about six months ago, enclosing *Landlocked* as a kind of afterthought. Thus it might be thought that a conflict of interest taints my favorable view of his verse, though I haven't read the dissertation yet—for all I know there may be harsh evaluations lurking in its imposing bulk. Nonetheless, literary conspiracy buffs should take note, and perhaps read no further.

However, I don't see much *explicit* evidence of my influence or anyone else's on his work. It's true there are echoes—which Michael Hofmann made rather too much of in his partly stern *TLS* review, finding Ford to be a creature afflicted with "vestigial Muldoon wings, Christopher Reid claws, Weldon Kees markings, Ashbery slither"—not unlike something Gustave Doré might have dreamed up for his Dante illustrations. Actually, Ford paints himself as just such a monster in the pathetic "Outing": "a huge green amphibian / made to inch my home-sick coils between the different counters / of your favourite store, taking all these fancy cautions / to keep my head down, and out of other shoppers' way. / Your ankles I can just make out. The cash till rings . . . "

Fortunately, Hofmann shifts gears in his closing paragraph, in an abrupt transition worthy of Ford's poetry and perhaps "caught" from it, concluding that "a fine and cultivated literary sense must be in operation here." And he is not far off the mark in his characterization of Ford's poems as "all surface, and all flaky, disintegrating surface at that . . . personal and phantasmagorical, punning and word-spinning, with a wide and arch vocabulary and a special stock-in-trade of phrases from sportscasts," though he seems to take a dimmer view of such goings-on than I do.

But about those echoes. Hofmann must be right, but if he is, he doesn't go far enough in identifying them. I've just been reading through Hugh Haughton's *Chatto Book of Nonsense Poetry*—perhaps not so coincidentally Chatto is Ford's publisher, and the "nonsense" Keats quatrain that serves as epigraph to *Landlocked* is included in the anthology—and I find in it pre-echoes of Ford wherever I look. So it's perhaps not so much a question of specific poets having influenced him but a whole tradition of which he is merely a late practitioner—one of the purest streams of poetry and a specifically English one, though it bubbles up everywhere. The anthology in fact contains two poems of mine that I didn't consider to be nonsense when I was writing them, but Haughton's introduction is at pains to dispel the term "nonsense" as a literary subgenre mainly intended for children, calling *Finnegans Wake* "our great nonsense epic" and noting Stevens's "gaiety of language," meanwhile summoning Freud as a witness for the defense: "Dreams, then, are often most profound when they seem most crazy. In every epoch of history those who have had something to say but could not say it without peril have eagerly assumed a fool's cap. The audience at whom their forbidden speech was aimed tolerated it more easily if they could at the same time laugh and flatter themselves with the reflection that the unwelcome words were clearly nonsensical."

And so it goes today. Even though Haughton locates nonsense in such unlikely places as Rimbaud's "Ô saisons, ô châteaux," John Crowe Ransom's "Captain Carpenter" and Paul Celan's "Todesfuge," the common reader of poetry, assuming he or she exists, relishes nonsense only when it is clearly labeled as such, and Haughton's anthology is, after all, titled *The Chatto Book of Nonsense Poetry*.

Ford's poetry is light and agile and sometimes sweet, but it also has a disconcerting way of turning sharp and naughty and even sinister—the turns, and not their direction necessarily, keep it alive on the page and sometimes aloft over it. John Bayley mentions Betjeman on the book's back cover, and there is surely something Betjemanish (and perhaps a reminiscence of Lear's "Uncle Arly") in the first stanza of "Cross-Section":

We all knew of his exploits—
The flowers from the Dean's wife for his overhead,
The chair carved into an oak tree bearing his name,
And the day he passed his driving test
Wine in hall for all.

But then the tone and the subject abruptly shift: this is the rest
of the poem:

A songster
Left out in the rain trills bleakly
It's morning: new habits for me too,
Sawing things palely in half on my saw-horse
Each Sunday afternoon.

Ambiguity steps in where drollery leaves off; how did the songster (a bird I assume) get left out in the rain, since birds are usually outdoors anyway? Since there's no period after "bleakly," is
the songster trilling that it's morning (nice concept that, a
"bleak trill," which could describe much of Ford's own music)?
And then why is it suddenly afternoon, and what are the
"habits" of Sunday afternoon: does "habits" mean clothes, one's
Sunday best perhaps? Or does it refer to "sawing" ("sawing
palely" somehow echoes "trills bleakly")? And "Sawing things
palely in half on my saw-horse / Each Sunday afternoon." What
is that? It seems vaguely to hint at "self-abuse," a common
enough distraction for a rainy Sunday afternoon, or even self-
mutilation: the speaker is at his saw-horse, sawing we know not
what. Something that results in a "Cross-Section," though that
title perhaps applies too to the life of the unnamed don or professor, of whom we know a few things, perhaps enough to constitute a "cross-section": the "exploit" of the Dean's wife's flowers for his "overhead" (some kind of canopy? business expenses?
some English sense of the word I'm unaware of?), the impressive oak-tree chair (which might be an appropriate place of repose for Uncle Arly, should he tire of his heap of barley), and
the undeniable exploit of passing his driving test. Was it the
"wine in hall for all" that produced the hangoverish seeming-
alienation in the voice in the second half of the poem? No one
need or should know the answers to these questions: I point to

them only to show how treacherous and irregular the terrain of a Ford poem is, even as one imagines oneself striding confidently over it.

Michael Hofmann also mentions (a shade reprovingly?) the "unmistakable mid-Atlantic" quality of Ford's poetry. Again I'm not sure what he means. Who are the "mid-Atlantic" poets? Does Michael Schmidt count as one? Muldoon maybe? I can think of American poets who have sojourned in England and vice versa without finding a voice that is an emulsion of English-English and the American kind. True, American place-names crop up in Ford now and then: the Adirondacks, Amarillo and the Pulaski Skyway (the latter in a darker than usual poem called "Snowfall," in which the poet is traveling by car with his mother on said skyway, a nightmarish elevated highway that connects New York to Newark Airport). But they exude local color no more than do mentions of Finsbury Circus or the Walworth Road in other poems. Rather, like Apollinaire's passing references to Galveston or Connecticut, they allude to the imaginary world of geography books, where, as Baudelaire said of Constantin Guys, "the observer is a prince who enjoys travelling everywhere incognito."

There is also the matter of the illustration on the cover of *Landlocked,* Fairfield Porter's painting *Broadway South of Union Square,* a somewhat odd choice for two reasons: New York cityscapes are an almost unknown genre in Porter's work (this one depicts a singularly dull urban stretch); second, Manhattan Island is scarcely landlocked. But then neither is the poet—born in Nairobi, educated in England, an occasional visitor to America and now resident in Japan. Perhaps in his choice of a cover illustration, as throughout his book, he is merely radiating insouciance—but that's the wrong word, for it implies enjoying oneself at someone else's expense; make that a fine and generous lack of consequence.

One would like to quote passage after passage, just for the pleasure of rolling them around on one's tongue, but you'll have to get the book, whose only shortcoming is that it's short—fifty-one pages and some of the poems are as short as blips (though a fine longer one, "A Swimming-Pool Full of Peanuts," has the nutty majesty of, say, Elizabeth Bishop's "The Monument," and shows that he can handle an expanded theme). I'll therefore limit myself to two, just to give the flavor. One is the middle of a three-stanza poem ("Then She Said She Had to Go"), which has a curious form: each seven-line stanza has a left and right column, but the fifth line is common to both and serves as a fragile but effective tie between them:

My new cow   Lunch is a strange experience
is loose in the field.   here. The big hall is
With her tail she   full of birds
swishes   swooping around—
away flies
and wanders   a carrot I
off happily to the fence   was about to eat.

Surely English poetry has few lines as wonderfully and weirdly attractive as

> away flies
> a carrot I
> was about to eat.

"The broken sheds looked sad and strange" from Tennyson's "Mariana" might be a close contender.

The last sample captures beautifully Ford's view of the world, which is hardly a worldview but a look at a small piece of it possessing a startling specific gravity. ("This view, for instance, includes // seven counties and a bull charging around in its paddock.") It's the end of a poem called "Winter Underwear."

> And a fresh snow covers the plains
> Above which newfangled aircraft constantly
> Manoeuvre, their vapour trails soft
> And brilliant as the white
>
> Winter underwear she is even now pulling on.

It may be that these lines are an illustration of the four that immediately precede it: "Until one day speech / Is merely syntax, and one's head / Is so full of stratagems / The tea freezes solid in its pot . . ." If so, Ford is being unkind to himself; that head full of stratagems has not, not yet at any rate, produced a nuclear winter, but a wintry world, ours in fact, where the beautiful and silly simultaneity of whatever is happening in it at a given moment has never been more touchingly, more joyously expressed.

Review of Mark Ford's *Landlocked* (London: Chatto and Windus, 1992). From *PN Review* (January–February 1993).

Introduction to Pierre Martory's
The Landscape Is behind the Door

Pierre Martory's poetry is unknown in his native France. There are a number of reasons for this, the principle one being that, save for a few poems which appeared in now-forgotten little magazines in the early 1950s, Martory has never tried to publish his work or showed it to anyone (myself excepted) who might be interested in it. His only published work in France, apart from articles on music and the theater written during a twenty-five-year stint at the weekly newsmagazine *Paris-Match*, is a novel called *Phébus ou le beau mariage* which the firm of Denoël brought out in 1953. Despite a favorable critical reception it was not followed by another, even though Martory continues to this day to write both fiction and poetry almost constantly.*

Before looking at his poetry, I have to give a few facts about his life, even though Martory shares an instinctive French antipathy for criticism mixed with biography and has asked me to keep his life out of this. But I think a little explanation in the form of a summary curriculum vitae is necessary in order for readers to approach a body of work that for me ranks with that of the finest contemporary French poets but has managed so far

*In America, Martory published a bilingual chapbook of poems titled *Every Question but One* (New York: Intuflo Editions—The Groundwater Press, 1990).

to escape attention even though the poet is now in his early seventies.

He was born in Bayonne in southwest France, of partly Basque ancestry. His mother died when he was two, after giving birth to a second son, Jean. His father soon remarried and had other children with his new wife. A career military officer, he was posted to Morocco, where Pierre spent much of his child-hood and where he was happiest, despite life with a stepmother and an authoritarian father who beat his children often and never allowed them to have any toys. Martory still visits Morocco frequently. He received his *baccalauréat* in Bayonne and in the fall of 1939 enrolled at the School of Political Sciences in Paris. In June 1940 he managed to get on the last train to leave Paris before the Germans arrived, and after a time spent at Bayonne and wandering through the south of France he traveled to Tunisia where he joined the French Army, which eventually joined forces with the invading U.S. Army.

After the war he worked at the unlikely-sounding Biarritz American University, then as an airline clerk in Bordeaux, before moving to Paris. Here for a while he was part of a loose-knit group of writers that included Hubert Juin and Hervé Bazin, who used to meet in a café on the Ile Saint-Louis and declaim their poems to one another. This was the only time he ever frequented a literary milieu. In 1952 he went to Munich for a year and a half, where he studied singing informally; on his return he found the group had dispersed. After the publication of his novel, which was overseen by the distinguished editor Robert Kanters, he wrote a second one which Kanters, himself a homosexual, rejected on account of its homosexual theme. (In those days, before the arrival on the scene of Barthes, Foucault and others, homosexuality was very much taboo in intellectual circles; today the climate is drastically changed.) Martory submitted a third novel to Kanters, who liked it but asked him to change the ending; in a fit of pique Martory withdrew the book and never tried to publish anything else. Years later, in his memoirs, Kanters wondered what had happened to the brilliant young author of *Phébus,* and Martory couldn't resist writing him a note reminding him that he had played a certain role in his withdrawal from the scene.

I first met Martory in 1956 while in France on a Fulbright scholarship. We soon became very close friends and remain so to this day. Pierre, a voracious and omnivorous reader with a preference for history, biography and memoirs (he reread those of Saint-Simon in their mammoth entirety after an improved Pléiade edition appeared), was the ideal guide to France and things French for an American; in addition, his take on them has something distinctly and irreverently American about it. He has always had more American friends (and Moroccan ones) than French, and claims that he loves France but detests the French.

Even with Pierre's help it took me a long time to become fluent in French, and thus I began to read his poetry only after we had known each other for a year or more. I was also reading other contemporary and classical French poetry, and as I became familiar with its tropes it began to strike me that his was quite different. He had assimilated the moderns, especially René Char, as well as the classical "canon" that French students are forced to ingest, but my still relatively unschooled eye could find no resemblances, or very few, between his poetry and French poetry of the past or present. In fact, with the exception of a few older poets such as Char and Ponge, French poetry in the decade following the Second World War was in a period of doldrums. Something similar had happened in England, where the thirties brio of W. H. Auden, F. T. Prince, Louis MacNeice, and Nicholas Moore had been supplanted by Larkin's austerity; and in America, where Delmore Schwartz and the early Jarrell and Berryman were eclipsed by Lowell and the later Auden, Berryman and Jarrell.

Looking today for antecedents to Martory's poetry I am forced to speculate, since for some reason we rarely discuss our work with each other. His fluency in German makes me aware of trace elements of Hölderlin, Rilke and Trakl (the latter especially in "Red and Black Lake"), though again these are only educated guesses. We both share an enthusiasm for Raymond Roussel, whose otherworldly landscapes are perhaps "behind the door," especially in a longish poem called "Evenings in Rochefort" which I translated for the review *Locus Solus* in the sixties, but which Martory preferred not to reprint in this collection. In the end the only fruitful comparison seems to be with Rimbaud, and not because Martory's poetry resembles his, but because both are similar in resembling no one else. It is difficult for French poets to escape the crystalline tyranny of the French language; even the Surrealists at their most fantastic built on classical foundations. Only in recent years, as younger French poets have become aware of new American experiments with language, and vice versa (thanks in some degree to the cross-pollinating efforts of *Américainistes* like Emmanuel Hocquard and Serge Fauchereau), has our younger generation begun to have an impact in France; meanwhile, a spate of recent translations has enabled English-speaking readers to assess the achievements of major figures such as Edmond Jabès and Michel Deguy, and of such innovative younger poets as Pascalle Monnier and Anne Portugal.

Whether Martory has been influenced by American models I don't know, though when we first met he was reading Emily Dickinson, Eliot and Gertrude Stein. He certainly hadn't read my poetry yet, though I find a curious prefiguring of it in poems of his written before we met, such as "Blues" and "Ma chandelle est morte." And after I began translating him, that is, after I began to realize that his marvelous poetry would likely remain unknown unless I translated it and brought it to the attention of American readers (fortunately this Sheep Meadow edition will be distributed in France in a French edition),* I have begun to find echoes of his work in mine. His dreams, his pessimistic résumés of childhood that are suddenly lanced by a joke, his surreal loves, his strangely lit landscapes with their inquisitive birds and disquieting flora, are fertile influences for me, though I hope I haven't stolen anything—well, better to steal than borrow, as Eliot more or less said. I can only hope that this first substantial gathering of Martory's poetry into a volume will be a revelation for others as well.

---

*This didn't happen. A French edition was printed by Sheep Meadow, but not distributed in France.

From Pierre Martory's *The Landscape Is behind the Door* (New York: The Sheep Meadow Press, 1994).

Introduction to a Reading by Robert Creeley and Charles Tomlinson

I'm very pleased to have been asked to introduce two of the leading poets of today, one English, the other American. Charles Tomlinson and Robert Creeley have been friends for many years. And they have been colleagues as well, despite apparent dissimilarities in their work.

Tomlinson indeed seems quintessentially British, a product of the industrial Midlands where he was born in 1927. Those tainted landscapes haunt his work as felicitously as they do the early poems of Auden. Unlike Auden, however, who seems never really to have come to terms with his adopted homeland, at least the part of it west of the Hudson River, Tomlinson has been a passionate visitor to and observer of America. One can think of few other contemporary British poets who have opened themselves to the American scene with such fortunate results. Thom Gunn, Nathaniel Tarn, and Lee Harwood have been pilgrims here, Gunn even a permanent one though his poetry has remained permanently English despite its exotic locale. One might conclude the same of Tomlinson, for he is certainly unmistakably English, yet I think closer inspection reveals the influence not only of the openness of the American landscape, such as that of New Mexico where he has lived, but the open-endedness of so much American poetry as well, particularly that of the Black Mountain School of which Creeley is such a fabulous representative. As Tomlinson wrote in a poem called "Small Action Poem," which he dedicated to Robert and Bobbie Creeley:

> The door
> is open now
> that before
> was neither
> open
> nor was it there.

It requires no great stretch of the imagination to conclude that he was describing what happened to him when he crossed the Atlantic and the American continent, and he puts it with a succinct elegance that matches Creeley's. But he goes farther still. His beautiful prose poem "Autumn" seems to have its starting point in a landscape that is English. I say this because of the presence of oak leaves and field mice, which, though they exist here, seem part of an English tradition. But the way the landscape turns itself inside out during the course of the poem is more reminiscent of American modernist poetry, and it would not, in my opinion, have come out this way without Tomlinson's very English brush with American poetry. He writes: "Peace? There will be no peace until the fragility of the mosquito is overcome and the spirals of the infusoria turn to glass in the crystal pond. These greens are the solace of lakes under a sun which corrodes. They are memorials not to be hoarded." The paradox of a memorial not to be hoarded seems very American to me; we Americans are constantly, for better or worse, rememorating and squandering memory at the same time, trying to have it both ways, as Tomlinson does so movingly in his transient, enduring poetry.

Almost fifty years ago Robert Creeley and I sat almost side by side at Harvard in a course on the eighteenth-century English novel. Not quite together, since the students were seated alphabetically and between us was one named Berlin. We never spoke—Creeley was much too forbidding-looking for me to attempt that, and perhaps I was too, but one of my keener lesser regrets is that we never sat down together and thrashed out the relative merits of *Pamela* and *Joseph Andrews*. At any rate, Creeley—we also participated in a poetry workshop where the future novelist John Hawkes was also a student—was a memorable presence on campus, though he didn't stay there long. Later on when one heard of him one realized that one knew one was going to all along.

I don't remember Creeley's poems in the workshop and wish I could forget my own, but we may well have realized then that we were on opposite sides of the poetic fence: me so European and maximalist, influenced by Auden and Stevens; he so American, with perhaps an Asian conciseness gleaned from Pound, stemming obviously from the Pound-Williams tradition to which

Olson's presence would soon be added. Yet I've never been able to think of Creeley as a minimalist, which some have called him. If cramming as many possible things into the smallest space with no sign of strain or congestion is minimal, then maybe he is a minimalist. But what strikes me most about his poetry is a sense of richness and ripeness, beautifully contained in a vessel which was made to order by the circumstance of writing the poem. As he writes in "Some Place":

> I resolved it, I
> found in my life a
> center and secured it.

And lest we misinterpret his accuracy for pride, he adds farther on:

> There is nothing I am
> nothing not. A place
> between, I am. I am
> more than thought, less
> than thought.

No one, I think, has ever stated what it is to be a poet more cogently and yes, more succinctly than Robert Creeley. But his succinctness is like the unfettered flashing of a diamond.

From a reading given at the New School, New York City (April 25, 1995). First published in *Poetry Pilot* (Summer 1995), the newsletter of the Academy of American Poets.

Robert Frost Medal Address

From the beginning there has been some difference of opinion between the Poetry Society of America and me as to what I should do to acknowledge the signal honor they have bestowed on me, the Robert Frost Medal. Just reading some of my poetry was ruled out from the beginning, just because poetry by itself is never enough—a dish without a sauce, or maybe a sauce without a dish. Every poet who reads his or her poetry before an audience is accustomed to the question and answer period that follows, which often ends with the question, "Are there any questions that haven't been asked that you feel you would like to answer?" The underlying thrust of all these questions is something like: "Please explain your poetry to me." Now it may be true that composers and painters and cineastes are also asked to explain their work, but if so their task is lightened somewhat by the fact that there is something there to explain. With a poem there is nothing, or there should be nothing if the poet has done his job successfully, and that is because the act of writing the poem *was* an explanation of something that had occurred to the poet, and demanded to be put into words which in turn formed a poem. To explain an explanation is a much more difficult, and in the end perhaps a hopeless task because it's doomed to redundancy. Yet I'm fully aware that I'll have to go on making repeated stabs at it for as long as I'll be asked to speak in public, and that this impossible feat is also a necessary one if only because people expect it, and it is normal and proper to give people what they expect.

In a calendar of events in this week's *New York* magazine I saw a mention of this occasion, which said it would include a retrospective poetry reading. That's fine: I can do retrospective poetry readings; indeed, I'm not sure there's another kind. Most poets, not just me, read not only from their work of the past week but also include some chestnuts even from the distant past which they've read countless times and for which they can reasonably expect a positive reception because it's happened that way before, though of course this isn't always the case. So fine: I'm going to read some old standbys and also make some "remarks," which is what I managed to persuade Elise Paschen would be a suitable alternative to a "lecture" which is probably what your invitations say I'm going to give. It also seemed natural that the subject of my remarks would be myself, or my poetry, since they—we—are what is getting honored here, though normally I go to extreme lengths to avoid talking about either of us, because I don't really know that much about us.

I grew up on my father's apple farm a couple of miles from a small farming village in western New York state with the melodious name of Sodus, which is apparently an Indian word meaning "moonlight on water"; at least that's what we were told. This region of piddling villages includes a number that are famous for something or are the capital of something. Nearby Baldwinsville is renowned as the Bird Dog Capital of America, and even nearer is the town of Phelps which revels in the title of Sauerkraut Capital, and at certain times of year offers pungent testimony to this distinction. But, as Kenneth Koch pointed out in his epic poem *Ko, or a Season on Earth,* "Some towns are famous for two things," and that is the case with Sodus, which is famous for having the largest bay on Lake Ontario, Sodus Bay, and the highest landmass on it, nearby Chimney Bluffs, which are quite picturesque. But, alas, Sodus remains largely unsung, even, cruelly, by me. The surrounding landscape does play a role in my work, though, as it does in most poets' work; indeed, W. H. Auden said somewhere that our childhood is all we have—rather odd coming from a poet with his reputation for intellectuality. Our farm was just a mile from Lake Ontario, which meant that we were in a mini-snowbelt where the snow was even heavier than it was just a few miles south, in the official snowbelt. And so snow is a constant in my poetry. "I hear America snowing" is a line in one of my poems, and one of my early long poems is called "The Skaters," even though I never learned to skate properly.

Actually, snow figured largely in my first poem, which I wrote when I was eight; it was called "The Battle," and was about a battle between the snowflakes and the bunnies. I can remember only two lines of it, which I will inflict on you to show that my poetry did too rhyme once upon a time, although I can't say that this couplet is all that felicitous. "To celebrate their victory" (I can't remember which side won); "To celebrate their victory they had a feast / Of turkey and dressing and cakes of yeast." Some feast. Anyway, I liked the poem, and it seemed so good that I didn't write another one until I was in high school. It also had the distinction of being read aloud at the Christmas Day celebration in the Fifth Avenue apartment of the best-selling novelist Mary Roberts Rinehart, whose son married my mother's cousin, and whose work I had already read in the *Saturday Evening Post*. I didn't think I'd ever be able to pull off another coup like that one, and so didn't try. Besides, what I really wanted to be was a painter, and for years attended art classes at the art museum in Rochester, and in fact did paint until I went away to college, where there was no space to do so in my dorm room. Like William Carlos Williams, who also began as painter, I discovered that it was "easier to carry a manuscript around than a wet canvas."

Painting has always been an influence on my poetry, though. The year after I wrote "The Battle," *Life* magazine did an article on Alfred Barr's celebrated show "Fantastic Art, Dada and Surrealism" at the Museum of Modern Art. I think it was at that moment I realized I wanted to be a Surrealist, or rather that I already was one. It was nice to know I was something and to know what that something was. For years I pored over that issue of *Life,* and then found some more examples in the museum library, including *View* magazine and a book about Joseph Cornell, who immediately became my favorite artist and has remained one to this day. I didn't know there could be Surrealist poetry, but a few years later my cousin in Buffalo gave me a copy of a poetry magazine called *Upstate,* published there by John Bernard Myers, who would, coincidentally, one day publish my first pamphlet of verse. The issue was devoted to Latin American poetry and included translations of Octavio Paz, whom I fell for immediately.

Around this time, I had won a contest in high school sponsored by *Time* magazine—a current events contest for students who would know about that week's current events as gleaned from *Time* magazine. You had your choice of five books, and they all seemed rather dull except for Louis Untermeyer's anthology of modern American and British poetry, which I chose. Almost from that moment on, I began to be fascinated by poetry and to gradually lose interest in painting. The first poets I liked were the easiest to understand—Robert Frost, Edna St. Vincent Millay, Elinor Wylie, Edwin Arlington Robinson, and of course Edgar Lee Masters. The more difficult poems attracted me without, yet, exactly appealing to me, notably those of Auden and Dylan Thomas. I remember going around in a permanently puzzled state trying to figure out the meaning of Thomas's line "The force that through the green fuse drives the flower," which now seems so open and beautiful. Similarly, Auden, who hardly has a reputation for obscurity anymore (perhaps because his later poetry tended to renounce it, and he was still writing his early poetry then), baffled me. Yet it was Auden who ultimately became for me *the* modern poet, the one I hoped most to emulate. What I couldn't understand in his poetry was how he could use colloquial language, and how he would leave you with a concrete image that he didn't explain or annotate, and that was supposed to *be* the poem. One of his most memorable passages for me, then and now, is the first stanza of "In War Time": "Abruptly mounting her ramshackle wheel, / Fortune has pedalled furiously away; / The sobbing mess is on our hands today." Even after I understood that "wheel" meant bicycle, and that he was punning cleverly on the idea of the wheel of fortune, I wasn't sure what to think, though today this image of an eccentric spinster climbing on to her broken-down bike and speeding away sums up the arrival of war more tellingly than any other passage I know.

So I began writing poetry out of a desire to emulate what was being done. At first I tried the traditional forms, sonnets especially, and used rhyme and meter, and then it began to dawn on me that poetry was more that that, that there was plenty of room to play around, that the conventions could be ignored just as Auden used popular speech, and that rhymes could be half-rhymes or assonance or no rhymes at all. My main ambition then was to get a poem in *Scholastic* magazine; they kept publishing poems by a young high-school student named Richard Avedon, and I thought my stuff was as good as his, good though he was. But though my English teacher would send in my poems, I never got further than pleasant, encouraging notes from the poetry editor. The last two years of high school I spent at Deerfield Academy; there I finally broke into print in the school newspaper. From there I went to Harvard, and during my second year met another young poet—a momentous occasion—Kenneth Koch. We showed each other our poems and became a mutual admiration society; Kenneth encouraged me to "go out for" the *Harvard Advocate,* and he indeed browbeat the other editors until they took me on. It was actually an exciting time to be a poet at Harvard: other students who were future poets were Donald Hall, Adrienne Rich, Frank O'Hara, Robert Bly, Robert Creeley and Peter Davison. Slightly older but on the scene and available if one wanted to talk about poetry were Richard Wilbur, Delmore Schwartz, John Ciardi and Ruth Stone and the critic F. O. Matthiessen, an inspiring teacher of modern poetry. And there were excellent poetry readings: while I was there I was able to hear readings by Auden, Marianne Moore, William Carlos Williams, T. S. Eliot and Wallace Stevens, who I believe only gave two readings in his lifetime.

I'm going to read one of my undergraduate poems, called "Some Trees," written in 1948; it was published in the *Advocate* and elicited a compliment from Richard Wilbur, a tremendous thrill—Wilbur's *The Beautiful Changes* had recently appeared to much acclaim. This poem, I think, was quite influenced by Marianne Moore, whose work I still love; her poem "An Octopus" is as fine as anything written in this century.

[Reads "Some Trees"]

You'll note the fashionable half-rhymes, which I was shortly to abandon; in fact, this poem, which became the title poem of my first book some eight years later, and which is perhaps my most widely anthologized poem, seems in retrospect like a farewell to "poetry as we know it." It rhymes, sort of; it tells a story, a sort of love story; and it seems, or seemed, modern in the nice, fresh, not-too-troubling way of that time—an artifact I was proud of and couldn't imagine how I had produced.

But after that, modernism led me farther afield—astray, perhaps? I had thought modern poetry gave the poet a license to be strange, but when mine was finally collected in a volume (I speak of my Yale Younger Poets book *Some Trees,* not of the pamphlet John Myers published, which was scarcely a blip on the poetry scene) and it was finally exposed to the gaze of criticism, though not many critics gazed its way, I got the distinct sensation that it was too strange, stranger than anybody else's, and though I thought I was writing in an acceptable if still controversial (from the standpoint of mainstream literature) tradition,

I had without meaning to gone too far. Of a handful of reviews, only one was really favorable, and that was written for *Poetry* by my friend Frank O'Hara, so I felt it didn't count; nevertheless, I was enormously grateful to him since both he and I had been finalists for the Yale award, with Auden (whom by that time we knew personally, though not well) choosing mine.

By this time I had been living in New York for several years; Kenneth preceded me here by a year and persuaded me to move here after graduation from Harvard. I was rather afraid of the place, but things were finally decided for me when I got turned down by the Harvard graduate school and accepted by Columbia. O'Hara joined us two years later, after getting a graduate degree at Michigan; by that time we were a group of poets, including Barbara Guest and the late James Schuyler; as well as painters, such as Jane Freilicher, Larry Rivers and Nell Blaine. It wasn't till quite a few years later that we poets were dubbed, somewhat to our surprise, the New York School of Poets; this was the idea of John Myers, whose gallery published our pamphlets and who thought that the prestige of New York School painting might rub off on "his" poets; he coined the term in an article in the California magazine *Nomad* in 1961, and it has stuck.

By the time *Some Trees* was published in 1956, I had gone to France on a Fulbright scholarship and would end up spending the next ten years there. I had worked at various menial jobs in publishing until then and was glad to go abroad, though the personnel manager at McGraw-Hill tried to persuade me I was making a big mistake renouncing my seventy-five-dollar-a-week job in the college advertising department. As soon as I got to Paris, I knew I wanted to stay, though when after several weeks I ran into Ned Rorem, who asked me how I liked it there, I remember replying, "After you've lived in Paris for a while, you don't want to live anywhere, including Paris." This remark eventually surfaced in one of his published diaries as "After you've lived in Paris awhile, you don't want to live anywhere else"—one of an ongoing series of misquotations of me that have appeared in his books, and which I'm glad to have the opportunity to correct now.

I made two very good friends shortly after arriving; one the French poet and novelist Pierre Martory, who's here today; the other the American writer Harry Mathews; both are still good friends, and in fact, the three of us had lunch in New York only last week. There were other friendships, and the city was then and is always a positive joy to be in—everybody knows that. But I was finding it difficult to write. First, I was satisfied on the whole with my book *Some Trees,* but I wanted to move on to something else and had no idea of what that would turn out to be. And living in a country where a different language than the one I was used to was all around me was a problem too; I began to realize how much the spoken American language, thanks to Auden's example of the colloquial, entered into my writing. For a long time I wrote little that I could value, though the first poem I wrote after arriving in France, still in the style of "Some Trees," has in recent years found favor with me that it didn't have originally.

[Reads "Thoughts of a Young Girl"]

For the next two or three years, I lived in a state of restless experimenting. Often I'd visit the American Library and leaf through popular magazines, looking for the tone of voice I felt was lacking. Or I'd buy magazines like *Esquire* and look through them, copying down random bits of phrases in a sort of collage technique—unaware that about the same time Burroughs, Allen Ginsberg and Gregory Corso were practicing doing "cut-ups" elsewhere in Paris. It's an odd coincidence that we all happened on this way of making writing at that particular time and place. I wasn't satisfied with most of my efforts, and they remain unpublished, but I did put some of them in my next collection, *The Tennis Court Oath,* published by Wesleyan in 1961. What happened was that John Hollander, whom I'd never met, had seen and liked my first books and asked me to submit to the Wesleyan poetry series. Most of the writing I had was experiments, not written with publication in mind since I didn't think I'd have another book published. But in fact, there were some poems in which I thought I'd achieved a satisfactory amalgam of my earlier style and whatever a new one might be; one of these is "To Redouté."

[Reads "To Redouté"]

Others are so fragmentary as to defeat most readers, I now see, though the group called Language Poets finds some of these my most valuable works. For them, unless I misunderstand, language is more or less an independent entity, a free-standing object not concerned with communicating. That position is to the left of my own; I wanted to stretch the bond between language and communication but not to sever it. Some of my influences at that time and since then were musical, particularly the music of Anton Webern which I heard in some historic concerts conducted by Pierre Boulez in the late fifties, most notably the two cantatas, Webern's closest approach to monumentality. Another was a work by Luciano Berio I heard on the radio, called "Omaggio a Joyce." In this homage, the composer took one of Joyce's poems and subjected it to a number of electronic operations, stretching out syllables, cutting and blurring the originals in a way I admired. These distortions of beautiful but rather simplistic poetry seemed to get at the heart of what I thought poetry was: one part shimmer, three parts shriek. A passage from my long poem of the time, "Europe," which has dismayed critics such as Harold Bloom and delighted the Language Poets, will give some idea of what I was after then.

[Reads part 52 of "Europe"]

I was inspired to write the poem after passing through a Paris Métro station called Europe, on a moving train. Somehow the sight of those ceramic letters set in a tile wall, with hordes of subway passengers passing by, made me realize for the first time that I was—Eureka!—in Europe.

I reserve judgment on these early experiments. In fact, they aren't works of mine I return to very often, or include in poetry readings. I'd just like to say that I didn't "do it to annoy, because I know it teases"; in fact, I never thought they would confront readers. I thought of them as a stage on the way to something else, which I knew nothing of then, when I would be able to reassemble language into something that would satisfy me in the way my early poems had once done but no longer did.

I felt this process beginning in a poem written in late 1961, after seeing an exhibition of Korean landscape scrolls at the Musée Cernuschi in Paris—by this time I had begun writing art criticism for the *International Herald Tribune,* and this was one of my assignments. The title, "Rivers and Mountains," alludes to the generic title for such landscapes; the full and correct title of such landscape scrolls is "Mountains and Rivers without End," which Gary Snyder coincidentally used as a title for one of his books at around the same time. This is my poem "Rivers and Mountains."

[Reads "Rivers and Mountains"]

Delivered at the National Arts Club, New York City (April 28, 1995), at the Poetry Society of America's eighty-fifth annual awards ceremony, with George Plimpton as master of ceremonies. The medal was presented to Ashbery by Kenneth Koch.

Introduction to Robert Mapplethorpe's *Pistils*

Mapplethorpe's flower pictures seem to be in danger of getting lost in the uproar that will probably always surround his name, though in my opinion they are far from being a minor interlude in his career. Together with the late self-portraits, they are one of its major moments. They have always been problematic, however, and not least so to the photographer himself. Again and again, when interviewers brought up the subject, he would insist on his indifference to or even dislike of flowers. "I don't love flowers and I don't like having them," he said in a conversation with the critic Anne Horton.

HORTON: "What don't you like about living with them . . .
the bother of watering them?"
MAPPLETHORPE: "Watering them and dripping on the floor."
HORTON: "And watching them die?"
MAPPLETHORPE: "And watching them die and feeling guilty
about them. I can't have part of my life devoted to flowers. But I can photograph them and get excited about
photographing them . . . I'll sort of force myself to photograph them before they die because I know I can get a
good picture of them."*

His concern for the flowers is almost touching; his dislike is
at least partly rooted in sympathy; he doesn't want the responsibility for their dying. This scarcely jibes with the image of Mapplethorpe as a calculating exploiter of his subjects. It does, however, coincide with his fanatical concern with perfection ("I'm
not after imperfections") and his equally obsessive horror of
decay and death. Not only does he want to be absolved of col-
lusion in the flowers' death but he senses the possibility of this
outcome as a kind of betrayal. From there it is only a step to
wishing to take revenge on the flowers for the transience of
their perfection. What better way to do this than to reveal the
cruelty that lies behind their seductive appearance? "I think the
flowers have a certain edge . . . I don't know if 'nasty' is the right
word—if you look at the picture of the orchid, to me it is a kind
of scorpion—it has a sharp edge to it." Having thus revealed the
nature of their mutual love-hate relationship, he expands on it:
"I get something out of flowers that other people don't get. . . .
I love the pictures of flowers more than I love real flowers."

Mapplethorpe's chosen environment was far from the light
of day, either in his darkened studio or the darkness of the S&M
bars where he hung out almost every night. Can one feel sympathy for an artist who hates not only flowers but sunlight too?
Well, yes. Not everyone appreciates the light of the sun. A sunny
day in winter calls attention to the moribund landscape; on
summer evenings too the excess of light can be unbearable, as
Thomas De Quincey noted in his *Confessions of an English Opium*

Robert Mapplethorpe 1986 (Cologne, West Germany: Kicken-Pauseback
Galerie, 1986). Catalogue with interview by Anne Horton.

Eater: "I find it impossible to banish the thought of death when I am walking alone in the endless days of summer." And there is also something wearying about flowers as art objects. Their extreme perishability makes them *mementi mori* without any intervention on the part of the artist. In seventeenth- and eighteenth-century Holland, painters like Ambrosius Bosschaert and Rachel Ruysch built up towering structures of flowers, often using varieties that would not have been in season at the same time; the monumentality of their volume is everywhere undermined by their fragility. Snails and caterpillars, creatures "of the earth, and intolerably earthy" in Vernon Lee's phrase, are very much at home here, reminding us of the precariousness of life. In the nineteenth century, Henri Fantin-Latour was as obsessive about capturing the precise moment of ripeness of bloom as Mapplethorpe would be in the twentieth; luscious as his paintings are, they radiate anxiety. Odilon Redon's otherworldly bouquets already have one eye on eternity, while the young Piet Mondrian was drawn to flowers that were fast fading or even dead.

So there are precedents for the chilly negativism one senses in Mapplethorpe's flower photographs. But their mood is negative for another reason as well: they are only one aspect, and an undernoticed one, of an oeuvre best known for its lurid depictions of violent sex. Scenes of fist-fucking and urine drinking, idolatrous studies of nude black men with huge penises (Mapplethorpe was looking for perfection here too: "If I photograph a flower or a cock, I'm not doing anything different"), are what has made his name a household word, and, at least in certain households, a synonym for all that is wayward and "degenerate" in contemporary culture. The fate and repercussions of the traveling show of his work, "The Perfect Moment," are well known. Of course, the flower photographs are not what made him simultaneously famous and unacceptable. They are, in the words of one of his dealers, "the tip of the iceberg." But because he is fashionable, because there is tremendous demand for his work and because so much of it cannot be shown in public, these presumably innocent photographs have been summoned to stand in for the others. It is impossible to look at them and ignore their context, and so they have taken on a further ambiguity: they are, in effect, calling attention to the pictures that are hidden from view. Like fig leaves for absent genitalia, they point to the scandal of what is not there.

This is perhaps an unfair burden for them, and one that, before the posthumous hullabaloo, wasn't in the original plan; at most Mapplethorpe was trying to make some money to finance other work that mattered more to him. He tried this in various ways, with fashion photography and celebrity portraits; once he even covered a chic house party in the Bahamas. The latter assignment was not a success, and Mapplethorpe loathed the result, not just because he was forced to forgo the strictly controlled studio conditions but because, as he repeatedly said, he was not a voyeur. This statement can seem strange coming from the photographer of scabrous sexual vignettes like *Jim and Tom, Sausalito*, but in fact it isn't: The silent "trust" that Arthur Danto cites as a vital ingredient of these exchanges between model and photographer is always implied. Even when not entirely immobilized, the figures have an iconic seriousness that is moving, regardless of the supposed squalor of the sex acts being recorded. Ingrid Sischy once tried to interest a publisher of pornography in Mapplethorpe's work only to have him refuse to look at it: "I know those pictures," she reports him as saying. "I've never liked them. They're so personal." Yet most pornography, dehumanizing though it may be, is positively clubby compared to Mapplethorpe's sexual panopticon. Eros has never seemed more generic, more mute.

In the last years of his life, his preoccupation with lighting became an obsession. His friend Lynn Davis recalls him asking for stronger and stronger light, to the point where you felt boxed in by power packs when you sat for a portrait. His sitters had to be elaborately made up and coifed; the concentration of light on their faces blots out wrinkles, producing an eerie marmoreal glow. Indeed, his still lifes now included marble busts whose whiteness is dazzling, and rigid arrangements of fruit and pottery with shadows of venetian blinds striping the wall behind. The artificial atmosphere is often claustrophobic, but there is no denying its provocation, which, subject matter aside, is even more shocking than that of the erotic pictures. Still, there are those who have no problem with Mapplethorpe's sexual imagery who find his work generally cold and empty. Without the context of scandal, does he even exist as an artist? And aren't many of the other works that complete his oeuvre a hairbreadth away from classy commercial photography?

I think that the malign brilliance of his erotic pictures is present throughout, and nowhere more than in the portraits of flowers, impassive but somehow conspiring in their own corruptibility. Their chic glossy-magazine ambience heightens the drama. We've all turned the pages of these magazines, ogled the luxury goods, envied the rich and famous, and then closed them newly conscious of our own mortality. *Vanitas vanitatum.* O rose, thou art sick!

Mapplethorpe approached flowers in the same way as his other subjects: by isolating them. Elaborate bouquets like those favored by the Dutch flower painters don't interest him, though he could produce an atypically sensual work like the photo of a mass of roses, wisteria, carnations and lilies of the valley that seems to float in mid-air. Usually, though, the flowers will be all one kind, as in a vase of tulips, more disheveled and past their prime than he usually allows his subjects to get, here perched perilously on the edge of a table; one tulip at far left is about to swan-dive into the abyss. It is one of Mapplethorpe's most haunting images. Another is a shot of a flat of tulips, a rare example for him of flowers that are still rooted and growing rather than cut, though they too seem *in extremis.* Their season will be short.

The most powerful photos are those in which he focuses on a single flower or just a few, pinning them almost cruelly under the lens. A bunch of carnations jammed into a constricting glass cylinder is one of many that hint at the voluntary constraints of S&M. Baby's breath, used by florists as filler in bouquets, looks almost startled to be the only subject in its frame, and its sparseness suddenly turns monumental. In another, a single rose placed next to its looming shadow evokes the "invisible worm" that had set its sights on Mapplethorpe as well. Even more highly charged are some calla lilies with teasing phallic pistils, perhaps derived from Georgia O'Keeffe, but to which he imparts a dangerous eroticism of his own.

It's when he uses color, which seems like such an unlikely medium for him (and which strangely complements the austere, limpid blacks of the late self-portraits), that Mapplethorpe really triumphs. Perhaps all the darkness and grit of his earlier work were a preparation for these sumptuous yet demonic explosions of light and light-saturated forms. The great white calla lily, whose horizontal lines serve as a foil to its proud gold erection, strikes an uncharacteristic jubilant note. It is an invitation to pleasure that will not be rebuffed. Equally forceful and steeped in sexuality are a study of a poppy, bathed in what looks like a sunset glow, and a much-bigger-than-life erect pink tulip against a brown background, placed at the exact center of the frame, with the stem bisecting its bottom edge. There is a sonnet by Théophile Gautier that boldly begins, "Moi, je suis la tulipe" (I am the tulip) and ends, "Nulle fleur du jardin n' égale ma splendeur, / Mais la nature, hélas! n'a pas versé d'odeur / Dans mon calce fait comme un vase de Chine" (No other flower of the garden equals me in splendor, / But nature, alas!, poured no scent / Into my calyx, shaped like a Chinese vase).

This image of splendor and sterility inextricably fused, of a flower fashioned to appeal to every sense save the one that matters most, is emblematic of these photographs. They are cruel and comforting, calm and disruptive, negative and life-affirming. For all the disillusion it enshrines, his work here paradoxically gives us back joy.

From Robert Mapplethorpe's *Pistils* (1996; New York: Random House, 1998).

Introduction to *Joe Brainard: Retrospective*

Joe Brainard was one of the nicest artists I have ever known. Nice as a person, and nice as an artist.

This could be a problem. Think of all the artists, especially those whose work you admire, who weren't all that nice. Caravaggio. Degas. Gauguin. De Chirico. Picasso. Pollock. Their art

257

isn't exactly nice either, but the issue seldom arises. In Joe's case, it does. He began around the time that Pop Art did. With Lichtenstein or Warhol there is a subtext of provocation, though the Pop Artists generally were too cool, too "down" as we used to say, to let this possibility become anything more than unspoken. In Joe's work, one of his pictures of pansies, for instance, there is confrontation without provocation. A pansy is a loaded subject. So is the effortless, seed-packet look of the painting. But there's no apparent effort on the artist's part to cause stress or wonderment in the viewer. With Joe, our relief and gratitude mingle in the pleasure he offers us. One can sincerely admire the chic and the implicit nastiness of a Warhol soup can without ever wanting to cozy up to it, and perhaps that is as it should be, art being art, a rather distant thing. In the case of Joe one wants to embrace the pansy, so to speak. Make it feel better about being itself, all alone, a silly kind of expression on its face, forced to bear the brunt of its name eternally. Then we suddenly realize that it's "doing" for us, that everything will be okay if we just look at it, accept it and let it be itself. And something deeper and more serious than the result of provocation emerges. Joy. Sobriety. Nutty poetry.

There are however no *histoires à l'eau de rose* here. Nor is Joe's book of "I remembers" for family viewing; some indeed seem to require a new rating for "humane smut," though they are so cleverly interleaved among others like "I remember wondering if I *looked* queer" and "I remember the rather severe angles of 'Oriental' lampshades" that one can't say for sure. One is "taken aback." The writing and the art are relaxed—not raging—in their newness, careful of our feelings, careful not to hurt them by so much as taking them into account. They go about their business of being, which in the end makes us better for having seen and lived with them; and better for not feeling indebted to them, thanks to the artist's having gone to such lengths for us not to feel that.

Joe was a creature of incredible tact and generosity. He often gave his work to his friends, but before you could feel obliged to him he was already there, having anticipated the problem several moments or paragraphs earlier, and remedying it while somehow managing to deflect your attention from it. Into something else: a compassionate atmosphere, where looking at his pictures and recognizing their references and modest autobiographical aspirations would somehow make you a nicer person without your realizing it and having to be grateful. It's for this, I think, that his work is so radical, that we keep returning to it, again and again finding something that is new, bathing in its curative newness.

Joe seems to have taken extraordinary pains for us not to know about his art. Either he would create three thousand tiny works for a show, far too many to take in, or be intentionally less prolific, as he was in the last decade of his life, indulging his two favorite hobbies, smoking and reading novels—mostly Victorian or Barbara Pym's. It's as though in an ultimate gesture of niceness he didn't want us to have the bother of bothering with him. Maybe that's why the work today hits us so hard, sweeping all before it, our hesitations and his, putting us back in the place where we always wanted to be, the delicious chromatic center of the Parcheesi board.

From *Joe Brainard: A Retrospective* (New York: Tibor de Nagy Gallery, 1997), the catalogue for a show that opened on February 6, 1997. Reprinted in *Joe Brainard: A Retrospective* (Berkeley: University of California Art Museum; New York: Granary Books, Inc.; in association with Mandeville Special Collections Library, University of California, San Diego, 2001).

Introduction to
Trevor Winkfield's Pageant

If all art aspires toward the condition of music, as Pater wrote, Trevor Winkfield must be counted among the most successful artists of all time. A picture such as his great, recent *Voyage II* totally fulfills that condition: the accuracy and surprises of great music, even its linear unscrolling, are what confront us. In fact its effect is the same one a musical score offers a person with some ability for reading music—"sight-reading." Each element in the painting has its precise pitch, its duration. It's as though seeing and hearing merged in a single act, and the "meaning" of the picture were lodged at the intersection of two of the senses, where one is pleasurably enmeshed, deliciously hindered. The strange erection on the left—a toy windmill with dysfunctional-looking paddles (isn't it from the coat of arms of some ancient and distinguished purveyor of something-or-other to the Royal Family?), firmly placed on a pedestal fashioned of bricks, tomatoes and other less namable objects, is there to cast the authority of its key-signature over the frieze on the right, whose elements include a harp, a seagull, some nautical-looking pennants, three table utensils tied together with a red bow, and at the far right some wave-like scallops and stylized drops of water that suggest the musical symbol for *da capo al fine*—go back and start all over again, you idiot! (One of the heroes in Winkfield's pantheon is Satie, author of a short piano piece called "Vexations" that is meant to be repeated 840 times.) There are also three identical hands, each one a different hue and each holding what may be an empty ice-cream cone (but the third cone has something attached to it that looks like a drooping slice of flan). There are two sculptural heads, one Greek, the other that of a medieval bigwig, Charlemagne perhaps; both are gazing to the left (westward), where the music is coming from, and each is bathed in a different light, for which no source is apparent. These are the describable things, but there are less identifiable ones on which the same amount of objective care has been lavished: three-dimensional grids; stripes and colored lines; some stylized leaves at the top; and the Greek figure's curious torso, like a child's top. The colors are those of brand-new but antique toys that have been randomly stacked together: intense pastel greens, banana-yellow, vermilion, chartreuse, Tabasco red, Kool-Aid grape: an assembly whose components ought to "scream at" each other, but which are instead intoning something ineffable, some music of the spheres, though the spheres appear to be rolling around on the floor of a nursery rather than in the heavens.

One could go on listing and describing, "to small purpose and with less effect," in the words of Winkfield's friend, the late

James Schuyler. What's clear is that there is no verbal equivalent for taking in the picture, just as there is none for assimilating a piece of music, which is as it should be. The experience in both cases amounts to what? Perhaps the very what in Jasper Johns's title *According to What.* Something is regulating everything and placing its parts in the proper relation to each other, but that thing is unknown: a blank, though a fundamental one. One reflects on how so much modern art is concerned with dropping things out: the momentous vacancies in Cézanne, in Cubist still lifes, in Henry Moore's holes, in Giacometti's erasures. And how an equally important activity has been filling things up again: how the ashen, empty glasses in Picasso's 1910 still lifes are brimming with violent-colored lemonade, Suze and cassis after 1911. Winkfield has somehow managed to combine both of these natural impulses to drain and to replenish, to build and to destroy. And he locates the core of creation precisely there, at the Plimsoll line where the glass is both half empty and half full, where ecstasy means having exactly enough.

From *Trevor Winkfield's Pageant,* text by Jed Perl (West Stockbridge, MA: Hard Press, 1997).

Frederic Church at Olana: An Artist's Fantasy on the Hudson River

"About an hour this side of Albany is the Center of the World— I own it," wrote the painter Frederic Church to his friend the sculptor Erastus Dow Palmer in 1869. The site he referred to was a 250-acre tract of land where Church was soon to begin building Olana, a Moorish-style mansion on a bluff overlooking the Hudson River some two hours by train north of New York City. The design and construction of the estate would be the culminating creative act of Church's career, occupying him from 1860 until 1900, the year of his death. By that time Church, crippled by arthritis, had all but ceased to paint, and his once towering reputation was ebbing. Olana was his final masterpiece.

Owned and operated by the New York State Office of Parks, Recreation and Historic Preservation, Taconic Region, and a New York State Historic Site since 1966, the house and its surroundings are being carefully restored to their appearance circa 1891 to 1900 under the guidance of manager James A. Ryan, whose dedication to this task recalls the devoted hero in such Henry James stories as "The Aspern Papers" and "The Altar of the Dead." (Ryan speaks of "Mr. Church" in a tone that suggests the master has just stepped out of the room for a moment.) Church's original gilt-and-polychrome stenciling is being recreated on the building's many cornices and its columned piazza. Twentieth-century "improvements" to the grounds (such as a formal rose garden with brick paths) have been removed, and hundreds of trees have been planted to replace those that Church's son and daughter-in-law had cut down to open out the view from the house to the lake below or that were destroyed in the 1938 hurricane.

To understand this remarkable residence and the somewhat patriarchal tone in which Church announced his annexation of "the Center of the World," one must look first at the man and his work. Frederick Edwin Church (he would drop the *k* from his first name in his twenties) was born to affluence in Connecticut in 1826; overcoming parental objections, he studied for two years with the English-born painter Thomas Cole, who was famous for dramatic, moralizing landscapes. Cole lived in Catskill, directly across the Hudson from the future site of Olana. Having sketched the view from "his" hill as a youth, Church returned there some fifteen years later after looking in vain elsewhere for a setting for what he would later call his "Feudal Castle . . . under the modest name of a dwelling-house."

By that time Church had achieved a celebrity never accorded an American artist before or since. Thousands queued up outside his New York studio to pay a hefty twenty-five-cent admission fee to view vast panoramic paintings like *Niagara* and *The Heart of the Andes;* the latter was sold for ten thousand dollars in 1859, then the highest price ever paid for a landscape in America. An American critic called *The Heart of the Andes* "the finest painting ever painted in this century, and one of the best ever painted," while in England the *Daily News* announced that "Turner himself, in wildest imagination, never painted a scene of greater magnificence." And, standing before *Niagara,* the renowned French academic painter and teacher Jean-Léon Gérôme grudgingly conceded: "Ça commence là-bas." Even as late as 1871 they stood "six deep" in front of Church's *Jerusalem from the Mount of Olives.*

Those were the years of Manifest Destiny, when the lush, sparsely peopled landscapes of America were taken as a sign of God's special benevolence toward the fledgling nation and a symbol of the spiritual and material blessings about to fall like manna on its people. Then the Civil War intervened; the mood of the country turned bitter, and as early as 1865 artistic backlash set in. Sublimity went rapidly out of style, and Church and his colleagues found themselves derisively dubbed the Hudson River School. (It seems strange today that this term, like Impressionism, was originally meant to be pejorative.) Genre pictures, the Barbizon School and the more plainspoken landscapes of Winslow Homer suited the post-Reconstruction period better than Church's rapt panoramas. He had to wait until late in this century for rehabilitation: *The Icebergs,* discovered by chance at a boys' school in England, set a record for an American painting (just as *The Heart of the Andes* had over a hundred years before) when it was purchased for two and a half million dollars in 1979 and donated to the Dallas Museum of Art; and Church loomed over his contemporaries in the Metropolitan Museum of Art's "American Paradise: The World of the Hudson River School" show in 1987. The 1989–90 Church retrospective at the National Gallery of Art in Washington confirmed his standing as one of the preeminent nineteenth-century American landscape painters.

As his reputation waned, Church devoted his energies increasingly to elaborating his fairy-tale fiefdom. ("I have made about one and three-quarters miles of roads this season, opening entirely new and beautiful views—I can make more and better landscapes in this way than by tampering with canvas and paint in the studios," he wrote to his friend Palmer in 1884, perhaps with a hint of regret.) In 1861 he began living more or less full time at a cottage, later named Cozy Cottage, built from plans by Richard Morris Hunt below the summit where the house now stands. He went on to construct a separate studio and various outbuildings while assembling the parcels of land that today make up the estate. After the hilltop was secured, Church and his wife, Isabel, embarked in 1867 on what was to become an eighteen-month voyage to Europe and the Middle East. By that time the property included a working farm and a "landscape garden" with an artificial lake and thousands of trees planted on what had only recently been raw farmland.

Apparently, Church had hired Hunt to draw up plans for a large house above the Hudson, and the architect had proposed both an Italianate mansion with "Persian" touches and a "French manor." On his return, however, Church commissioned Calvert Vaux (Frederick Law Olmstead's collaborator on Central Park) to come up with something in the "Middle Eastern" style. Ultimately the design was largely Church's (about three hundred of his architectural sketches and numerous letters relating to the construction survive). Vaux's role was that of engineer; his structural and design knowledge allowed Church's ideas to take shape.

In a letter from the Middle East, Church had praised flat-roofed houses surrounding a central court with patterned marble pavements; Olana has these features, which were, of course, adapted to the harsher climate of upstate New York. The east façade, which greets the visitor, is a vast masonry wall pierced at ground level only by an ogival entrance and a narrow window, conferring a sense of mystery and inaccessibility on the oriels and balconies above. The south façade, which looks down the river, is more hospitable. A "piazza" of slim gilt pillars connects the main mass of the house (dominated by a tower with a truncated pyramidal roof and an observation platform whose balustrade has finials in the form of teapots) to a smaller pavilion, built at the edge of the cliff, which contained Church's studio and an observatory above it. The ensemble is breathtaking, and despite the proliferation of architectural elements and polychrome tile decoration, it is not busy but solemn and wildly fanciful, like Church's painting.

Once inside the vestibule, one looks straight down a one-hundred-foot vista to the studio, where a huge plate-glass window trimmed with Islamic fretwork frames the distant trees on the west bank of the Hudson. The first-floor plan is more or less Palladian, with four rooms radiating off a large central hall that Church unabashedly called the Court Hall. Cluttered with comfortable furniture and collections of treasures such as Persian armor; Chinese and Japanese pictures; a Mexican Madonna; mounted birds of paradise, quetzals and iridescent butterflies; and two life-size bronze cranes perched atop turtles, it is the spiritual core of the house. At the bottom of the stairway is a raised platform that was used as a stage for amateur theatricals. Dramatic entrances were possible from left and right and down from the landing; kilims hung from a brass rod could close off the stage. Turning to the right, one can see the distant panorama of the Catskills to the west. Straight ahead the view is to the south, through a room called the Ombra, a kind of shadow-box parlor whose window focuses the seemingly infinite downriver perspective. It is as though a moral and aesthetic lesson (on the order of Hopkins's line "The world is charged with the grandeur of God") was being wordlessly expounded.

Throughout the house, a complicated and subtle scheme of surface patterns and interrelated colors, which Church himself mixed on his palette, draws one forward. The strongest color is a rich, muted purple that appears in the entrance hall and is taken up later in the stencils of the Court Hall and the sitting room. The quiet gray of the walls of the formal reception room is heightened by the silver arabesques ornamenting its doors. (Both the gold and silver of the stenciling are tarnished by time, since Church used powdered bronze and aluminum to obtain them, but when new they glittered enough to cause a reporter to exclaim: "One feels as if transported into the orient when surrounded by so much of Eastern magnificence.") The salmon color in the arches of the Court Hall reappears in the pink-marble fire surround in the sitting room and, above it, in Church's painting of the pink-sandstone temple of El Khasne at Petra— the one important picture of his that he kept at Olana.

Naturally, the house is chiefly oriented toward the west and south to take advantage of the views, but, strangely for an artist, north light seems to have bothered him. Though his studio does have a high north window, the room gazes longingly west-ward. A number of windows, including the north-facing ones of the staircase landing, are fitted with amber-tinted glass against which cutout-paper latticework is silhouetted, as though the house's owner felt the northern light of the Hudson Valley clashed with Moorish sensuousness. In the picture gallery/dining room, vaguely medieval with its gray-green-and-maroon-plastered walls, brass-and-teak fireplace and mixed bag of heavily framed "old master" paintings (acquired by Church in Europe and hung here to create the atmosphere of a room "toned down to 400 years back," in his words), the north-facing windows are too high to afford a view. The room was meant for evening use, when the artist could play lord of the manor at the long and beautifully appointed banquet table. On the second floor (not open to the public), the Moorish motifs extend to the bedroom suites of Mr. and Mrs. Church, though these private rooms were never as elaborately decorated as the reception rooms on the first floor. The most remarkable feature there is the south window of Isabel Church's bedroom—a large, single pane framed in amber glass to give the impression of a changing painting of the view downriver.

For a long time the name Olana was thought to be a translation of sorts of an Arabic word meaning "our place on high"—a definition first quoted in an 1890s *Boston Herald* article and accepted ever since. However, art historian Gerald Carr, author of the 1994 catalogue raisonné of Church's work, found the name in a volume by the Greek geographer Strabo, a Christmas gift from Isabel Church to her husband in 1879 that is still in his library. There the word is cited as the name of a fortified treasure house on a hillside in Artaxata, an ancient Mesopotamian city that was one of the supposed sites of the Garden of Eden. Doubtless this was the meaning Church had in mind: a fortress, to protect his fragile family (two children had died in infancy); a treasure house because it sheltered not just the glittering trophies he brought back from his travels but that family itself—his wife and their four surviving children. According to James Ryan, it was in this sense that the house was, for Church, a work of art in just the way he meant his paintings to be: a noble artifact designed to instill notions of artistic and moral superiority.

To this end Olana still raises its proud, but not haughty, bulk high above the admittedly grander spectacle of the great river that inspired Church and his fellow artists, in the halcyon days when nature could still be read as a message of hope set down in God's cursive, unfaltering hand.

From *Architectural Digest* (June 1997).

Introduction to a Reading by
Charles North

Charles North was born in New York City and continues to live here. It will come as no surprise to most of you that he is Poet in Residence at Pace University. Among other distinctions he has been the recipient of a National Endowment for the Arts Creative Writing Fellowship and awards from the Poets Foundation and the Fund for Poetry. The poet James Schuyler called him "the most stimulating poet of his generation"—no mean feat, considering the horde of stimulating and over-stimulated poets that comprises this generation. William Corbett mentions his generosity of spirit and an intelligence that never outsmarts its subject but is there to serve it and the reader. And Ann Lauterbach, commenting on his recent book of critical essays, *No Other Way,* reminds us how North knows that "clarity begins at home."

I would like to add that he is one of the most *accessible*—dread word—of contemporary poets. I don't mean this in the negative way critics of poetry tend to use the word as a club to beat the poets they don't like; i.e., that modern poetry is out of touch with its audience, and nobody reads poetry anymore because poets for some reason refuse to be accessible. Alas, the world is full of poets who are accessible in that definition and yet nobody reads them either. Could it be because they insist on telling the reader something he or she already knows?

North, however, has attained a plane where accessibility really means what it says: he takes us there, and we are participating with the writing and learning as we read. Take for instance his calm but devastating rewriting of the history of poetry, which begins, "Open poetry died with Whitman. / Closed poetry died with Yeats. / Natural poetry was born and died with Lorca / And Clare, also with France's Jean de Meung." In other words, we have only to settle down, look about us, open a book and start seeing as we never did before. Charles North is the ideal guide for such a journey, as the poems you are about to hear will soon demonstrate.

From a reading given for the annual Dyson College of Arts and Sciences Lecture in the Humanities at Pace University, New York City (April 16, 1998).

Obituary for Pierre Martory

Pierre Martory, a French poet, journalist and fiction writer, died suddenly on October 5 at his home in Paris.

Born on December 1, 1920, in Bayonne to a father who was a career army officer and a Basque mother who died when he was two, Pierre-Jean Martory (he seldom used the middle name, perhaps because a brother, Jean, was born scarcely a year later) spent the first years of his childhood happily pampered by poor but doting aunts and grandparents. All this changed some six years later when his father, a harsh disciplinarian, returned from assignment in North Africa, remarried, and took the two boys back to Morocco with him. Although Pierre loved that country and visited it often in later years, he was now living with a stepmother and soon several half-brothers and -sisters. His father had broken off all contact with the Bayonne relatives and even falsely told him that his grandparents were dead.

He was delighted to find them alive and loving as ever when the family moved back to Bayonne in the late thirties. After taking his baccalaureate there, he entered the School of Political

Science in Paris in the autumn of 1939. He escaped Paris on the last train to leave before the Germans arrived in June 1940, a harrowing journey that included the sight of the station at Tours in flames (it had been bombed by the Italians) as the train passed through. After a journey on foot across the unoccupied zone and a brief stay in prison in Lyons because his papers weren't in order he succeeded in joining the French (soon to be Free French) Army in Morocco and wound up fighting alongside the Allied forces in the Tunisian campaign.

After the war Martory suffered from a deep depression for which he was hospitalized for a while. He drifted through a variety of jobs: teacher at the short-lived Biarritz American University for GIs (housed in what was rumored to be a former brothel with a ceiling decorated by Matisse); airlines clerk; assistant to the anthropologist Marcel Griaule; parliamentary secretary and eventually editor at *Paris-Match,* to which he contributed a weekly page on the arts. Meanwhile he had published a novel—*Phébus ou le beau mariage*—a Mauriac-like tale of an embittered provincial family—with the firm of Denöel in 1953; his editor was the esteemed Robert Kanters. The book was well reviewed and seemed to augur a successful career as a novelist for Pierre. But Kanters turned down Pierre's second novel. He was willing to publish Martory's third novel but proposed changes Martory was unwilling to make.

I first met Pierre in March 1956, having recently arrived in France on a Fulbright scholarship. We became instant friends, and soon began living together, an arrangement that lasted until my reluctant departure from France in 1965. Thereafter we visited each other often in the U.S. and France, and talked twice weekly on the telephone. He led a solitary life, his main friends a young Moroccan family whose children he adored, and Denis Demonpion, a journalist at *Match* who is now editor of *Le Point* and author of a biography of the actress Arletty. Another friend was Francis Wishart, with whom Pierre collaborated on a volume of text and etchings entitled *Père Lachaise*—the cemetery near which he lived and where his ashes are now scattered.

Since Pierre shunned literary politics and people in general (though in social situations his charm could be irresistible—the poet Ann Lauterbach said recently that his charm devolved back to the original meaning of "spell"), I began translating his poems so as to make them known at least in English. This produced a pamphlet, *Every Question but One*, and a more substantial collection, *The Landscape Is behind the Door*, published by Sheep Meadow Press in New York. There were some good reviews, and his poetry soon began to appear in such magazines as *Poetry* (Chicago), *American Poetry Review*, and *The New Yorker*. American colleges and other poetry venues began inviting him to give readings, and he was particularly gratified when a poster at the Institut Français in Boston billed him as a great poet still undiscovered by the French. This situation seemed about to change: in 1997 Sheep Meadow Press published *Veilleur de jours*, a volume of his poems in French, which was to be distributed in France by Alyscamps Press, a publisher of English books in Paris. But for unexplained reasons the distributor dropped the project, and the copies have never been put on sale.

Martory suffered a stroke in New York in 1995, which left him slightly lame; another in the spring of this year was more severe. He fell frequently; on October 4 when we last spoke on the telephone I suggested he get a beeper that would allow him to summon help. He replied, "Je suis un vieux loup sauvage. I don't want help. When I die it'll be an unpleasant affair of ten minutes; puis c'est tout." Scarcely twenty-four hours later he was found dead in his apartment.

It's difficult to describe the flavor of Martory's poetry. To begin with it is located somewhere between Paris and New York. He used to say, "I love France but I hate ze French." Conversely, though he had more American friends than French ones and had probably seen more American films than most other Frenchmen (starting at the age of five with Lon Chaney's *Hunchback of Notre Dame*), he mistrusted America and her political institutions. In my preface to *Every Question but One*, I wrote that his poetry "doesn't seem to derive from any of the modernist (or postmodernist) French schools, though there are echoes of 'fringe' Surrealists like Reverdy and the chameleon-like Raymond Queneau." The austerity of Jouve's poetry and the cloudy fantasy of Supervielle's also come to mind. There is a touch of the gaiety of Charles Trenet and of René Clair's early films; of the blues of his favorite singers Florel and Piaf. Both the humor and the sadness in his poems are always rendered with an unemphatic clarity that is like that of Mozart, his favorite composer. A poem from the early fifties, "Blues," epitomizes the childish expectancy and the jaundiced *spleen de Paris* that mingle in the best work of this extraordinary poet.

Blues

The bed of the railway links me to these days of hell
The bed of the railway just one night can do it all

Love of the others you wear me out with great strokes of a
    stiff brush

In a station of Paris is there a true love that smiles?
In a station of Paris everything begins and everything fails.

Love of the others you suck the young blood of my life

And the words of my big brother I still hear them on my cot
And the words of my big brother can it be he forgot?

Love of the others you are slow to promise a reward

So be it my child some people are never satisfied
So be it my child some win some fall by the wayside

Love of the others you put out my eyes by dint of fevers.

Goodbye is a big handkerchief a big handkerchief of paper
That you throw in the sewer once it's been spoiled with
    tears

Love of the others you leave in my mouth a taste of clay.

An edited version appeared in the *Guardian,* London (November 18, 1998). "Blues, " translated by John Ashbery, is from *The Landscape Is behind the Door* (New York: Sheep Meadow Press, 1994).

Foreword to Mark Ford's *Raymond Roussel and the Republic of Dreams*

It is unlikely that Raymond Roussel ever read John Keats's more-than-accurate prediction: "I think I shall be among the English Poets after my death." Yet in his posthumous book *Comment j'ai écrit certains de mes livres,* published in 1935, two years after his death, he offers a similarly modest and touching estimate of his work: "I may perhaps gain a little posthumous recognition for my books." Both the extravagantly impoverished Keats and the extravagantly wealthy Roussel were destined to die in a foreign land (Italy, in both cases) with a single friend for company and doubtless with little real confidence that their genius would indeed be recognized by posterity.

Keats, however, had a certain measure of fame during his lifetime. Roussel had only notoriety, the result both of the absolute strangeness of his work and the vast fortune he dissipated in trying to draw attention to it. Perhaps he might have been more successful if he had been poorer, but it is more likely that, as with Proust, we should never have heard of him if his means hadn't allowed him the leisure to devote himself entirely to his writing, and, in Roussel's case, to publishing it. Another advantage was that his financial adviser happened to be the father of the future Surrealist writer Michel Leiris, who, beginning in 1935, published a remarkable series of essays on Roussel's work (eventually collected in a volume called *Roussel l'ingénu* in 1987, and reprinted in 1998 in *Roussel & Co.*). Thus his name, at least, was kept alive by the Surrealists and a few others until the 1960s, when a sudden explosion of interest gave birth to what can only be called a "Roussel industry." Though the fame that has resulted would have pleased him far more than the attentions of the Surrealists, whose works baffled him, it seems that misunderstanding of a different, albeit benign, sort has supplanted the scorn with which the world viewed him during his lifetime. From being always *le mal aimé,* he became almost too well loved, not only in the domain of literature but by the mass media as well, though it is chiefly his bizarre biography that interests the latter.

Though Jean Ferry's book-length study, *Une étude sur Raymond Roussel*, appeared in 1953, interest in Roussel had pretty much congealed by 1958, when I decided to do research on him with the aim of producing a doctoral dissertation at New York University. I had already spent three years in France, trying to learn the language chiefly in order to read this writer whose work had fascinated me since 1951, when Kenneth Koch had brought back some of his books after a Fulbright year in France. Even their physical aspect attracted me, published as they had been by the firm of Lemerre, whose heyday in the late nineteenth century had long passed and whose pale-yellow volumes of the likes of Leconte de Lisle and José-Maria de Heredia emitted an appealing air of desuetude. One book in particular, Roussel's *Nouvelles impressions d'Afrique*, a long poem interrupted by sets of multiple parentheses and illustrated with curiously banal drawings like the ones in my high-school French grammar, intrigued me. It seemed impossible that I would ever be able to read it with any understanding, but for a long time it was the thing I most wanted to do. So I learned French with the primary aim of reading Roussel.

Eventually I began my research by writing to Michel Leiris, who kindly invited me to have a drink at his sumptuous digs on the Quai des Grands Augustins. He produced a stack of postcards from Roussel that he had received over the years, starting in childhood, which I began to devour eagerly—too eagerly, as I later realized. Although I am not exceptionally uncouth, I committed the faux pas of copying down some of the postcard messages, without, as I recall, even asking Leiris's permission. I suppose I thought that he, as the principal guardian of the flame, would welcome the interest of a fellow Roussel enthusiast, or *roussellâtre* as they were called even during the master's lifetime. How could I have been so stupid as to forget that tenders of flames rarely feel the need of outside assistance? After a cordial hour, Leiris withdrew the pack of postcards and announced that they were the only Roussel documents in his possession. This proved to be false, and when I ran into him several years later, and after the publication of a volume of Roussel's miscellanea called *Épaves* (Flotsam) that included several other previously unpublished texts from Leiris's collection, he said, "But you know those were the last papers of his that I owned."

Leiris did, however, give me the last address he had for "Madame Dufrène," Roussel's sole companion, who had played the role of his mistress so as to shield his homosexuality from public knowledge. Eventually I was able to find her in 1960 at a public nursing home in Brussels, a far cry from the elegant flat near the Champs-Élysées she had occupied during Roussel's lifetime. During the course of several visits she told me of her platonic relationship with him and gave me a couple of photos—an elegant "official" portrait of the supposed couple and a passport photo of Roussel. (Soon afterward I mentioned her destitution to Leiris, who had her placed in a comfortable private residence where she lived till her death in 1968, aged eighty-eight.)

Meanwhile I had begun to pester everyone I could find who might have had a connection to Roussel, to the point where I became known (in the words of Paule Thévenin, a onetime friend of Antonin Artaud) as "ce fou d'Américain qui s'intéresse à Raymond Roussel"—an indication of the state of Roussel's reputation at that time. Being American was, however, useful in at least one instance, since I was able to establish relations with Roussel's nephew and sole heir, Michel Ney, Duc d'Elchingen, who had hitherto refused to discuss his uncle with anyone, considering him the disgrace of the family. But an inquiry from America was welcomed, since it raised the prospect of possible revenue from Roussel's hitherto unsaleable writings.

In the early 1960s Roussel's stock began to rise. Michel Foucault's first book, a study of Roussel, was published in 1963. Alain Robbe-Grillet and Michel Butor, creators of the *nouveau roman,* acknowledged their debt to Roussel, and essays on him by Leiris, Breton and other Surrealists continued to appear. Michel Ney was now more than willing to talk about his uncle to anyone who would listen. He had remarried in the early 1960s and his new stepson, François Lorin, happened to be a writer who subsequently contributed an essay to a special Roussel number of the review *Bizarre.* Ney had, it seemed, kept nothing in the way of documents or mementos that might be of use to researchers. He did contribute recollections and some family photos to François Caradec's groundbreaking biography of Roussel which appeared in

1972. Meanwhile, Roussel's books were being reprinted by Pauvert, Gallimard and the Livres de Poche series. The Roussel revival was on, but the trail had grown cold. It seemed unlikely that any unpublished writings or further biographical materials would ever come to light. (I had meanwhile abandoned my project of a dissertation and returned to America for personal reasons.)

Then in a *coup de théâtre* worthy of Roussel's play *La poussière de soleils* (which deals, like so many of his works, with a search for hidden treasure), a trunk filled with boxes of manuscripts, letters, photographs and other memorabilia was discovered by accident in a Paris warehouse where it had been deposited shortly after Roussel's death, probably by Ney, and had been gathering dust ever since. The warehouse was itself moving house, and the trunk and its contents might well have been discarded had an alert workman not noticed a sumptuously bound volume of Roussel's great novel *Locus Solus,* in which he had written that it be bequeathed to the Bibliothèque Nationale. The library was notified, and most of the trunk's contents are now in its possession in a specially created Fonds Roussel. (I couldn't help feeling pangs of jealousy—when I was attempting to do research there some thirty years before, the subject index of the card catalogue, consisting of handwritten fiches, had progressed only as far as the letter M and was therefore of limited use to someone investigating a writer whose name began with an R, not to mention the normal bureaucratic roadblocks seemingly set up on purpose to discourage scholars in that once antiquated but now futuristic institution.)

So, valuable new studies of this great and elusive writer are now being made. Publication of the thousands of newly discovered manuscript pages is proceeding, albeit at a snail's pace. Two enormously long previously unknown early works have already appeared with the firm of Fayard/Pauvert. François Caradec, the grand master of *rousselâtres,* has published a new and vastly enlarged version of his earlier biography. And now Mark Ford has written the first major work on Roussel in English (Rayner Heppenstall's brief and cursory study of 1966 doesn't really count). It's to be hoped that out-of-print translations of the works will be reissued and new ones undertaken, so that a new generation of Anglophone readers can discover what the fuss (created by a small but energetic minority of Roussel freaks) is all about.

I have purposely avoided describing the work since Mark Ford has done it so brilliantly. In particular, his intensive analysis of Roussel's famous *procédé*, the gimmick at the core of his writing, sheds light not only on the passages where it was employed (insofar as they are known) but on his writing as a whole, and on its potential for writers to come. (It has already borne fruit in works of writers of the Oulipian group, most notably in major novels by Italo Calvino, Georges Perec and Harry Mathews.) Perhaps it's necessary only to add that readers proceed with caution: Cocteau was correct in noting something "dangerous" in Roussel's writing, a "charm" against which he had to build "defenses." Pierre Loti's writing was like a drug for Roussel, of which, he said, he had to have his daily dose. But Roussel's is far more addicting. Caveat lector.

From Mark Ford's *Raymond Roussel and the Republic of Dreams* (London: Faber and Faber, 2000; Ithaca, NY: Cornell University Press, 2001).

Introduction to an Exhibition
Catalogue: Lynn Davis

When the first traveler-photographers of the nineteenth century began bringing back and displaying their finds in the capitals of Europe and America, audiences must have found these artifacts doubly puzzling. First there were the subjects themselves: the Pyramids, Yosemite, the Taj Mahal, the Dead Sea, as few had ever seen them, in all their awkward, unapologetic grandeur. But perhaps even more surprising was the fact of photography itself. This new, ill-understood medium for capturing the "wonders of the world" was itself one. In a few short decades, of course, every family would have its Kodak, and snapshots of the Sphinx with Aunt Clara in the foreground would be a feature of many a parlor. The novelty of photography quickly became a commonplace.

Lynn Davis's images take us back to the dawn of epic photography, when the shock of seeing remote sites hitherto only imagined was compounded by the astounding technical means that brought them into view, so that the dew or pollen of earliness still stippled their surfaces. She has sought out not only extraordinary constructions—buildings or monuments whose reason for being is often enigmatic—but constructions of nature which can seem even more so. An enormous dune in the "empty quarter" of Saudi Arabia whose grandeur and proportions seem excessive even for the geological forces that created it, or a vast, solitary iceberg whose stature and presence look as purposefully intimidating as an intact temple far from any human settlement—these are phenomena she has not only captured but in a sense helped to create by isolating them for our attention.

Her most recent photographs are mostly of contemporary, manmade objects, but they are no less astonishing than the remote sites she has been drawn to previously. *Abandoned Missile Site, Cavalier County, North Dakota,* has the Ozymandias-like mystery of some of her desert photographs: only gradually does it dawn on us that this is a recently built and abandoned temple in our own "heartland," and that the Pentagon official responsible for its being there might have meant something far different from Shelley's legendary king if he had bothered to leave behind the inscription: "Look on my works, ye Mighty, and despair!"

One might be tempted to intuit a political subtext here, but Davis's work is political only insofar as the act of looking is political. Even *Very Large Array #2, New Mexico* (and I think I'd just as soon not know what a "Very Large Array" is) seems ominous at first (a vast machine in the desert whose use we assume to be military), but immediately after that achingly beautiful—a colossal waterlily (or Venus flytrap?) holding itself tremblingly open to the dark, storm-infused sky that seems about to empty itself into its cup. A sexual image, too, perhaps, yet why try to stick a label on work that is so various and so utterly involving as hers? She has re-created the unconfined forces of nature (including human nature) that are around us, wherever we look, and made us look at them, and at ourselves in relation to them. The final experience of her work is perhaps not a comfortable one, but intoxicates by letting us recognize the real dimensions of the world we live and think in.

From the catalogue for an Edwynn Houk Gallery show, New York City (November 11, 2000–January 13, 2001).

On Jane Freilicher's *View over Mecox* *(Yellow Wall)*

Throughout her long career, Jane Freilicher has always seemed equally fascinated by the medium she happens to be using and the prospect before her, which is frequently the same one: an interior or exterior view in her studios in New York and Water Mill, Long Island. (Not such a limited one in fact, since it can include the Atlantic Ocean and adjacent Mecox Bay, and the landscape of lower Manhattan, including glimpses of the Hudson River and the New Jersey heights beyond it, as well as the mysteriously luminous night sky over the city.) Still, her landscapes, like Courbet's forest scenes, seem less interested in conveying a strong sense of *genius loci* than a general sense of the components of landscape: grass in all its grassiness, trees without the poetry of "Trees" but as objects in the prospect, water that suggests the sweep but not necessarily the skittering surface of, say, Mecox Bay. We have seen such things countless times and don't need to be reminded of how they looked at a specific moment. They are apprehended by Freilicher somewhere between that moment and the generalizations of eternity. Mecox Bay in her painting of it bears a family resemblance to Mecox Bay the place, but the family relationship isn't a very close one—more like that of a first cousin once removed.

This may be due to a democratic urge to avoid the solemnity of "privileged moments" in favor of a feeling for how nature and objects just keep plugging along—it's that, perhaps, that makes them ultimately important to us. And there is as well her constant awareness of the materials she is using—oil (as here), pastel, charcoal, whatever. The pigment that stands in for water is as much an object of delectation as the water itself. It has to be humored, nudged, helped along to awareness of its materiality even if that means forgetting subject matter for a moment. Of course she always returns to the subject—one can even sense her taking a few steps backward toward the end of the painting session, squinting to make sure it all checks out and holding the brush horizontally to see how it compares to the horizontality of the horizon. (If they don't quite match, that's okay too.) The end result, for me, is a continual *joie de vivre* whose source is light breaking out of the canvas, as though it has filled every crevice to overflowing. The painting sings a song of thingness, whether that of the swatch of nature sitting for its portrait or the paint that's helping it to become itself even as it casually poses for its own portrait.

From *Voices in the Gallery: Writers on Art,* edited by Grant Holcomb (Rochester: University of Rochester Press—Boydell and Brewer, 2001).

Introduction to James Schuyler's
Alfred and Guinevere

Although James Schuyler's reputation rests chiefly on his poetry, his first book was the present novel, published in 1958. At that time he was all but unknown as a poet, despite a few poems published in magazines such as *The New Yorker, Partisan Review,* and *Accent.* Reviewers, coming on his name for the first time, didn't know quite what to make of *Alfred and Guinevere.* Nor had the publisher, Harcourt Brace, helped by commissioning quite superfluous line-drawing illustrations, which caused the *New York Times Book Review* to treat it as a children's book. Only Schuyler's friend Kenneth Koch was able to make the connection between the novel and the poetry (and poetic prose) which preceded and followed it. His review in *Poetry* treats it as a further expression of the voice we find in the poems, which is always both nostalgic and ironic, but still tinged with humbleness before nature and the many-colored minutiae of daily life. Schuyler's humorous and playful side would later enliven the novels *A Nest of Ninnies* (on which he and I collaborated) and *What's for Dinner?* His darker nature would surface in the poetry, especially in the magnificent long poems "The Morning of the Poem" and "A Few Days," and also in many shorter lyrics, though even there the somber subtext is often undercut by Schuyler's particular brand of mordant wit, which sustained him throughout periods of mental illness and emotional withdrawal.

James's life seemed destined from the start to be a troubled one. He was born in Chicago, on November 9, 1923. His early childhood was happy, but when he was six his parents separated and three years later his mother married a man whom her son would come to loathe. The father, Marcus Schuyler, had been a journalist for the *Washington Post;* James would later describe him as "an enchantingly wonderful man, a heavy, jolly, well-read man [terms which could be just as well applied to the son during the happier periods of his life]. Unfortunately he was a compulsive gambler, which my mother found hard to take." After Marcus and Daisy Schuyler separated, Daisy's mother, Ella Connor, came to live with her daughter and grandson. She taught James the names of flowers and birds, and delighted in taking him on visits to museums, such as the Freer Gallery, the Corcoran and the Smithsonian. James probably used her as a model for Alfred and Guinevere's Granny Miller, though that character's more irritating characteristics sound more like his descriptions of his mother.

Daisy married Fredric Berton Ridenour, a building contractor, in 1931, and the family moved to the town of East Aurora, New York, near Buffalo. The town had been made famous by the pop philosopher Elbert Hubbard ("A Message to Garcia") and his arts and crafts colony, Roycroft. The couple had a son, Fredric Jr., in 1933. Schuyler's frequent disputes with his stepfather (who disapproved of his stepson's love of reading, and confiscated his library card, though James managed to get it back) contributed to the misery of growing up sensitive (and gay) in a small town. The glamorous autobiography Guinevere fantasizes may well be an echo of James's determination to escape the confines of home, while her sudden (and unexplained) remark to Alfred: "I'm sorry Daddy hit you"—one of the rare allusions to violence in the novel—casts a shadow over the pastel-hued accounts of children's pastimes and conversations. James briefly attended Bethany College in West Virginia (where he got mostly bad grades except for a course in Victorian literature), enlisted in the Navy in the Second World War and got discharged for going AWOL, and made his way to New York, where he found a job doing clerical work at NBC. He was befriended by Chester Kallman and his lover W. H. Auden (he would later type the manuscript of Auden's book *Nones* for him), and for a while lived with them in a building on Lexington Avenue and Twenty-seventh Street. Using a small inheritance, he traveled to Italy and spent about a year and a half there, partly at Auden's home on Ischia. He met a number of Auden's artist and writer friends, including Christopher Isherwood, Stephen Spender, Rosamond Lehmann, William Walton, and John Richardson.

It was a promising milieu for a promising young writer. But after returning to New York he suffered the first of what was to be a series of mental breakdowns, and was hospitalized at the Bloomingdale Sanitarium in White Plains, where he would be confined again some twenty years later. This was, I believe, in 1950. He and I met the following year through John Bernard Myers, an art dealer and a friend of Auden's, who also introduced him to Frank O'Hara and the dance critic Edwin Denby, with whom he had an affair. Denby in turn introduced him to Arthur Gold, of the two-piano team Gold and Fizdale. Much to Denby's chagrin, Schuyler and Gold embarked on a love affair which was to last about five years. (One result of their relationship was Paul Bowles's "Picnic Cantata," set to a text by Schuyler, for which Gold and Fizdale arranged a commission.)

In about 1952 Schuyler moved in with the two pianists, who were sharing a romantic Victorian house overlooking the Hudson in the pleasant village of Snedens Landing, close to New York

but somehow insulated (as it is today) from the surrounding suburban sprawl. It was here that he began writing *Alfred and Guinevere*. Until then he had written only poetry and a few prose tales
such as "The Home Book" and "The Infant Jesus of Prague," in a
vivid but jarring style influenced by Surrealism and perhaps by
some of Auden's early, atypically surreal prose. Partly at Gold's
suggestion, he abandoned this style so as to produce something
with commercial possibilities (the Gold-Fizdale ménage lived elegantly but was chronically short of cash). He now turned again
to the *Kinderscenen* he had evoked bitterly in "The Home Book,"
this time writing about the past with tenderness and humor, influenced by Firbank, Benson's "Lucia" novels, and George Gros-
smith's comic masterpiece, *The Diary of a Nobody*. (Reviewing our
collaborative *Nest of Ninnies* in the *Times Book Review*, Auden
rightly pointed to the latter book as a likely influence, which it
was—except that at the time I hadn't yet read it, but James had.)
The result is a timelessly idyllic comedy of manners, whose English models are inflected by 1930s small-town life in America, as
seen through the gauze filters of the movies and children's literature. (James had a special fondness for the Nancy Drew books,
where character delineation is supplanted by descriptions of the
heroine's clothes and hair styles; he was especially amused by
their endpapers, which showed the tireless girl detective
sleuthing by moonlight with the help of a magnifying glass.)

Nevertheless, in addition to the "Daddy hit you" passage,
there are other disturbing hints that there is more to these children's lives than dress-ups, storytelling, walks in the rain and
cookies after school. In a letter to Dan Wickenden, his editor at
Harcourt Brace, Schuyler gave some clues to his intentions for
the novel: "Now what has happened (in the story) is that two
white middle-class children had their first direct experience of
death: a dead Negro in a park (Rock Creek Park, to be precise)
[the incident is alluded to on pages 6–7 of the novel]. There is
a black thread that goes through the book, but that is a fear (an
animal fear, one might say) of death, and not necessarily xeno-
phobia [by which he apparently meant racism]. 'I like Lily but I
don't love her': Alfred, chapter one. . . . Alfred in the simplest
sense does love Lily. He is also very aware of how the 'grownups'
respond to stimuli. At any rate, because of that, I'm trying to

make the last chapter (it's well under way) a big relief: like a faux [*sic*] d'artifice."

Schuyler was, then, very aware of the tensions, racial and other, that he had planted so far beneath the novel's benign surface. But his letter also leaves much unclear. Was the incident of the dead man in the park something that he, as well as his juvenile characters, had experienced? Rock Creek Park is in Washington; neither place is mentioned in the novel, nor is the name of the city where the Gates family lives, but Schuyler had spent part of his childhood in Washington. The issue of Lily's race also bothered him: elsewhere in the letter he worried that the name Lily might suggest a "colored" maid, and says that he is afraid of offending his black friends; nevertheless he keeps the name and avoids mention of her race. Lily at first seems the affectionate, cookie-baking black caregiver of white mythology, though toward the end she is said to be complaining to Mrs. Gates about not getting paid (one of several hints that the family is struggling financially). In the final chapter, the "dead colored man" (one is at first inclined to read it as "dead-colored man") is discussed in greater and more disturbing detail. The children are on board a ship, talking to a Mrs. Perlmaster:

> "Most likely," Mrs. Perlmaster said, "he was dead drunk."
> "He was stone cold as a fish."
> "Don't pretend you touched him," Guinevere said.
> "That's gilding the lily. He was dead, though, you could tell from looking at him and the way the men acted. I used to dream about him almost every night, isn't that funny? The first time was the night Alfred had his attack . . . "
> "I got appendicitis the same day I saw him. It will probably always be the day the most things happened to me on."

This, in the chapter Schuyler meant as "a big relief," is as close to a catharsis as anything in the fragile weft of the novel.

It should be noted that Lily and the other "grownups" are barely characters, barely anything but names. Nor is the rudimentary (but ambiguous) plot much more than an armature to support Guinevere's diary entries and the children's conversations, some of them very funny. At the beginning, eight-year-old (more or less) Alfred is recovering from appendicitis in a hospital; he is visited by his slightly older sister Guinevere and their Granny, who tells them they will be coming to live with her and their Uncle Saul in the town of Fairview. Their father has gone to New York to be interviewed for a job in Europe, followed by their mother who will apparently not be accompanying him further. The children's stay is to be a long one, since the family home has been sublet. At Fairview Guinevere is befriended, somewhat, by "stuck-up" Betty and the even more obnoxious Lois, and Alfred makes friends with young Stanley. After a time their mother joins them, the "absent father" is still absent and the parents might be contemplating divorce—at least, that is the impression one gets from Guinevere's admittedly one-sided diary. Money problems are hinted at. Guinevere precipitates a crisis by confiding her suspicions in Betty, who publicly calls her "daughter of divorce," after which Guinevere punishes her by causing her to slip on the ice (though that is Guinevere's laundered version of events). The gossip gets circulated by grownups and Mother stops speaking to Guinevere. At the end the children, Mother and (for some reason) taciturn Uncle Saul are on a liner bound for France, the father having relocated to Paris. We take our leave of them in mid-ocean, and Alfred's last snippet of bedtime repartee with Guinevere is the familiar childhood conjuration (a sort of verbal missile shield): "I'm rubber and you're glue so anything you say to me will bounce off of me and stick to you. Good night"—which somehow brings the family's saga full circle.

Schuyler's later fictions—the two novels mentioned previously and the short story "Current Events"—a wonderful parody of high-school journalism which chronicles a class outing to the state capitol—are more substantially furnished with novelistic particulars than "Alfred and Guinevere." By comparison, the latter seems more like a deftly dashed-off sketch from the hand of a master. In each of them, however, Schuyler is mainly concerned with language used as a precision tool to further the ends of poetry. As Kenneth Koch wrote in his review of the novel for *Poetry:* "It is NOT, not at all, 'poetic prose'—any more than is Jane Austen's. It is, rather, prose as poetry really should be: among other things fresh, surprising, artful, and clear; and with a great deal of its joy and shock arising from language."

Schuyler's art is a kind of localized, domestic magic, and all the more powerful for being so. It is good to have this book, a talisman for many who know it, available once again.

From James Schuyler's *Alfred and Guinevere* (New York: New York Review of Books, 2001).

Introduction to a Reading by Tony Towle

Thinking about how I would introduce Tony Towle, I remembered that we first met at a party given by Frank O'Hara. As soon as I remembered this, a book arrived in the mail: Tony's new memoir of the years 1960–63. There I found the date it happened: August 21, 1963. I had just arrived for a visit in New York after spending five years in France without returning. When I left, in 1958, I left behind a group of friends who were poets: Frank, Kenneth Koch, James Schuyler, Barbara Guest. When I returned, I found that we were now kind of famous, a "school" in fact, soon to be called, though not by us, the New York School of Poets. I hadn't really been aware that this was happening. I also found that we were no longer young poets, but had grown up to be "younger" poets. There were new young poets, who gravitated around Frank's magnetic self. At the welcome-home party he gave for me, a number of them were guests: Ted Berrigan, the dapper Jim Brodey, Ron Padgett, Joe Brainard, and one Tony Towle. It was pleasantly surprising to find that these young writers seemed to have taken the ball we had tentatively played with and were running with it.

One of those who ran the farthest and is still doing so is Tony. Over the years, his poetry has become more and more luscious and complex, while still retaining a vernal freshness. What I like about it is how he will start with a simple statement or proposition, weigh it, turn it this way and that, and then suddenly we are in a new parallel space which completes the one we were sitting in when we began reading the poem. The world itself has just this way of blossoming into unexpected exfoliations, sad or funny, always exciting just because they are a change. Here is an example from a brief poem of his called "Long Island Pastoral" which Tony wrote for Tatyana and Maurice Grosman, his longtime employers at Universal Limited Art Editions (he always enjoyed the firm's oxymoronic name). The first of the poem's nine lines is: "Again and again there is something to see," almost a Wallace Stevens gambit, which is furthered by the next-to-last line, "the world as we think we know it," and deliciously subverted and expanded by the last line, "images active in the constant sea." Of course, the world as we think we know it keeps going on and on, which is basically all it knows how to do. But next to it, or nearby, or maybe far away, is the sea, continuous and full of active images that are the substance of our world, even though we don't see them and may not even be aware of them.

That seems to be how his poetry works: first by demonstrating how things happen, then by smashing or changing this demonstration so that it no longer quite fits the model we began with. The elegant simplicity of the universe is derailed by the refractory kernel of our living in it, so we now see our lives in 3-D and hear them in stereo. That's what you'll be hearing as Tony Towle reads his poems.

From a reading given at the Library of Congress, Washington, D.C. (November 8, 2001).

Larry Rivers Was Dying. He Asked to See Friends.

On August 7, I found myself in an unusual situation—headed for the Hamptons with my friend the playwright and librettist Arnold Weinstein, in a chauffeur-driven town car. Normally I go there by jitney exactly once a year, to visit my friends Joe Hazan and his wife, the painter Jane Freilicher, at which point they throw their annual party. Since my birthday and Labor Day aren't that far apart, it's never entirely clear whether it's a birthday party or a Labor Day party, which makes it easier on those who don't wish to bring a present.

But there would be no party this summer, a summer of sorrow. Less than a month earlier I had made the same trip out to attend a small memorial service for the poet Kenneth Koch, arranged by his wife, Karen, in the garden of their house in Bridgehampton. Kenneth was suddenly given a diagnosis of leukemia in July of last year. Just as it became apparent that his time was finally running out, we heard that Larry Rivers, whose retrospective had recently opened at the Corcoran Gallery of Art in Washington, D.C., was being treated for liver cancer at a hospital in New York.

Nobody knew what his condition was and no visitors were allowed, thanks to controls quickly put in place by Larry's assistant, John Duyck, who was now managing Larry's departure (at seventy-eight) as capably as he had managed most aspects of his life for twenty-three years. It was John who had broken the news the night before our trip: Larry was back from the hospital but didn't have long to live. He wanted to see friends. John would send a car the next day to pick up Arnold and me for what would surely be our last visit to our great, old, rambunctious friend and occasional adversary.

On the way out, we talked about what we might expect to find. Surely Larry wouldn't have lost his capacity for aggravation, the one constant in his volatile personality. Arnold was bringing Larry a gift, a CD by the jazz saxophonist Ben Webster.

Jazz was Larry's other career; he had begun playing sax with a small outfit in 1945. After a gig in Stockbridge, Massachusetts, a fellow musician announced that the evening's music had been provided by Larry Rivers and his Mudcats. Until then, his name had been Irving Grossberg, though it began as Yitzroch Loiza Grossberg. Briefly there was a third pseudonym which Larry gets wrong in his memoir, *What Did I Do?*, along with about 60 percent of the teeming facts in that fascinating, salacious and barely readable book. It was Jack Slocum—not Jack Harris, as he reports—a name he adopted for a job drawing customers' portraits to demonstrate a new kind of pen in Hearn's Department

Store—not Bloomingdale's—at Christmas, 1953. He did one of me for free—two dollars was a large sum in those days—and, alas, I no longer have it.

When Arnold and I arrived at Larry's modest house, long considered an eyesore by Southampton neighbors, he greeted us faintly but cheerfully, and with some surprise; no one had told him a parade of friends would begin dropping by. Arnold slipped on the CD and we heard "Tenderly," played in a straightforward, unjazzlike manner. Immediately Larry was alert and kvetching. "He's not playing the tune! That's *not* the tune!"

Knowing next to nothing about jazz, I tried to argue with him: "But isn't that the way jazz is supposed to be?"

"No, it's not the tune! That guy's not playing jazz!"

Arnold and I had trouble suppressing giggles: our contentious pal, master of the unforeseen objection, had outflanked us once again.

After decades of being considered one of America's top avant-garde painters, beginning in the mid-fifties when the Museum of Modern Art bought his outsize *George Washington Crossing the Delaware* and then set the cat among the pigeons by hanging it alongside the cerebral abstractions of Mark Rothko, Barnett Newman and Philip Guston (Were they trying to send a message? Was abstraction *over*? Wasn't this kitsch?), Larry's critical reputation began a slow decline around 1980. Or, more accurately, critics got bored and moved on to the next big thing. Larry seemed not to notice, or at any rate not to mind. He continued to show at the Marlborough Gallery (an exhibition is scheduled there for next winter), but as a free agent, meaning he could sell his work elsewhere if he wished, and accept the lucrative portrait commissions that often came his way.

Occasionally he would gripe that he had painted flags before Jasper had, or soup cans before Andy, but mostly he ignored the art world and concentrated on making work: big sprawling accumulations like *The History of the Russian Revolution, From Marx to Mayakovsky* (which is at the Corcoran through tomorrow), or a series about Primo Levi, or the series on African animals ("I grew up in the Bronx Zoo," he used to say, and in fact he was born across the street from it), or another series based on Japanese ukiyo-e prints.

Much as he enjoyed a scuffle (like the fist fights with the critic Clement Greenberg, which were almost de rigueur for New York artists in the fifties), he was far more preoccupied with patient investigating and inventing. He could do brilliant pastiches of classic styles of the past: Ingres and Rembrandt as well as the "Dutch Masters" cigar labels derived from Rembrandt, which could morph into the forbidding jowls of Daniel Webster, another cigar-box icon.

His 1968 Velázquez riff, *Silver Infanta,* is to my mind more beautiful than any of Picasso's forays into the same territory. One of my favorites of his "concentrations" is the "Social Patterns" series, based on a cousin's wedding photographs from the thirties, complete with warning that all proofs must be returned, at which time "blemishes, wrinkles, etc. will be removed." Needless to say, Larry ignored the warning and added a lot of "blemishes" of his own. The slick results, suggestive of a still from an Astaire-Rogers film like *Roberta,* are as buoyant and teeming with technical tricks and subtle stylistic juxtapositions as anything he ever did.

Perhaps he was meditating a return to this series, sans the bravura, in his last large painting, which I happened to glimpse in his studio the day I visited him. Apparently done from a photograph, it's a black-and-white oil and charcoal sketch of his family: his wife, Clarice; their daughters, Emma and Gwynne; and Emma's two children, sitting and standing on Clarice's porch and smiling the way people on porches smile for the camera. Clear and candid, it's one of his most beautiful works.

Naturally, in churning out everything from historical *machines* (as the French call labored nineteenth-century storytelling paintings), to portraits of his kids and of wealthy clients, to literally just about anything (another recent group I saw in the studio was a flock of plaster chickens painted crazy colors), he was bound to produce a lot of clunkers along the way, beginning with the early inept-though-touching Bonnard knockoffs that Greenberg had once said were better than Pierre Bonnard, before recanting and saying they "stank." But the sheer volume of masterful work in many mediums (including storm windows, on one of which he once painted a portrait of Jim Dine) is staggering. Critics are going to have a field day tracking down, sorting

out, categorizing and labeling (good luck!) this glittering bo-
nanza of stuff, much of it unseen by anybody. I have a feeling
the process may have just begun.

From the *New York Times* (August 25, 2002).

New York? Mais Oui!:
Rudy Burckhardt

At first glance Rudy Burckhardt's photographs of New York in
the thirties and forties resemble those of other contemporary
documentarians: Dorothea Lange, Russell Lee, John Vachon—
even the eccentric Weegee. But Rudy's have less social bite
(though that is certainly an element), less wistful poetry
(though that is there too), and more sly comedy. The latter is
present not only in his candid shots of distracted passersby (a
tubby guy in T-shirt and suspenders walking past a storefront an-
nouncing that it "will reopen soon, under same manage-
ment"—is that good?), but also in the crazy geometry of New
York. The bland checkerboard tiles in that picture form a witty
counterpoint to the man's rotund silhouette. Elsewhere, a pattern of opaque glass tiles in a sidewalk rhymes melodiously with
the pattern of circles in a woman's skirt. And sometimes the narrative is purely abstract, like the black-and-white tiled counter of
an on-street soft-drink stand surmounted by two erect and very
businesslike soda faucets.

Rudy was amused and in love with the haphazard look of
things in America, by the ways we have of inventing how to look
and walk and talk, by the fanciful nomenclature that comes nat-
urally to us. He used to live near a Chelsea firm called the Atlas
Protexit Company, which plays an important role in his film
Mounting Tension, where a girl mistakenly knocks on Larry
Rivers's door and asks, "Is this the Atlas Protexit Company?"
These names pop up throughout his photographs of New York,

where signs proclaim the virtues of Fixt Waffles, Jeris Hair Tonic, Mais Oui toiletries and Blood and Sand Worms (for sale as bait). In one subway scene, an old man seated beneath an ad for Kellogg's All-Bran glares ominously at another man who doesn't see him. There may be a story here, but it's all the better for being barely hinted at.

It's unlikely that many of the harried and abstracted New Yorkers traipsing through these pictures found much that was amusing in their surroundings. For that they would have had to wait for Rudy's version: splendidly wry and witty, but never patronizing, and in fact deeply empathetic and humane. Few other photographers have seen as deeply into the way streets and people look, and been able to report back that the news is good: we're all in this thing together, and that is just as it should be.

From *Rudy Burckhardt: New York Photographs,* the catalogue for a Tibor de Nagy Gallery show, New York City (May 1–June 6, 2003).

Foreword to Mark Ford's *Soft Sift*

Ever since I first happened on Mark Ford's poetry, some fifteen years ago, it has struck me that it is a kind of poetry unlike any other being written in English. This may be in part because of his having been brought up in various parts of the world. Born in Nairobi in 1962, Ford also spent time in Nigeria, Sri Lanka, Hong Kong, Bahrain, and the United States, where his father was posted for ten years. He spent two years in Japan as a visiting professor at the University of Kyoto. One might have expected to see repercussions of the latter sojourn in his poetry, but he has said that during that time he produced only ten lines—the beginning of "Looping the Loop," the first poem in *Soft Sift,* though he feels that "my experiences of Japanese landscapes and cities, culture and poetry, sift softly through the entire collection." By way of explanation he cites a famous haiku of Buson: "A tethered horse / snow / in both stirrups." Such are the devious ways of influence, and it would be wrong to measure Japan's importance in his work by the quantity of lines produced there.

Not that it sounds particularly Japanese. But then, how *does* it sound? To the English, I imagine it sounds American, perhaps because of the occasional dash of U.S. local color (mentions of the Pulaski Skyway and Grandma sitting on the front porch with her hounddog, though she appears in the lines written in Japan!), or an occasional New York School riff ("A Swimming-Pool Full of Peanuts" is the title of the longest poem in his first book, *Landlocked*). Maybe it's the continual determination to experiment with words, which is certainly not a trait of most contemporary British poetry. But Ford's tense, deliberate experimentation isn't American either: its seriousness, though little else about it, connects it to Larkin and his disciples, rather than to the anxious glitter of early W. H. Auden and prewar British poetry, when camp and politics coexisted somewhat uneasily. Neither element, as far as I can tell, plays much of a role in Ford's work.

One important influence is certainly that of the French novelist and poet Raymond Roussel (1877–1933), on whom Ford has written the definitive study in English (*Raymond Roussel and the Republic of Dreams*), and whose works are the product of experiments of an almost forbidding intensity. (Roussel was a wealthy recluse whose means allowed him to devote almost his entire life to his writing. Though he attracted the attention of the Dadaists and the Surrealists, the attraction wasn't mutual, and their nihilistic playfulness has no parallel in his work.) Ford has written: "I think of the extreme formal rigor—or rather, varieties of rigor—of the poems in *Soft Sift* as analogous to Roussel's compositional methods. It came to seem to me as if words, experiences, could only ever hope to enter the looking glass realm of art by first passing through some narrow, predetermined aperture like that of Roussel's *procédé* [a stratagem, too complicated to summarize here, that Roussel devised by replacing words with their homophonemes]—or that of the rondeau, the haiku, the sonnet, the couplet, the eight line stanza, or whatever. Emily Dickinson makes a related point in the lines used as an epigraph to Part II of this book: 'And through a Riddle, at the last— / Sagacity, must go.'"

Thus the path to the "looking glass realm of art"—and how courageously right he is to locate the realm of art there, despite those who would insist that bloody chunks of reality should be transferred directly to the page, like meat to the butcher's waxed paper—is a *porte étroite,* a narrow way through which life is transformed into poetry by a process something like dying. Alice's looking glass is reached via Emily's riddle. And only then can we take the measure of life, after it has been transformed into its opposite, its reflection—more real, it turns out, than the expectant viewer posted in front of the mirror. The riddle is not a game, but a dead-serious operation which is sagacity's only chance of being reborn—as enlightenment—in the poem. The paths to this outcome can seem as devious, or irrelevant, as a translation of a fragment of the remote Apuleius or the fragile Charles d'Orléans. It takes a poet to uncover these unlikely trails, and we recognize him by the results of his search, the "beast in view." Ford's poetry is the real right thing; it matters little how it came to be that way.

When I said that Roussel's writing is devoid of playfulness, I didn't mean that it lacks humor. Humor is a central element in his work and also in Ford's, but it is of a peculiar kind, the by-product of an extreme seriousness that's not without overtones of lugubriousness. Roussel wrote that he sometimes spent an entire day trying to compose a single sentence. In practice this could mean trying to get rid of a single superfluous word: succinctness was perhaps his chief aesthetic concern, but it was a highly verbose concentrate that resulted, leaving one to guess at all that had been left out so as to arrive at writing that has an incredible specific gravity. The monumentality of what has been left out is the key to the humor. In his novel *Impressions d'Afrique,* Roussel describes a prisoner whose punishment is to weave exquisite mosquito-traps out of gossamer-fine filaments of fruit while reciting an enormously long mantra, which is not unlike the tasks Roussel imposed on himself: ridiculously complicated but often culminating in a thing of bizarre beauty, and, in this case, usefulness, that couldn't have been achieved by simpler means. And of course there is something funny about such a contraption. Ford's methods are simpler but no less awe-inspiring, and they somehow leave one feeling good, which is after all what poetry should do. His grotesque self-portrait as a "green amphibian" slithering along the floor of a department store and out the door (in *Landlocked*'s "Outing") has morphed into darker and more realist grotesques in *Soft Sift*, like "the errant protagonist" in "Brinkmanship." But diagnosing and describing a hitherto unknown form of pain can produce invigorating aftershocks. He is locating and enlarging on new kinds of living that we recognize, in the looking glass world, as what we have been doing all along without realizing it. And he does so with superb grace, generosity and wit.

From Mark Ford's *Soft Sift* (New York: Harcourt, 2003).

Preface to Paul Killebrew's *Forget Rita*

Among a number of unusually promising poetry manuscripts forwarded to me by the Poetry Society of America, Paul Killebrew's *Forget Rita* stood out for several reasons. First for its length—one isn't accustomed to twenty-three-page poems by young, relatively unknown poets. Second for its title—who the heck is Rita, anyway? We never find out, and though we are told to forget her, we couldn't remember her if we tried. Then for the poem's aggressive rhythms—short but dense lines that float like a flag lifted by a breeze and then snap taut, all nerves and focused attention. At that point, still unaware of much else, I found myself mesmerized.

Killebrew buttonholes us like the Ancient Mariner, urging our complicity in his dark tale of anxiety and/or intimacy. We seldom learn exactly what happens, but we get a strong sense of how it happens—the telling of the story is the story. His technique is cinematic, though the cinema is hardly Miramax but more like the epic chronicles of crushing ordinariness thrust on us by Chantal Akerman or Bela Tarr. Killebrew's camera is hand-held and has a zoom lens that keeps slipping in and out of focus, homing in on the parking lot instead of the expected used-car salesman, like a first-time auteur's inept home movie. *America's Funniest Home Videos* comes to mind, except that here the humor can abruptly turn savage, and the viewer feel that he has become the film's subject.

The poet's slow-swaying lines mimic the movements of a wrestler in the ring as he paces back and forth, trying to fake his opponent by ignoring him before dashing in for the kill. The décor—carpools, swimming pools, offices, junkyards, "shattered shop windows," "buckling sidewalks"—is middle American, blighted but still functioning. (Dubuque, Iowa, is one of two place-names mentioned in the poem, reminding us that *The New Yorker* was founded to defeat the expectations of "the old lady from Dubuque.") "Pity the statuary completing its daily circle at noon, / because midday is sad. Lunch is a goddamn tragedy." A dog keeps us company for a while; then we are voyeurs in a situation between two lovers, one of whom may well be Rita. A passerby complains that the penny ought to be discontinued. Eight-year-old Sammy is anxious on a fishing trip with his father, Phil. "Sisters punch each other the whole ride to Memphis." "Passionate RVs [are] turning into the quiet state park." "It's raining like the weatherman said it would."

Then suddenly the poet is in your face, telling you why you are listening to him, which you probably knew already and dreaded to hear. "What have we done that our great unity is grief?" he asks. As I was reading this, troop ships were moving into the Persian Gulf and our Secretary of State was saying on TV: "Once they're there, they pretty much have to do something," or words to that effect.

I don't understand all of Killebrew's decisions, such as why he chooses to reiterate the phrase "in the end" six times near the beginning of the poem, or why in another place he uses contractions, like "fin'ly" and "fev'rish." At times the mood is almost too bleak. Granted that the air of his post-industrial wasteland is stifling, isn't he skirting the forbidden zone known in France as *la délectation morose?* Still, the dazzling authority of 95 percent of this long, strange trip is such that I'm willing to suspend any lingering shades of disbelief. He plunges us into a world we inhabit but seldom notice, forcing its horror on us but also reminding us why we go on coping with it, why we're in for the long haul, wherever the carpool takes us. "You are rich in treasures commonly discarded," he proudly informs his readers, "but nonetheless, you are rich."

From Paul Killebrew's *Forget Rita* (New York: Poetry Society of America, 2003).

On the Poetry of Joan Murray

One of the poets of the forties whom I most enjoy rereading is Joan Murray, author of the 1947 volume *Poems* in the Yale Series of Younger Poets. (She is not to be confused with the contemporary poet Joan Murray, author of *Queen of the Mist, Looking for the Parade,* and *The Same Water.*) Very little is known of her life, and what little biographical information I have comes from George Bradley, who did research on her when compiling the *Yale Younger Poets Anthology* (Yale University Press, 1988). I haven't had a chance to consult her archives, which are at the Smith College Library and are said to be rather sparse.

Murray was born February 12, 1917, in London, apparently of Canadian parents who had met in Toronto. Her father, Stanley, was a painter. Her mother, Margaret or Peggy, had aspirations to become an actress and advertised herself as a *diseuse* or monologist, a genre whose most famous exponent was the American Ruth Draper. The couple soon separated and by 1927 Peggy and young Joan were back in North America, living in Chatham, Ontario, and Detroit (where Peggy had a sister), and eventually in New York. Joan's health was always frail; she had rheumatic fever in 1930 and thereafter, and eventually died of a heart valve infection on January 4, 1942, a month before her twenty-fifth birthday, in Saranac Lake, New York.

In New York Joan studied dance and acting, the latter at the School of Dramatic Arts under the famous Russian actress Maria Ouspenskaya. In the fall of 1940 she studied poetry with W. H. Auden at the New School. They became friends and Auden chose her posthumous volume as the first during his tenure as judge of the Yale Younger Poets series, which lasted from 1947 to 1959. (Her finest poetry was all written in the scant year and a half between meeting Auden and her tragic early death; Bradley says "the great outpouring of high-quality work all happened within a year.") The book was edited by a little-known poet named Grant Code, a friend of Peggy's who hadn't known Joan. He admitted that he did so with a rather free hand, but we have only his versions of most of the poems; a box containing the original manuscripts was lost by moving men when the archives were shipped to Smith College some time in the 1960s.

Although it seems unlikely that Code could have improved on the originals, we are lucky to have his versions; my impression is that Murray's poetry was powerful enough to stand up to the ministrations of a well-meaning but somewhat heavy-handed editor. The volume seems not to have attracted much attention when it was published. Bradley, who calls it "one of the high points in the series," says that reviewers were "puzzled." William Meredith, however, gave it a mostly laudatory review in *Poetry* (September 1947), saying that the book "introduces a powerful and distinctive voice. The distinction is not achieved without sacrifices, often of clarity, sometimes of music, but all the cost is justified by the fresh excellence of the best of Joan Murray's poems. These make strong reading."

Grant Code said that she left most of her poems untitled, and that he therefore chose the first line of a poem as its title in many instances, using her title if there was one, and occasionally supplying one of his own. Using the first line turns out to have been a good idea; just reading the table of contents gives one an idea of the strength and sharpness of her work. Here are a few titles: "If Here in the City," "There Are Shapes Out of the North," "The Young Host of Rockledge," "As the Summer Sun Comes Down into the Autumn Trees," "You Spoke of Windmills," "Not That I Had Ever Laughed Too Much," "Talk of People in Warning," "Here Where I Tamper with the Inverted Walls of Tomorrow," "I Feel Only the Desolation of Wide Water," and "Even the Gulls of the Cool Atlantic."

These I think demonstrate her power of abruptly inducting the reader into the poem *in medias res*. In fact the second, third, and succeeding lines often veer in quite other directions. In "Here Where I Tamper . . ." we scarcely get a chance to wonder about the nature of "the inverted walls of tomorrow" or what "tampering" with them could involve; the poem is already off and running. The second stanza is typical of her whirlwind trajectories.

> Leave the head to its particular swimming
> The hand as fist where it belongs, the finger to its
> skimming.
> Know the new, and meet again the adult,
> Walk the path with men and women, and consult
> The attitudes of little children,
> Treat with gravity the statements of the parrot and the hen,
> Run with your hands in pockets, whistling, and listen to
> sharp wisdom
> From your own spontaneous play, even from
> The clip of your heels under night lamps and on in the
> dark,
> While hieroglyph trees are marked thin and bare about the
> winter park.

Here we have her fondness for unexpected rhymes (children / hen; wisdom / from), perhaps as a result of Auden's influence, and for lines of unequal length, suggestive of waves washing up on a beach, with every so often an unusually long one, like the wave that surprises you when you're walking by the ocean, making you run to escape it. (The sea is often a backdrop for her poems, though I am not aware if she ever lived near a seacoast.) What is most startling here and elsewhere in her work are the abrupt transitions and changes of scene: the head and its particular swimming, the finger skimming, the attitudes of little children, the statements of parrot and hen, running with hands in pockets, the clip of heels under night lamps in the winter park. How did we get from there to here, and what have we been told? As so often, this remains partly or even largely mysterious. What we are left with is the sense of an act accomplished, an act of telling, and a feeling that we must take this communication away to study it; something important is hidden there. Repeated readings may not reveal it, but the mere act of reading Murray's poetry always seems to be pushing one closer to the brink of a momentous discovery.

Men and Women Have Meaning Only as Man and Woman

Men and Women have meaning only as man and woman.
The moon is itself and it is lost among stars.
The days are individual, and in the passage
The nights are each sleep, but the dreams vary.
A repeated action is upon its own feet.
We who have spoken there speak here.
A world turns and walks away.
The timing of independent objects
Permits them to live and move and admit their space
And entity and various attitudes of life.
All things are cool in themselves and complete.*

---

*From *Poems* by Joan Murray (New Haven: Yale University Press, 1947).

From the *Poetry Project Newsletter* (October–November 2003).

On Val Lewton's *The Seventh Victim*

Like Paris, New York is always ready for its close-up. Somehow the city never fails to look good on the screen, where it quickens excitement the way the place itself does. This is sometimes true even when the film is obviously shot in a studio. The "Riverside Drive" backdrop in an early scene of everybody's favorite cheapo film noir, *Detour,* adds a note of romance, though it is obviously a photograph and a crude one at that. And at least two of Val Lewton's low-budget programmers for RKO, *Cat People* and *The Seventh Victim,* convey a haunting New York ambience, though they were shot thousands of miles away.

Lewton's films, in a genre awkwardly labeled "psychological horror," are cult favorites today, but in their time (the early

1940s) they were considered B-movies. Though Lewton was billed as a producer, it was he who imposed a distinctive style on his films. Besides the two mentioned above, *I Walked with a Zombie* and *The Body Snatcher* have become classics of the genre. My favorite, however, is *The Seventh Victim.*

I first heard of it when a fellow Harvard student, Edward Gorey, recounted its plot in his unforgettable delivery, constantly interrupted by strangulated giggles and gasps, a few years after its 1943 release. In those pre-TV and -VCR days, if you missed seeing a B-movie when it first came out, you had pretty much lost your chance of ever seeing it. Television, of course, would soon arrive and begin recycling Hollywood's archives, so that children born after the forties grew up with a cinema literacy that those born in the twenties like me missed out on. It wasn't till the mid-eighties and my first VCR that I was able to buy a commercial VHS cassette of *The Seventh Victim* and find out what Ted Gorey had been gasping about all those years before.

Directed by neophyte Mark Robson (who would go on to commercial fame with the likes of *Peyton Place, Valley of the Dolls* and *Von Ryan's Express*), it tells the eerie saga of young Mary Gibson (the late Kim Hunter in her first role) as she leaves her boarding school to go to New York in search of her older sister, Jacqueline (the obscure Jean Brooks, sporting a dazed expression and Morticia Addams hairdo). After the obligatory, always electrifying logo of the RKO radio tower (accompanied by the opening notes of Beethoven's Fifth Symphony), Roy Webb's angst-laden score (recently released on a CD) surges forth to accompany a quotation from John Donne: "I runne to Death and Death greets me as fast / And all my pleasures are like yesterday." The opening shot is of a staircase (borrowed from the set of *The Magnificent Ambersons*) at Highcliffe, a boarding school. Mary is confronted by a tide of prattling schoolgirls as she makes her way up to the headmistress's office. The latter explains that Jacqueline is behind with Mary's tuition; Mary says she has been without news of Jacqueline and wants to go to New York to question her associate, Mrs. Redi. The headmistress doubts that she'll learn anything from "that woman," but gives Mary permission to go, offers to help with her expenses and says she can always return to school as a teacher. After Mary leaves the office, the headmistress's assistant, Gilchrist, follows her to the staircase and warns her not to come back, saying that she had once been in a similar situation and rued having returned to Highcliffe; she is cut short by the headmistress's angry call of "Gilchrist!" Mary goes down the staircase and out the door, pausing to bestow an affectionate smile on the big grandfather clock in the hall.

This short scene contains a number of the small anomalies that finally make the film such a disorienting experience and contribute to the fascination it has held for its fans (including Carol Reed and Jacques Rivette, who reportedly screened it for the cast of his movie *Duelle*). The headmistress is actually being kind. But her appearance and tone are sinister. We wonder in passing what she knows about "that woman," Mrs. Redi, and how she knows it, though we soon forget this detail as the story unwinds. Nor do we learn why Gilchrist urges Mary to leave, nor why the headmistress summons Gilchrist back with such urgency. (Neither actress appears in the film again.) Mary's affection for the grandfather clock is also unexplained.

We soon learn more about Jacqueline's disappearance and the satanic cult she has become involved with in Greenwich Village, but these mysteries tend to get sidetracked by small discrepancies of plot and motivation, and by erratic strands of dialogue. Tom Conway, the real-life alcoholic (and brother of George Sanders) who plays Dr. Judd, at one point irrelevantly remarks to a receptionist that he doesn't treat alcoholics: "Dipsomania can be rather sordid." We hear nothing further of dipsomania or the receptionist's problem (her father drinks), but this odd exchange contributes to our sense throughout the film that people are saying anything that comes into their heads, and that the apparent mysteries of the plot are perhaps only a smokescreen for other, ill-defined ones. We gradually get the feeling that the ground under our feet is unstable.

To make matters worse, the original film was cut clumsily to fit into its second-feature slot, adding to the narrative chaos. Some of these cuts are evident; others are not. Natalie (Evelyn Brent), leader and hostess of the sedate devil-worshipping cult that meets in her Greenwich Village duplex for tea and classical music (shades of *Rosemary's Baby*), has only one arm. It has been suggested that missing footage would reveal that she was once a dancer who lost the arm in an accident, which drove her to satanism, but the story seems more engrossing when you don't know this detail.

After arriving in New York, Mary calls on Mrs. Redi, a proper-seeming matron who has taken over Jacqueline's cosmetics factory, La Sagesse ("Wisdom"; its trademark is a satanic emblem). Redi claims not to know Jacqueline's whereabouts, though the latter is in fact being kept prisoner in the factory for having revealed occult secrets to her psychiatrist Dr. Judd and, it turns out, is facing execution: six other cult members have been similarly condemned and Jacqueline may well become the "seventh victim."

The spiraling complications of the plot take Mary on a scary trip through a studio-bound Manhattan which, as so often, seems more realistic than location filming would have produced. Particularly memorable is the Fourteenth Street station of the IRT subway, where Mary boards a train at night and is soon fleeing from two formally dressed revelers who are supporting the corpse of a murdered man. She dines with a poet, Jason, and a lawyer, Gregory Ward (who turns out to be Jacqueline's husband; he is played by Hugh Beaumont, the future Ward Cleaver of the sixties sitcom *Leave It to Beaver*), in a Perry Street Italian restaurant called the Dante, which features a mural copied from Henry Holiday's famous painting of Dante's first encounter with Beatrice along the Arno. Beatrice in the mural is a dead-ringer for Mary, but, as usual, this coincidence is left unexplored, while red herrings continue to pile up. (A curious one is a scene outside the "Ivy Lane" theater, obviously an allusion to the Village's still-extant Cherry Lane Theater, above which Kim Hunter lived in later life!)

In the film's most famous scene, Mary is confronted in her bathroom shower by Mrs. Redi (brilliantly played by an actress named Mary Newton), who has come to tell her to stop looking for her sister and return to school. While Mary listens naked under the dripping nozzle, Mrs. Redi, wearing a hat and coat, looms as a menacing shadow against the shower curtain, her voice cold and ominous. (It has been said that Hitchcock, who knew Lewton, got the idea for the shower scene in *Psycho* from this episode.) Eventually Jacqueline is summoned before the assembled Palladists and told she must drink poison from a wineglass. Just as she is about to do so, young Frances, who is loyal to Jacqueline, smashes the glass and bursts into tears. (This cameo is magnificently acted by Isabel Jewell, the hard-boiled blonde in a hundred forgotten and otherwise forgettable B-movies.)

Jacqueline is allowed to leave, but told she will soon have to pay the price for her betrayal. A member of the group follows her through the oddly empty streets, at one point seizing her wrist and brandishing a knife. Jacqueline breaks free and makes it back to her room above the Dante. In the final moments of the film, Mary and Ward declare their love for each other, Mary insisting that it can never be consummated on account of Jacqueline. Jacqueline's neighbor Mimi (Elizabeth Russell, who produced a memorable frisson as Simone Simon's nemesis in Lewton's *Cat People*) emerges coughing from her room in evening dress, determined to go out for a last desperate night on the town, just as a thud from Jacqueline's room tells us that she has finally committed suicide with the noose she kept suspended for that eventuality. We hear a woman's voice intoning the Donne couplet that prefaced the film.

Muddled yet marvelous, *The Seventh Victim* is one of the great New York noir movies. (Though it is classified a horror film, the horror is kept under wraps; as in all the Lewton films, there is barely a splash of gore.) Even though the backgrounds are artificial they have a compelling authenticity. In his 1929 Surrealist novel *Hebdomeros,* de Chirico wrote: "A false beard is always more real on the screen than a real beard, just as a wooden and cardboard set is always more real than a natural setting. But try telling that to your film directors, avid for beautiful locations and picturesque views; they won't know what you are talking about, alas!" Despite its second-tier cast and modest production values, *The Seventh Victim** captures the weird poetry of New York in a way that few films have ever done.

---

*The Seventh Victim (Turner Classics, RKO Collection; VHS, 70 min.).

From *Modern Painters* (Autumn 2003). Reprinted in *City Secrets: Movies,* edited by Robert Kahn (New York: Little Bookworm, 2004).

On F. T. Prince's "The Moonflower"

F. T. Prince is a poet who deserves to be better known. Born in South Africa in 1912, he studied there and at Oxford and matured in England in the 1930s. It was an exciting period for poetry: Auden, MacNeice, Spender and others were producing their finest work. Prince was just a few years younger than they and participated in the scene, though always somewhat on the fringes. His first book, *Poems,* was published in 1938 by Faber and Faber.

He was distanced from his contemporaries by a number of factors, including temperament. He led a fairly isolated life with his wife, Elizabeth, in Southampton (having taught at Southampton University for many years). Growing up far from the centers of poetry, he was free to form his own poetic allegiances. Unlike Auden, for instance, who lived in Germany and seems to have had little use for French poetry, he was drawn to the work of Rimbaud and Valéry, and to T. S. Eliot's translation of St.-John Perse's epic prose poem, *Anabase.* He also read extensively in Italian literature of the Renaissance, which resulted in a classic study of the Italian elements in Milton's verse (Milton being another poet who was out of favor in 1930s England).

"The Moonflower," the early poem I have chosen, is a flawless gem, like several scattered throughout English poetry: one thinks of the anonymous ballad "The Unquiet Grave," of Southwell's "The Burning Babe," of Keats's "grasshopper" sonnet, of Emily Dickinson's "Because I could not stop for Death." Like those, it is both very simple and mysterious. The hushed, almost oppressive nocturnal sweetness suggests Keats's "Ode to a Nightingale." But Prince is more oblique. From the very first line—one of the greatest first lines in English poetry, I submit—one wonders: What are those secret drops? What exactly is this moonflower, that "squanders" its scent, and is left "the weaker" by the night that draws out its perfume? And what exactly is the role of the night? It provides the poet, both weary and ecstatic, with a haven, a medium for the caress of the moonflower: "Delicate, serene and lonely, peaceful, strange / To the intellect and the imagination"—an isolated place indeed!

The last stanza is the most mysterious and, paradoxically, the most rewarding. All being (along with the moonflower) is dissatisfied—dissatisfied for the dark kiss that only night gives. Strange, to be dissatisfied *for* something. And the final couplet compounds the mystery. Does night give only to the soul that waits in longing, and lives in that (i.e., the soul)? Or is it the soul that waits and lives only in longing? I suppose it's the latter, but the wording is such that it might indeed be night that needs to live in the longing soul. I think that it's probably a functional ambiguity: the soul and the night depend on each other, can only live within each other. In any case, the ecstasy seems not unlike that of St. John of the Cross (whose poetry Prince has translated): sacred and profane woven together in a single strand.

The Moonflower

The secret drops of love run through my mind:
Midnight is filled with sounds of the full sea
That has risen softly among the rocks:
Air stirs the cedar-tree.

Somewhere a fainting sweetness is distilled:
It is the moonflower hanging in its tent
Of twisted broad-leaved branches by the stony path
That squanders the cool scent.

Pallid, long as a lily, it swings a little
As if drunk with its own perfume and the night,
Which draws its perfume out and leaves the flower
The weaker for its flight.

Detached from my desires, in an oblivion
Of this world that surrounds me, in weariness
Of all but darkness, silence, starry solitude,
I too feel that caress—

Delicate, serene and lonely, peaceful, strange
To the intellect and the imagination,
The touch with which reality wounds and ravishes
Our inmost desolation.

All being like the moonflower is dissatisfied
For the dark kiss that the night only gives,
And night gives only to the soul that waits in longing
And in that only lives.

From *Dark Horses: Poets on Lost Poems,* edited by Joy Katz and Kevin Prufer (Champaign: University of Illinois Press, 2004). "The Moonflower" by F. T. Prince, from *Collected Poems, 1935–1992,* copyright © 1993 by F. T. Prince. Reprinted by permission of Sheep Meadow Press.

Biographies

John Ashbery was born in Rochester, New York, on July 28, 1927. He received a B.A. from Harvard (1949) and an M.A. from Columbia (1951), went to France as a Fulbright Scholar in 1955, and lived and worked there for most of the next decade.

He has published more than twenty collections of poetry, beginning in 1953 with *Turandot and Other Poems* (Tibor de Nagy Editions). His *Self-Portrait in a Convex Mirror* (Viking, 1975) won the three major American prizes: the Pulitzer, the National Book Award, and the National Book Critics Circle Award. His most recent volumes are *Wakefulness* (Farrar, Straus and Giroux, 1998), *Girls on the Run* (Farrar, Straus and Giroux, 1999), *Your Name Here* (Farrar, Straus and Giroux, 2000), *As Umbrellas Follow Rain* (Qua Books, 2001), and *Chinese Whispers* (Farrar, Straus and Giroux, 2002).

He began writing about art in 1957, served as executive editor of *ARTnews* (1965–72), and as art critic for *New York Magazine* (1978–80) and *Newsweek* (1980–85). A selection of his art writings was issued by Knopf in 1989 as *Reported Sightings: Art Chronicles 1957–1987,* edited by David Bergman (Harvard University Press, 1991).

The novel *A Nest of Ninnies,* written with James Schuyler, was first published in 1969 (Dutton) and has been reissued several times. The collection *Three Plays* (Z Press, 1978) includes *The Heroes,* which was first produced in New York by the Living Theater in 1952. Ashbery's numerous published translations from French include works by Raymond Roussel, Max Jacob, Alfred Jarry, Antonin Artaud, and two collections of poems by Pierre Martory, *Every Question but One* (1990) and *The Landscape Is behind the Door* (1994). His own work has been translated into more than twenty languages.

Ashbery was Professor of English and co-director of the MFA

program in Creative Writing at Brooklyn College (CUNY) from 1974 to 1990, and Distinguished Professor from 1980 to 1990. He delivered the Charles Eliot Norton Lectures at Harvard in 1989–90, published as *Other Traditions* (Harvard University Press, 2000). Since 1990 he has been the Charles P. Stevenson, Jr., Professor of Languages and Literature at Bard College in Annandale-on-Hudson, New York.

He has been elected to membership in the American Academy of Arts and Letters (1980) and the American Academy of Arts and Sciences (1983), and served as Chancellor of the Academy of American Poets from 1988–99. The winner of many prizes and awards, he has received two Guggenheim Fellowships and was a MacArthur Fellow from 1985–90. He holds honorary doctorates from Southampton College of Long Island University, the University of Rochester (NY), Pace University, and Harvard University. International recognition for his outstanding career achievement includes the Horst Bienek Prize for Poetry (Bavarian Academy of Fine Arts, Munich, 1991), the Ruth Lilly Prize for Poetry (*Poetry* magazine, Modern Poetry Association and the American Council for the Arts, 1992), the Antonio Feltrinelli International Prize for Poetry (Academia Nazionale dei Lincei, Rome, 1992), the Robert Frost Medal (Poetry Society of America, 1995) the Grand Prix des Biennales Internationales de Poésie (Brussels, 1996), the Gold Medal for Poetry (American Academy of Arts and Letters, 1997), the Walt Whitman Citation of Merit (State of New York and the New York State Writers Institute, 2000), the Signet Society Medal for Achievement in the Arts (Signet Associates, Harvard University, 2001), and the Wallace Stevens Award (Academy of American Poets, 2001); in 1993 he was made a Chevalier de l'Ordre des Arts et des Lettres by the French Ministry of Culture, and in 2003 he was named Officier of the Légion d'Honneur of the Republic of France by presidential decree.

Eugene Richie teaches in the English Department at Pace University in New York City, where he is the Director of Writing. He has worked with John Ashbery for twenty years as a secretary, as research assistant for the Charles Eliot Norton Lectures, and as an editor. He is currently collecting and editing a volume of Ashbery's selected literary translations from the French.

With Edith Grossman, he co-translated two volumes of poems by Jaime Manrique—*Scarecrow* (Intuflo Editions, 1990) and *My Night with / Mi noche con Federico García Lorca* (Painted Leaf Press, 1997; University of Wisconsin Press, 2003). He is also translating, with Raimundo Mora and Margaret Carson, a volume of stories of the Venezuelan writer Matilde Daviu.

His poems are collected in *Moiré* (The Groundwater Press, 1989) and *Island Light* (Painted Leaf Press, 1998). He has also published poems written with his son, Joseph Richie, in the chapbook *Endless Enchantment* (2000) and with his wife, Rosanne Wasserman, in *Place du Carousel* (2001). Together they founded The Groundwater Press, which publishes work of emerging writers from the United States and abroad.

Index

Duard, Émile, 37
Duchamp, Marcel, 34, 37
Dufrène, Madame, 36, 39, 274
Dullin, Charles, 25
Dumas, Alexandre, 126–27
Duncan, Robert, 92–94, 164, 205, 206
Dunsany, Edward Lord, 102
Durrell, Lawrence, 92
Dusk to Dusk (Wheelwright), 138, 140
Dust of Suns, The (Roussel). See *poussière de soleils, La*
Duyck, John, 287

"Easter" (O'Hara), 132
Eddingsville (Johns), 71–72
Eliot, Thomas Stearns, 3–4, 19, 137, 180, 192, 215–16; M. Moore and, 83–84, 88, 109; O'Hara and, 81, 129
Elliott, Richard, 225
Elmer, Edwin Romanzo, 76
Elmslie, Kenward, 114, 159–63
El Topo (film), 142
Éluard, Paul, 21, 38, 89
Emerson, Ralph Waldo, 137, 145, 146, 205
"Empathy and New Year" (Schuyler), 210
"End, The" (Borges), 102
Endgame (Beckett), 156
En vrac (Reverdy), 24
Épaves (Roussel), 273
Ernst, Max, 154, 155, 157
Esquire (magazine), 67
ètoile au front, L' (Roussel), 37, 43, 221
Étude sur Raymond Roussel (Ferry), 44, 197, 273
Europa, Rape of, 50–54
"Europe" (Ashbery), 55–56, 66–67
Every Question but One (Martory), 270
existentialism, 106
Experimental Review (magazine), 92

Exquisite Corpse, The (Chester), 97, 99

Fabergé, 104, 126
Fabian, Françoise, 149
Fables (La Fontaine; trans. M. Moore), 108, 109, 111–12
"Familiar" (Wheelwright), 140
Fantin-Latour, Henri, 254
Fantômas (Allain and Souvestre), 183–90; Feuillade and, 183, 185; Surrealism and, 187–88
fantôme de la liberté, Le (film), 153
Fayard, Arthème, 184
Feldman, Morton, 115, 131
femme 100 têtes, La (Ernst), 157
Ferdydurke (Gombrowicz), 104–6
Ferry, Jean, 49, 53, 197, 273; *Étude sur Raymond Roussel*, 44, 50
Feuillade, Louis, 150, 152, 183, 185, 188–89
"Few Days, A" (Schuyler), 280
"Few Leaves, A" (Porter), 182
Ficciones (Borges), 100
"Filling Station" (Bishop), 123
film, 3, 20, 22, 25, 34, 35, 39, 123, 125, 148–53, 172, 183, 185, 187, 188–89, 290–91, 299–303. *See also specific filmmakers, actors, and films*
Firbank, Ronald, 129, 173
Fire Island (New York), 78, 80, 175
"Fish, The" (M. Moore), 110–11
Fitzgerald, Robert, 73, 76, 138, 178
Flaubert, Gustave, 16
fleurs du mal, Les (Baudelaire), 130
Flio (Roussel), 45
Flow Chart Foundation for Bard College, 7
Folder (review), 80
Ford, Mark, 2–4; Hofmann on, 232–33, 235; *Landlocked*, 231,

315

Objectivist poets, 113, 217–18
O'Brien, Flann, 129, 173
"Octopus, An" (M. Moore), 111, 248
"Ode to a Nightingale" (Keats), 304
Oeuvres complètes (Artaud), 25
Ogier, Bulle, 149
O'Hara, Frank, 4, 78–83, 114, 203, 249, 285; *Biotherm*, 82; *Collected Poems*, 4, 128–34; Elmslie and, 159–60; reminiscence of, 171–75; Schuyler and, 281
O'Keeffe, Georgia, 256
Olana, 261–67; Church paintings and, 262–63; Hudson River and, 261–66; origin of name of, 266
"Old Amusement Park" (M. Moore), 86
Olmstead, Frederick Law, 264
Olson, Charles, 92, 103, 131, 206, 243
"Omaggio a Joyce" (Berio), 67, 251
Ommateum (Ammons), 144
"One: Many" (Ammons), 147
Op art, 71
Opium (Cocteau), 34, 39
"Oranges" (O'Hara), 132
Orchid Stories, The (Elmslie), 159, 162
Other Traditions (Ashbery), 3, 4
Ouspenskaya, Maria, 296
"Outing" (Ford), 232
Out One / Spectre (Rivette), 148–53
"Over 2,000 Illustrations and a Complete Concordance" (Bishop), 5–6, 121–23, 169
Oxford University, 5

Pabst, G. W., 25
Pace University, 7
Pageant (Winkfield), 259–61
"Painter, The" (Ashbery), 5

painting, poetry and, 57, 59, 79, 211–16, 246. *See also specific painters and paintings*
Palace at 4 A.M. (Giacometti), 42
Palmer, Erastus Dow, 261
Palmer, Michael, 216–18
Pannini, Giovanni, 18
Paris Conservatory, 35
Paris-Match, 237, 269
Parisot, Henri, 31
Partisan Review (magazine), 5, 122
Pascal, Blaise, 34
Paschen, Elise, 244
Passion of Joan of Arc (Dreyer), 25
Pasternak, Boris, 4, 81, 129, 131
"Pastoral" (N. Moore), 193
"Pastoral" (Moss), 77
Patchen, Kenneth, 92
Pater, Walter, 259
"Paul Bannows Thinks of His Honeymoon" (N. Moore), 196
Paulhan, Jean, 59
Pavilions (Elmslie), 159
Peasant of Paris, The (Aragon), 27, 89
peau de l'homme, La (Reverdy), 23
Péguy, Charles, 16
Perec, Georges, 105
Père Lachaise, 269
Perse, St.-John, 180
Persistence of Memory (Dali), 212
Personal Anthology, A (Borges), 100–101
Phébus ou le beau mariage (Martory), 237–38, 269
photography, 252–57, 290–91
Picabia, Francis, 37
Picasso, Pablo, 20, 128, 130, 261
"Picnic Cantata" (P. Bowles), 281
"Pierre Ménard, Author of Don Quixote" (Borges), 100, 101, 126, 205
Pierrot le fou (Godard), 123
"Pilgrim's Progress" (Bunyan), 94
Pistils (Mapplethorpe), 252–57
plaisirs et les jours, Les (Proust), 35
Plan of the City of O (Palmer), 217